DICKENSLAND

DICKENSLAND

THE CURIOUS HISTORY OF DICKENS'S LONDON

LEE JACKSON

YALE UNIVERSITY PRESS
NEW HAVEN AND LONDON

For information about this and other Yale University Press publications, please contact:
U.S. Office: sales.press@yale.edu yalebooks.com
Europe Office: sales@yaleup.co.uk yalebooks.co.uk

Set in Adobe Caslon Pro by IDSUK (DataConnection) Ltd
Printed in the United States of America

Library of Congress Control Number: 2023938167

ISBN 978-0-300-26620-7

A catalogue record for this book is available from the British Library.

10 9 8 7 6 5 4 3 2

CONTENTS

ILLUSTRATIONS

ACKNOWLEDGEMENTS

I would like to thank Professor Juliet John (City University, formerly Royal Holloway) and Dr Cindy Sughrue (Director of the Charles Dickens Museum) who offered me an opportunity to think about Charles Dickens and heritage, as part of PhD research generously funded by the Techne AHRC Doctoral Training Partnership. Staff at the Charles Dickens Museum, past and present, have also been consistently helpful and welcoming, including curators Louisa Price, Emily Dunbar and Frankie Kubicki. This book, of course, builds on a long tradition of enquiry and research into Dickens and Dickensiana and, therefore, owes a great debt to the Dickens Fellowship, Dickens Society and the worldwide community of Dickens scholars. Thanks, as ever, must also go to Heather McCallum and everyone at Yale, who make the business of publishing a pleasure; and to my dad, Ken Jackson, who has always appreciated Boz and offered helpful suggestions. Lastly, my love and gratitude to Joanne and Clara, although I cannot forgive them for not allowing me to christen the cat 'Mr Dickens'.

1

DEAD: TO BEGIN WITH

Charles Dickens died at his home in Kent on 9 June 1870, having suffered a stroke the previous evening. Within twenty-four hours of his passing, innumerable tributes to the great author appeared in the press. Many began with the same exclamation – 'Charles Dickens is dead!' – capturing a widespread sense of astonishment and disbelief.[1] The talk was of a national loss that simultaneously felt like a personal bereavement. For Dickens had established a profoundly intimate connection with his readership. His recent public reading tours, where he had acted out both comic and tragic scenes from his fiction, had only cemented this bond. Audiences in both Britain and America had responded to his performances 'with an almost painful intensity of feeling'.[2] Such was the strength of this attachment, the power and reach of his work, the extent of his fame, that his death seemed almost unthinkable. Obituarists concurred that the world had been deprived of a titan of English literature, perhaps second only to Shakespeare, 'utterly unmatched for originality and greatness of heart'.[3]

There was some debate about arranging a fitting funeral. Dickens himself had hoped for a simple burial in Rochester, not far from his country retreat at Gads Hill. Nonetheless, John Forster (his friend and biographer), his son Charley and the Dean of Westminster conspired to ensure that he was buried in Westminster Abbey, albeit with a private service.[4] The general public were then permitted to file past the open grave in 'Poet's Corner' and pay their respects. The spot soon had to be protected by a temporary wooden barrier, lest it disappear from view amidst multitudinous flowers and wreaths. The modest inscription on the memorial tablet would simply read:

CHARLES DICKENS
BORN 7th FEBRUARY 1812
DIED 9th JUNE 1870

Of course, Dickens never really departed. Literary immortality, predicted during the author's lifetime, was amply realised after his death. Print editions multiplied, much to the satisfaction of the book trade (as one contemporary put it, 'to quote a term used in the trade, "Dickens is still alive"').[5] Theatrical and then cinematic adaptations, likewise, kept his famous novels fresh in the public imagination. His characters, meanwhile, seemed to acquire a life of their own. Charitable Dickens-themed pageants, balls and bazaars, where people dressed as Little Nell, Mr Pickwick et al., became remarkably popular in the late Victorian and Edwardian period. Rochester even hosted a 'Dickens Fancy Dress Roller-Skating Carnival'.[6] Advertisers, meanwhile, had their own particular uses for Dickens's familiar creations. Mr Micawber can be found in turn-of-the-century advertisements for cork linoleum; Serjeant Buzfuz makes the case for Gordon and Dilworth's Tomato Catsup; a sketch of Nicholas Nickleby endorses a mail-order secretarial course ('"I want to get on," said Nicholas' being the tag line).[7] Dickens's highly individual characters also readily lent themselves to being turned into gifts and collectibles. The Charles Dickens Museum in Bloomsbury holds a variety of these curios, from silver bookmarks to figurine pin cushions (imagine a miniature porcelain Pickwick or Bumble, garlanded with a sort of puffball skirt). In 1912, Gamage's Department Store in Holborn installed a mocked-up 'street in Old London of Dickens' Time'. This was part of their Christmas offering, selling 'reproductions in brass of interesting and historical subjects', including Pickwickian pipe-stoppers and an Old Curiosity Shop door knocker.[8] The celebrated author and his fictional world seemed to offer boundless possibilities for marketing and merchandising. Dickens had become a commodity, a brand, a visitor experience. This sort of commercial appropriation, in fairness, had some precedent. A review of *The Pickwick Papers* from 1837, for instance, makes passing mention of 'Pickwick chintzes [which] figured in linendrapers' windows, and Weller corduroys in breeches-maker's advertisements'.[9] Nonetheless, there was a growing sense that Dickens had created an entire imaginative universe which could now be freely exploited for pleasure and profit. This included excursions into 'Dickens's London'.

From the 1880s onwards there was a remarkable boom in Dickensian tourism, evident in the publication of dozens of books, travelogues, and newspaper and magazine articles. Professional guides offered to take metropolitan visitors on 'Dickensian Rambles'. Lecturers armed themselves with magic lantern slides of 'Dickens views' and toured the nation's public halls and meeting rooms.[10] Places mentioned in Dickens's fiction suddenly seemed to exert an extraordinary fascination. The pitch was simple: *these famous fictive locations actually exist in the real world – dozens of them – and so why not visit them for yourself?* The delineation of touristic 'Dickens's London' was partly the work of diehard fans, dubbed 'The Dickens Cult' in the popular press, for whom making a literary pilgrimage was one way of keeping the author's memory alive. But the general public were soon to be found stalking the Inns of Court in search of Pip's lodgings; window shopping at the so-called Old Curiosity Shop on Portsmouth Street; and admiring the author's former homes and haunts. Guides and guidebooks touted novel touristic experiences, some of which I discuss in this book: discovering the hospitality of archetypal 'Dickensian' coaching inns; locating the neglected burial ground which featured in *Bleak House*; standing upon London Bridge's riverside steps at midnight, reimagining Nancy's confession to Mr Brownlow; enjoying a 'Dickens shave' in Poll Sweedlepipe's barbershop (or, at least, its real-world 'original' in Kingsgate Street). There was now a modicum of money to be made from proclaiming that a business had Dickensian associations. Shopkeepers, hoteliers and publicans all benefited from the Dickens tourist craze and shaped its progress. Members of public could also, of course, explore the territory at a more leisurely pace, from the comfort of their own armchair, merely by perusing articles such as 'Charles Dickens in Southwark' or 'The Haunts of Sarah Gamp', or books with titles such as *Dickens's London*, *A Pickwickian Pilgrimage* or *The Real Dickens Land*.[11]

Some literary topographers – a term I will use throughout this book for creators of works of literary tourism – preferred 'Dickensland' (or 'Dickens Land') to 'Dickens's London'. It possessed a certain imperialist swagger, as if the great man had stamped his name on vast swathes of conquered territory. Not everyone, however, was impressed by such pretensions to literary dominion. One journalist, writing in 1903, noted sardonically:

> ... where Dickens posted his first manuscript – where he had a red hot chop – where he looked out of a window, and what he saw when he looked out. It is all recorded. He might be a dead king with a vast empire still of loyal subjects who will hardly believe he is dead. At the worst, they can make a vice-regent of one of his old hats, and reverence that. He has been canonised and his shrines are everywhere.[12]

'Dickensland' also conveyed a sense of enchantment, redolent of the obligatory 'transformation scene' in Victorian pantomime, in which an ordinary place became a magical 'fairyland'.[13] Indeed, many literary topographers suggested that the appeal of Dickensian tourism was mentally conjuring up favourite moments from the novels *in situ*, a 'transformation scene' of sorts. To modern ears, of course, 'Dickensland' sounds more like a theme park – an apt association. For the most visited real-world sites were themselves moulded by commercial interests, adapted to meet the demands of eager visitors. Canny entrepreneurs, at places such as Wood's Hotel (formerly Furnival's Inn, where Dickens lodged as a young man) or the George Inn (a typical Borough coaching inn), made the most of their Dickensian credentials, as I have already hinted. Moreover, when those credentials were underwhelming, they embellished or invented them. The Old Curiosity Shop – undoubtedly the most popular destination of all – had not the slightest connection to the novel, nor to its author. 'Dickens's London', in other words, was always something of a construct, not merely a collection of historic buildings but a tailor-made 'Dickensland'.

This might seem counter-intuitive. Surely the literary tourist always seeks out the 'real' place, the authentic original building which inspired or informed the author's work? The line between the authentic and the manufactured in literary tourism, however, is often rather blurred; and the general public are not necessarily overly troubled by the distinction. Representations and recreations of 'Dickens's London' are instructive in this regard: topographically themed Victorian bazaars; the stage sets of televisual and cinematic adaptations; even the failed Dickens World theme park in Chatham. Such ersatz places – avowedly artificial 'Dickenslands' – have a good deal in common with the most popular 'real' sites. The principal difference is that they are *explicitly* manufactured to suit the public taste. This is not to say that literary tourists place no value on visiting authentic buildings and locations, but they are often content to overlook a degree of simulation and fakery. One is reminded of the famous witticism about sincerity, attributed to the comedian George

Burns ('The secret to success is sincerity. If you can fake that, you've got it made'). Manufactured authenticity, likewise, can prove very appealing.

***

'Dickens's London' flourished as a tourist experience *c.* 1870–1930, and, of course, although public interest has waxed and waned, it can still be enjoyed to this day. The origins of the phenomenon, however, are quite complex. Obviously, Dickens's own topographic specificity is fundamental. He seems to have regularly prowled the streets of London, scouting for suitably interesting locations that he might use in his fiction. Whilst writing *The Old Curiosity Shop*, he famously penned a note to John Forster which read, 'intended calling on you this morning on my way back from Bevis-marks, whither I went to look at a house for Sampson Brass' (the venal solicitor in the novel).[14] This reference to Bevis Marks also highlights his interest in the older parts of the metropolis. Situated on the border of the City of London, the run-down district was particularly quaint, containing a number of Elizabethan buildings, such as the timbered, gabled Blue Pig public house, on the corner of St Mary Axe and Bevis Marks, later known as the Golden Axe.[15] In fact, a fascination with old buildings runs through Dickens's fiction and was noted by his critics. John Ruskin, writing in a private letter shortly after the great author's death, criticised Dickens for being 'a pure modernist ... with no understanding of any power of antiquity except as a sort of jackdaw sentiment for cathedral towers ... [who] uses everything for effect on the pit'.[16] The accusation was that Dickens appropriated historic locations as picturesque scenic backdrops for his novels – a superficial engagement with the past. Walter Bagehot, similarly, imagined the author drawing upon an extensive memory bank of (real-world) 'old buildings and curious people'.[17] Bagehot, however, differed from Ruskin, praising Dickens for assembling a peculiar sort of modernist literary collage. The novels, he argued, recalling these random and curious facets of the metropolis, reflected the fragmentary nature of urban existence. Bagehot's notion of the author pulling together disconnected elements – an old building here, an eccentric character there – nevertheless echoes Ruskin's jibe about 'jackdaw sentiment'. I hope to demonstrate that Dickens was not quite so random. For there are biographical, historical and contemporary (nineteenth-century) resonances in his choice of particular London localities which suggest a very purposeful approach to place (see, in particular, my discussion of 'Nancy's Steps' in Chapter 6).

In terms of the literary topographers who actually produced the travelogues and tourist guidebooks, there was no single guiding hand. Some of this material, certainly, was initially generated by literary acolytes, such as Percy Fitzgerald (1830–1925), one of the young writers whom Dickens himself had encouraged and championed whilst editing his magazines *Household Words* and *All the Year Round*. Various other writers and journalists, also tried their luck. John Rose Greene Hassard (1836–88), for example, literary editor of the *New York Tribune*, published the first series of articles charting 'Dickens's London' for American readers in 1879.[18] Predictably, professional tour guides also contributed, such as Robert Allbut (1832–1915), who penned a Dickens guidebook, *London Rambles "en zigzag" with Charles Dickens* (1886), whilst working for a London travel agency. But one did not have to be a *litterateur*, or even involved in the tourism industry. Thomas Edgar Pemberton (1849–1905), author of the first complete book of Dickens tourism, *Dickens's London* (1876), found time to write plays, pantomimes, the occasional novel and theatrical biographies but was also the manager of his family's brass foundry. William R. Hughes (1830–99), author of *A Week's Tramp in Dickens-Land* (1891) and one of the first great collectors of Dickens's first editions and memorabilia, was treasurer of the City of Birmingham. Admittedly, there was not great social diversity amongst these figures. The majority, as readers will have gathered, were middle- and upper-middle-class men, often financially comfortable men of advancing years, for whom Dickensian topography was something of a pleasant hobby.

Solitary men, of course, could wander the streets of the capital, particularly its less salubrious districts, with much greater social freedom than their female counterparts. Nonetheless, middle-class women also played a lively and active part in Dickensian tourism, even if constrained by the requirement to be chaperoned. In fact, another famous author, Louisa May Alcott, a self-styled 'spinster on the rampage' in mid-Victorian London, has good claim to be the first documented Dickensian literary tourist/topographer. Alcott records making a 'Dickens pilgrimage' in her diary entry for June 1866 and would chronicle her adventures in a lightly fictionalised account published the following year.[19] Later fictionalised travelogues, also written by female authors, similarly hint at American enthusiasm for 'Dickens's London' as both an imaginary place and a real-world tourist destination. The heroine of Elizabeth Williams Champney's *Three Vassar Girls in England* (1884), for example, sees the London crowds as akin to 'a grand Dickens carnival'.[20] The heroine of Susan Coolidge's *What Katy Did Next* (1886) likewise finds London 'just like a dream or a story', part of a 'Story-Book England' (although she wonders why Dickens made so much of muffins, 'a great disappointment, tough and tasteless').[21] We might also note that the Lady Guides Association (LGA), founded in 1888 by Edith A. Davis to provide employment for 'intelligent gentlewomen', included tours of Dickensian sites for its exclusively female clientele. Some of the LGA's female guides actually made this their speciality and became 'acquainted with every single place of which mention is made in the great novelist's works'.[22] The intention was to satisfy knowledgeable and rather exacting American fans. The LGA laid on numerous other tours and visits, with Davis even arranging for female-led tours of Jack the Ripper's Whitechapel.[23] Nevertheless, 'Dickens's London' was perennially in demand, particularly among her transatlantic clients.

I would argue, however, that the more rewarding question is not so much who created touristic 'Dickens's London' – who wrote the books or gave the tours – as under what circumstances it flourished. The Victorians' burgeoning interest in London's built environment as urban heritage was critical. During the late nineteenth century, what were once merely everyday old buildings increasingly came to be seen as valuable survivals, preservation-worthy cultural assets. The Dickensian tourist trail was an important part of a new heritage metropolis of commemorative plaques and authenticated 'historic' buildings. Mentally summoning up Dickens's scenes and characters *in situ* exemplified the possibilities for rich imaginative engagement with place in this 'newly old' capital.[24] This relationship was not, however, entirely straightforward. Some questioned whether 'Dickens's London' was worthy of preservation. The author's patent interest in the seamier side of London life – the slum and the back alley – was particularly problematic for progressives, such as the members of the newly formed London County Council (LCC), established in 1889. The Council was both self-appointed guardian of the capital's history and heritage and yet simultaneously engaged in redevelopment work that involved the wholesale demolition of 'old London'. For the LCC, 'Dickensian' streets were places not to be commemorated but to be wiped from the map. Indeed, a good deal of Dickens's literary territory would be obliterated by the turn of the twentieth century, laid waste by schemes for urban improvement.

The general popularity of literary tourism was, of course, another important factor that nurtured Dickensian tourism. The practice of visiting sites associated with authors and their work has a long history. For example, during the 1520s, tourists sought out real-life locations in the south of France which were associated with Petrarch's sonnets of unrequited love. They were assisted by 'the publications of maps [...] the construction of museum-like collections [...] the rise of more or less organised tours'.[25] Most academic studies of the subject, however, look to the continental 'Grand Tour' in the seventeenth and eighteenth centuries as the precursor of not only modern mass tourism but also literary tourism. The Romantics' enthusiasm for venerating creative genius and finding imaginative stimulation in historical/picturesque localities also fostered a growing interest in 'literary pilgrimage' in the early 1800s.[26] Suffice to say, by the mid-Victorian period the literary tourist was a familiar figure. Some travellers sought out the homes of literary celebrities, inspired by books such as William Howitt's *Homes and Haunts of the Most Eminent British Poets* (1847). In Scotland, excursion trains and coach tours took visitors to destinations found in the works of Walter Scott, the likes of Melrose Abbey and Loch Katrine.[27] The publication of Mrs Gaskell's *The Life of Charlotte Brontë* (1857), two years after Charlotte's death, similarly brought a constant stream of tourists to Haworth, determined to see the Brontë parsonage and experience the surrounding moorland. The influx of visitors reportedly produced 'quite a revolution' in the district, not least in the price of food and accommodation at local inns and hotels.[28] Touristic 'Dickens's London', therefore, was part of this pre-existing tradition, but it was, I suggest, rather unusual and distinctive. For a start, there had never been such an extensive *urban* literary territory, charted by so many interested parties. Literary tourism was traditionally associated with the remote, rural and picturesque, a legacy of Romanticism. 'Dickens's London', moreover, went largely unexplored during Dickens's own lifetime (unlike, for instance, the Scotland of Walter Scott, or the Lake District of Wordsworth). Dickensian tourism was part of a tradition but it was also a historically specific cultural phenomenon, with its own particular origins in the late nineteenth century.

Certain individuals, of course, have always been keen to encounter famous living writers, and even Dickens's removal from London to Gads Hill did not deter sightseers hoping to catch a glimpse of the famous author. One local recalled that American tourists were wont to park their carriages outside the raised front garden 'and there sit and gloat and nudge one another if a daughter of a maid servant came out of the dwelling and picked a flower'.[29] Dickens's reading tours also pandered to, and doubtless boosted, a demand for making a personal connection with the author. Nonetheless, aside from those who hoped to catch a glimpse of the man himself, few seem to have been interested in Dickensian tourism before the 1880s. We do know that individual readers would occasionally query the real-world correlate of places in his fictional world. Sarah Hammond Palfrey, a writer who met Dickens en route to America in 1867, quizzed him on the location of the burial ground in *Bleak House* and was later treated to a letter which described its location near Drury Lane Theatre (a site which I will discuss in detail). Louisa May Alcott, as already noted, included Dickens-related literary sites in her tours of the capital. But Alcott, writing in the mid-1860s, whose strolls through mid-Victorian London made her feel 'as if I'd got into a novel', was rather ahead of her time.[30] While a trio of American articles containing topographical content marked Dickens's death, and T. Edgar Pemberton's guidebook/travelogue *Dickens's London* was published in 1876, they made little immediate impact ('a reverential, but as far as we can see, useless piece of work', remarked a reviewer of Pemberton).[31] It was not until the 1880s that similar books and articles began to be produced in large numbers and organised guided tours began to appear.[32] Percy Fitzgerald regretted that he had never spoken to Dickens about Pickwickian topography while the great author still lived, remarking, 'But, at that time, no one much cared. The thing was assumed to be concluded. It was enough to read your "Pickwick" then without troubling about details – a sensible course enough, after all.'[33] Fitzgerald would nonetheless become one of the most assiduous chroniclers of 'Dickens's London'.[34]

This prompts the question: what changed? There is no doubt that Dickens's death and his induction into the national literary pantheon at Poet's Corner provided some impetus to chart his literary territory. For literary pilgrimage had long been associated with notions of communing with the dead, a means of forging a spiritual connection with famous figures from the past. As William Godwin put it at the start of the nineteenth century, 'let us visit their tombs; let us indulge all the reality we can now have, of a sort of conference with these men'.[35] But one can also trace broader trends which stimulated the Dickens tourism boom, not least the Victorians' fascination with history and heritage, to which I have already alluded – an interest increasingly centred on the metropolis. 'Dickens's London' thus became part of the 'old city' that needed to be documented, commemorated, perhaps even saved from demolition, in the face of ongoing urban redevelopment. The peculiar immersive pseudo-cityscapes of international exhibitions – particularly the 'Old London Street' of the 1884 International Health Exhibition – also increased public interest in 'virtual' urban exploration. There was not much difference between 'stepping back in time' at the Health Exhibition, where visitors could walk through a meticulous recreation of medieval streets and imagine themselves in Tudor London, and stepping into 'Dickens's London', guided by the literary topographer. Both required a particular sort of imaginative engagement with place and promised similar imaginative rewards.

Perhaps the most significant factor fuelling the Dickens tourism boom, however, was the remarkable passion for all things Dickensian among American tourists. By the 1880s, ever-growing numbers of wealthy Americans were visiting the capital and they were particularly enamoured of the quaint places mentioned in Dickens's fiction ('[they] especially love to trace the localities ... they may be met, guidebook in hand, wondering which were the grimy chambers in Barnard's Inn where Pip and Herbert Pocket lived').[36] Britons were often rather condescending when they encountered such brazen enthusiasm, declaring themselves mystified why such spots were 'especially prized by our American cousins'.[37] American tourists also provoked a degree of anxiety. Rumours circulated that the Portsmouth Street Old Curiosity Shop might be demolished and rebuilt in the United States as an attraction managed by P.T. Barnum.[38] Transatlantic visitors reportedly regularly made cash offers for the 'Little Wooden Midshipman' of Leadenhall Street (a real-world wooden figurine which Dickens appropriated as a street sign for Sol Gills's fictional shop in *Dombey and Son*).[39] Americans, in the British imagination, were proverbially acquisitive; and it is true that they did make some purchases of Dickens relics. For instance, a bed from the infamous East End opium den of *Edwin Drood* fame was sold to a collector.[40] But, as a scholar of Shakespearean heritage has noted, condemnation of greedy foreign tourists also neatly shifted responsibility for the tawdry commercialisation of British cultural sites onto a convenient transatlantic scapegoat.[41]

***

Modern-day Dickens fans may legitimately ask why I have limited my research to London. Naturally, I must concede that a complete survey would extend beyond the metropolis. Rochester, Chatham and their surrounds, associated with Dickens's childhood, feature in several of his books, and he resided at nearby Gads Hill from 1857 until his death. This corner of Kent, therefore, has long been a site for Dickensian tourism. By the turn of the twentieth century, for example, Thomas Cook was laying on tours of Rochester and its environs entitled 'A Day's Pilgrimage to Dickens' Country'.[42] Growing interest in 'Dickens's Kent', in particular, went hand in hand with the late Victorian cycling craze and then, a decade or two later, the advent of the motor car, opening up the county to new waves of visitors. Motoring, in fact, breathed new life into Kent's 'Dickensian' coaching inns, which had teetered on the brink of extinction (as well as resulting in some peculiar advertisements, such as Mr Pickwick advertising the likes of the Bean Tourer, a 1920s automobile).[43] I do make a brief diversion to Gads Hill, and I take a tour of Chatham's Dickens World, but a full exploration of the county's ties with Dickens is beyond the scope of this book. Any complete study of

Dickensian tourism, in any case, would have to go much further. The Charles Dickens Museum – whose origins I will discuss – holds Dickensian tourist guides to Yorkshire (home to the infamous Mr Squeers and his school in *Nicholas Nickleby*); Portsmouth (Dickens's birthplace, also in *Nicholas Nickleby*); Bath (featured in *The Pickwick Papers*); Italy (described in *Pictures from Italy* and an important backdrop in *Little Dorrit*) and numerous other localities. Hefty pictorial volumes, such as *Charles Dickens's England* (2009), nestle beside niche pamphlets such as Edwin Harris's *The Hundred of Hoo and Its Dickensian Associations* (1921) and Edward Preston's *Hastings in Dickens and Dickens in Hastings* (1988). But this is all too much. I have, therefore, largely confined myself to selected sites in London, the metropolis which Dickens did so much to define in the popular imagination as a 'special correspondent for posterity'.[44]

Readers must also forgive me for not arranging this book strictly chronologically. Rather, I have settled on some key sites, investigating their relationship with Dickens's fiction, heritage and literary tourism on a place-by-place basis. Hopefully this provides a clearer insight into the subject. I begin with coaching inns – a suitable point of entry into the great metropolis and a type of building well known to Dickens as a young man. For the budding author worked as a parliamentary reporter in the early 1830s, covering local elections and public meetings for London newspapers, including the *Morning Chronicle*. This involved regular travel to the provinces, and he would later vividly recall transcribing his shorthand notes as the mail coach rattled back to the capital, 'writing on the palm of my hand, by the light of a dark lantern, in a postchaise and four, galloping through a wild country'.[45] He thus became familiar with the character of numerous coaching inns and his pen portrait of these institutions in *The Pickwick Papers* remains the definitive description of what the late Victorians nostalgically dubbed 'the old coaching days'. The inns which Dickens described, rendered somewhat obsolescent by the coming of the railways, would, in turn, come to fascinate the literary tourist.

2

GREAT RAMBLING QUEER OLD PLACES

In the Borough especially, there still remain some half-dozen old inns, which have preserved their external features unchanged, and which have escaped alike the rage for public improvement and the encroachments of private speculation. Great, rambling queer old places they are, with galleries, and passages, and staircases, wide enough and antiquated enough to furnish materials for a hundred ghost stories, supposing we should ever be reduced to the lamentable necessity of inventing any, and that the world should exist long enough to exhaust the innumerable veracious legends connected with old London Bridge, and its adjacent neighbourhood . . .[1]

Dickens's first novel, *The Pickwick Papers*, was originally published in serial form between March 1836 and October 1837. The book recounts the picaresque travels of a club of bumbling middle-class gentlemen, led by the cherubic, kind-hearted Mr Pickwick. Coaching and coaching inns feature prominently in the narrative, with characters making road trips to Kent and East Anglia, Bath and

Birmingham. Dickens, however, singles out the ancient inns which lined Borough High Street in Southwark for particular attention. Their old wooden balustrades, courtyard galleries and winding staircases are inextricably associated with a litany of 'ghost stories' and 'veracious legends' that almost adhere to the buildings. Dickens clearly has a strong sense that run-down antiquity prompts the imagination, akin to the suggestive power of the ruin. To quote John Forsyth, author of *Remarks on Antiquities* (1802), 'we must fancy what a ruin has been . . . we rebuild and re-people it, we call in history, we compose, we animate, we create'.[2] The allusion to stories and legends is also a typically self-referential touch. Dickens knows that *The Pickwick Papers*, his own traveller's tale, will add a new layer of narrative, a new set of associations belonging to these 'great rambling queer old places'. Mr Pickwick and his companions will become part of the fabric.

But how long would that fabric actually survive? Dickens's fictional portrait of coaching and coaching inns captured a world on the brink of extinction, even though great improvements had recently been made in road transport. By the early 1800s, better road surfaces, improved coach suspension, regular changes of horses and fierce competition amongst rival companies had produced mail coaches capable of averaging eight miles an hour. This was considered a remarkable achievement. Nevertheless, as one nostalgic historian of the period put it, this new road network, 'just as it was perfected, apparently, was rendered useless'.[3] The first railway line in London, from Deptford to Spa Road in Bermondsey, opened only a month before the first episode of *Pickwick* appeared; and both London Bridge and Euston stations would open while the novel was still being serialised. Coaching would soon be in decline and many of the old inns would, indeed, fall victim to those powerful forces of improvement and speculation. By the 1860s, the old-fashioned coaching inn had all but vanished from contemporary life; and *Pickwick* seemed like a historical document. As an anonymous journalist, writing shortly before Dickens's death, noted, 'Half the fun and the humorous description in "Pickwick" is about mail-coaches and drivers, and guards, and country inns, which the young Londoner of today never saw even in a picture.' Indeed, the whole milieu of *The Pickwick Papers* now seemed thoroughly quaint and antiquated, 'older than the Elgin marbles'.[4] Dickens's literary topographers, consequently, would come to paint him as a sort of accidental historian of this bygone era.[5] A review of the 1886 'Jubilee edition' of *Pickwick* (an annotated edition of the novel, complete with historical and topographical footnotes) remarked that coaching inns had been 'frightened away by the whistle and roar of the steam engine' and expressed gratitude that Dickens had fictively preserved them.[6] John Camden Hotten, an early Dickensian biographer, likewise claimed that the great author had gifted posterity with the best possible description of 'those old coaching days and that old tavern life that have passed out of actual existence, to live forever in Dickens's pages'.[7]

London's coaching inns, of course, were particularly hard hit by the coming of the new railway termini. Their generous galleried yards which allowed coaches space to turn, robbed of their trade in passengers, would generally come to serve as goods depots for the railways and local hauliers, before being demolished altogether. Inns situated outside the capital, on the other hand, tended to have greater longevity, facing less pressure from the railway and land-hungry developers and still serving local communities as large public houses. Regardless, by the latter part of the nineteenth century, those old inns which stubbornly clung to life were increasingly hailed as rare historic survivals. Tourists began to seek them out, both in London and beyond. Literary tourists, in particular, were keen to discover the 'great rambling queer old places' which Dickens had so eloquently described and to mentally populate them with Dickens's characters.

This chapter considers three examples of Dickensian inns: the White Hart Inn in Southwark (demolished in 1889), the King's Head in Chigwell (nowadays a restaurant) and the George Inn in

Southwark (still a public house). Their histories hint at themes that run throughout this book: the threat posed to 'Dickens's London' by urban redevelopment; how individual literary shrines were not simply places visited by a curious public but were shaped and promoted by canny interested parties (such as pub landlords); and how willingly literary tourists embraced somewhat confected Dickensian destinations. For the George Inn, owned by the National Trust, a proverbially 'Dickensian' tavern in the heart of London, has very little connection to the author or his work.

***

Not everyone, it must be said, was enamoured of the old-fashioned coaching inn. The writer Albert Smith would pen a damning portrait entitled 'Of the Good Old Coaching Days' in his satirical magazine *The Month* in 1851.[8] The article does not mention Dickens but Pickwickian nostalgia is plainly in the author's sights.[9] Coaching inn dinners, according to Smith, were coarse; fellow passengers usually drunk (the only way to get through the trundling rigours of the journey, even when vehicles were fitted with the latest in spring suspension); the accommodation wretched. Indeed, Smith lists every possible inconvenience belonging to antiquated coaching inns, from the soap ('that little inconvenient latherless cube'), to ineffectual wax candles, to airless rooms dominated by a single giant four-poster bed, with the poor traveller barely able to move or draw breath (a 'heavy expensive, elaborate mass of serge, chintz, feathers, mahogany, horsehair, sacking, holland, ticking, quilting, winch-screws, brass rings, castors and watch pockets'). Smith documents his sundry discontents in minute detail – the article even includes a diagrammatic plan of the typical cramped room – before concluding that, for the benefit of the public, 'Every inn ought to be entirely burnt down every ten years'.

The various inns depicted in *Pickwick*, in fact, are not treated identically. Some are cosy and welcoming, such as the Saracen's Head in Towcester, with its blazing hearth, where 'everything looked (as everything always does, in all decent English inns) as if the travellers had been expected, and their comforts prepared, for days before-hand'.[10] The faults of the bustling White Horse Cellar in Piccadilly are patent but are treated with comic indulgence ('The travellers' room at the White Horse Cellar is of course uncomfortable; it would be no travellers' room if it were not').[11] The Great White Horse at Ipswich, on the other hand, is described more unfavourably, savouring of a disgruntled nineteenth-century Tripadvisor review ('Never was such labyrinths of uncarpeted passages, such clusters of mouldy, ill-lighted rooms . . .').[12] But the tenor of the novel is relentlessly cheerful, carefree and jolly; and this is what lingers in the memory. *Pickwick* was fondly remembered for its charming portrayal of 'coaching days' because of this enduring effervescent mood. But, of course, literary tourism demands specific locations. Where were Dickensian tourists to find the 'great rambling queer old places' so beloved by the great author?

The most obvious candidate in the metropolis was the White Hart Inn, one of the antique Borough inns described in *The Pickwick Papers*. The original public house on this spot served as the head-quarters of Jack Cade's popular rebellion of 1450, as dramatised by Shakespeare in *Henry VI, Part 2*. Destroyed by fire in 1676, it was rebuilt along similar lines and, at the start of the nineteenth century, remained a notable example of a traditional galleried coaching inn. Pickwick arrives there in the novel on the tail of the conniving scoun-drel Mr Jingle, who has eloped with the naïve spinster Rachel Wardle and taken a room at the inn. Dickens paints a meticulously detailed picture of the building:

A double tier of bedroom galleries, with old clumsy balustrades, ran round two sides of the straggling area, and a double row of bells to correspond, sheltered from the weather by a little sloping roof, hung over the door leading to the bar and coffee-room. Two or three gigs and chaise-carts were wheeled up under different little sheds and pent-houses; and the occasional heavy tread of a cart-horse, or rattling of a chain at the farther end of the yard, announced to anybody who cared about the matter, that the stable lay in that direction.[13]

Here, Pickwick also meets the 'boots' (boot cleaner) of the inn, Sam Weller, a fast-talking, indefatigable individual who swiftly becomes his servant and cherished companion on his travels. The scene is illustrated by Phiz, showing the galleried inn courtyard with its latticed windows and wooden balustrades, an enormous goods wagon, and Pickwick and his companions addressing Sam, the cheeky Cockney with his hat tipped rakishly askew. It is notable that late Victorian literary tourists would often seek out scenes which had originally been illustrated in Dickens's novels. The translation from printed text to image seems to have suggested the further possibility of encountering the place in three dimensions. Hence the act of illustration itself made the White Hart a likely destination for literary pilgrimage.

Sam Weller, of course, would become one of Dickens's most memorable characters, the Sancho Panza to Pickwick's Don Quixote. Weller was soon recognised as a literary phenomenon and a crucial factor in turning *Pickwick* into a bestseller – 'the prime character in the whole book'.[14] His comic sayings or 'Wellerisms' were endlessly copied and reproduced, his character given pride of place in stage adaptations (such as W.T. Moncrieff's farce 'Sam Weller, Or the Pickwickians', which played at the New Strand Theatre in June 1837). The initial encounter at the White Hart Inn, therefore, would be remembered as a key scene in the novel purely for its introduction of the irrepressible Cockney bootblack. Theatrical adaptations, in turn, rarely scorned reproducing the coaching inn yard. Moncrieff's farce opened at the White Hart Inn ('Entrance to Coach Yard of the White Hart Inn – Bar and Coffee-Room on one side – Staircase, leading to a range of bedrooms, on the other').[15] When a desultory stage version of *Pickwick* appeared at the Lyceum Theatre in 1871 – described by one critic as a three-hour-long insult to the recently deceased author – the only saving grace was the 'scene painters and dress-makers [who] have made such diligent study of Phiz's pictures that they succeed in ticking the reminiscences of the spectators'.[16] Naturally, this included an excellent representation of the old coaching inn.

In short, everyone knew where Pickwick and Weller had met – they had read about it and seen it represented on stage – and so why not have a look at the original building? Unfortunately, one side of the inn's courtyard was knocked down and rebuilt in the late 1860s to create a restaurant. But Victorian visitors in search of antiquarian delights were assured that they could still see 'pretty much the same appearance as that which Mr Dickens photographed with such literal exactness'.[17] Dickens was often said to have such an eye for small detail that his prose descriptions resembled, as it were, a photographic likeness. The literary tourist, therefore, could go and compare that likeness to nature. There is a sense that the visuality of Dickens's prose, alongside Phiz's illustration, suggested the possibility of seeing the place for oneself. Alfred Rimmer, author of *About England with Dickens*, visiting in 1883, found the remains of the inn satisfying enough. His account describes the red Dutch tiles that top the roof as 'eminently picturesque' and details various curiosities. The traveller's room, for example, the inn's common room for guests, still contains 'a fireplace several centuries old and a groined apartment that certainly dates back to the time when Canterbury pilgrims used to rest here'.[18] The modern restaurant, moreover, is worth a visit ('steaks and chops of the very best . . . [and] a dinner of half a grouse with bread sauce, for eighteenpence, including the vegetables that were in season').

But Rimmer also regretfully informs his readers that the rest of the ground floor has been occupied by a curer of bacon (one contemporary photograph shows a painted sign reading 'James Pidgeon's

Bacon Stoves', another 'H. Spencer, Bacon Dryer'), and that the galleries and their rooms have been converted into shoddy flats for the poor.[19] The stables are in ruins; the yard is half filled with rubbish, only frequented by flocks of birds. Furthermore, a collection of old wagons rot in a second yard at the back. Rimmer learns from the proprietor that he hopes to recondition the wagons as quaint advertising vans or exhibit them as historical heritage artefacts, but there seems little likelihood of this happening. The place is clearly in decline, its days numbered. Percy Fitzgerald, visiting the following year, would paint a similar picture, describing not only the bacon drier's shed but also washing lines strung across the yard – something Fitzgerald might have celebrated, given there is a clothes line in Phiz's original illustration – and 'squalid women' hanging about the galleries. Overall, the place is 'black, grimed, rusty and decayed'.[20]

Both these accounts of the White Hart Inn are plainly tinged with melancholy and disappointment. The grim spectacle of the decaying inn seems a long way from the jolly world of Pickwick. Rimmer and Fitzgerald thus find themselves encountering an altogether different sort of 'Dickensian' experience, more redolent of the slums than the cheerful inn of the novel. By 1889, in fact, the roof had been reduced to rafters, the facade was partially demolished and the building was in the process of being replaced by a hops store (Southwark had a long history of both trading in Kentish hops and brewing). The inn swiftly vanished, with only the street name of White Hart Yard commemorating its passing.

***

While the White Hart disappointed the likes of Rimmer and Fitzgerald with its slum-like dereliction, another more prosperous inn on the outskirts of London actively cultivated its association with the great author and welcomed literary tourists: the King's Head in Chigwell. This ancient tavern was reputed to have provided inspiration for the Maypole Inn in *Barnaby Rudge* (Dickens's fictional account of the Gordon Riots of 1780). The King's Head was situated in Epping Forest on the London–Essex borders but it was easily accessible by train and formed part of any thorough late Victorian tour of 'Dickens's London'. Metropolitan tourists were very willing to make the modest pilgrimage from Liverpool Street station because no other public house features quite so prominently in the narrative of Dickens's novels.

The Maypole Inn has such an imposing presence in *Barnaby Rudge* because it carries a good deal of symbolic baggage. Dickens makes clear, from the very beginning of the book, that the inn represents 'Old England'. The pub is named after the traditional emblem of village life and its architecture is archetypical and evocative of a fondly imagined Elizabethan past: oak-panelled rooms, generous bay windows full of diamond-pane latticed glass, heavy oak beams, ivy-coated walls, and a misshapen bulging upper storey projecting over the pavement. There is a similar building in *The Pickwick Papers*, Manor Farm, the Wardles' family seat. The Wardles' Tudor manor house – a model of cosy old-fashioned English domesticity – is situated in 'Dingley Dell', a fictional Kentish village. The name is redolent of the fairy dell, hinting at its magical status, a wonderland where time has somehow stood still. There are echoes of this fairy-land at the Maypole, with its front door guarded by a pair of high-backed wooden benches 'like the twin dragons of some fairy tale'.[21] But whereas Dickens seems to delight in conjuring up a comforting nostalgic vista in *Pickwick*, he gives us a far bleaker vision of Old England in *Barnaby Rudge*. The Maypole tavern differs from Manor Farm in being described as sleepy and even senescent, with its brick-work 'grown yellow and discoloured like an old man's skin'.[22] The pub possesses the 'melancholy aspect of grandeur in decay'.[23] The publican, John Willet, is likewise a sleepy, pompous, conservative fellow who almost resembles part of the furniture. He does not like travel – a great irony, given that he maintains an inn – and prides himself on the building's unchanging antiquity. We learn, later in the novel, that he even opposes stage coaches: he does not take bookings and ignores their approach ('restless, bustling, busy, horn-blowing contrivances, quite beneath the dignity of men, and only suited to giddy girls that did nothing but chatter and go a-shopping').[24] Willett, however, will face a very rude awakening. *Barnaby Rudge* is the story of the Gordon Riots, and Willet's rustic retreat will ultimately be overrun by rioters spilling out from the metropolis, shattering his rather empty-headed equanimity.

This violent overturning of the old inn is significant and symbolic. The implication is that one cannot remain cosy and cosseted in the past. Willet's antithesis in the novel, the sensible locksmith Gabriel Varden, remarks at one point: 'We all change, but that's with Time; Time does his work honestly ... Use him well, and he's a hearty fellow, and scorns to have you at a disadvantage.'[25] Willet clearly has not learned this universal truth and he must suffer for it. But this is not merely a personal matter. The pub and its landlord represent conservatism and nostalgia as a form of national malaise. They constitute part of Dickens's musing on the inevitability of historical progress and the pent-up sociopolitical forces behind the Gordon Riots. The dangerous chaotic energy of the rioters is an inevitable horrific reaction to a backwards-facing, stultifying vision of Old England symbolised by the old inn and its drowsy landlord. There is no doubting the pub's charm, but Dickens makes one thing clear: one cannot live in the past.

Interestingly, like the inns which Dickens describes in *The Pickwick Papers*, the Maypole also has 'veracious legends' attached to it. Hence we learn at the very beginning of the novel that Queen Elizabeth once stayed the night and then had an altercation with a neglectful page while mounting her horse. Dickens hints that locals have their doubts about the truth of the story. But Willet always points to the pub's mounting block (a simple stone on which one could stand to get on a horse) as if it provides conclusive proof of the queen's visit ('the landlord of that ancient hostelry appealed to the mounting block itself as evidence, and triumphantly pointed out that there it stood in the same place to that very day').[26] This piece of stone, for Willet at least, serves as an icon of historical stability and continuity, a tangible link back to olden times. His own sense of self-importance seems to rest, at least in part, upon this solid rock and its supposed connection to royalty (another unchanging institution). The mounting block's solidity is what 'proves' the veracity of Queen Bess's visit, guaranteeing the Maypole's historic pedigree. The reader, however, is given to understand that this is a form of self-delusion. There is no guarantee of continuity and permanence in these comforting stories of the olden days, as the rioters will ultimately demonstrate. It is also no coincidence that the legend about Queen Bess also includes an act of casual aristocratic violence (she 'boxed and cuffed an unlucky page for some neglect of duty'). Dickens hints that the past is no better than the present – it was merely governed by despotic violence, as opposed to the fearful coming violence of the mob. When we cleave to the past, we are only clinging to what is brutal and primitive. In other words, he does not want readers of *Barnaby Rudge* to think he is merely painting picturesque scenes of the olden days.

In fact, throughout his novels, Dickens is often at pains to point out that the reality of 'olden times' was cruel, despotic and violent. The Chuzzlewit family's claim to be an 'old family' in *Martin Chuzzlewit* can only connect them to ancient times of 'violence and vagabondism'.[27] Temple Bar is ironically described as 'headless and forlorn in these degenerate days' in *Little Dorrit* (referring to the heads of traitors once displayed on the gateway).[28] We might also note Dickens's publication of 'The Bemoaned Past' in *All the Year Round*, an article which mocks, amongst other medieval fantasies, pre-Raphaelite visions of medieval chivalry ('Oh! those "feasts in hall and bower"... Alas, they were rather different to what the illustrators of silly ballads and the mock worshippers of the olden times would have us think ... vilely drunken orgies').[29] Mrs Skewton's tone-deaf appreciation of Warwick Castle in *Dombey and Son* – 'their delicious fortresses, and their dear old dungeons, and their delightful places of torture, and their romantic vengeances, and their picturesque assaults and sieges' – clearly falls into the same category, as well as mocking the picturesque tourist.[30] The description of Cloisterham in *Edwin Drood* (a lightly fictionalised Rochester) likewise seems like an admonition about the romanticisation of antiquity. Cloisterham, full of historic remains from every era, is an antiquarian's dream but it is also muddled, drowsy and stagnant – not unlike the Maypole. Dickens knew where he stood on such matters. He famously had a set of fake books made up for his library at Gads Hill which bore the series title 'The Wisdom of our Ancestors', with volumes entitled 'I. Ignorance II. Superstition III. The Block. IV. The Stake. V. The Rack. VI. Dirt. VII. Disease'.[31]

The symbolic importance of the Maypole in the novel may also help to explain why George Cattermole's accompanying illustration bears little resemblance to the tavern described in the text. Cattermole's drawing of a remarkably lofty Tudor baronial mansion strikes a suitably impressive note of decaying grandeur, capturing the spirit rather than the detail. Dickens himself told Cattermole that he adored it, although he may have been constrained by having a relatively close personal friendship with the illustrator (letters were generally comically addressed 'Dear Kittenmoles'). Regardless, Dickens's descriptive powers and Cattermole's evocative illustration would render the Maypole highly appealing to literary tourists. They tended, however, to treat Dickens's depiction of the Maypole as a straightforward paean to 'Old England', an excuse to seek out an archetypal 'Old English inn'. Dickens's implicit warnings about the dangers of conservatism and nostalgia, ironically enough, resulted in the creation of a literary heritage site.

But where in the real world was the original of the timeless ancient tavern described in the novel? Literary pilgrims were assured that the answer lay in the village of Chigwell.

***

The first substantive published account of Dickens tourists seeking out the Maypole appeared in an American journal, *Harper's New Monthly Magazine*, in 1878. This comic piece by James Payn, 'An Adventure in the Forest; or Dickens's Maypole Inn', tells of the author attempting to shepherd some American friends to 'the old Maypole Inn at Chigwell, drawn so beautifully by Cattermole in Dickens's *Barnaby Rudge*'.[32] Payn suggests that Americans are generally better acquainted with English literature than his own countrymen and confesses to be personally clueless as to the location.[33] Nonetheless, together, they hope to find the old inn:

> more antique than even when the great novelist described it, with its huge porch and carved oak parlours, and gracious associations, such as cling around the picturesque abodes of old. And there would be, methought, if not a venison pasty and a blackjack of ale, still some good homely fare . . .[34]

There is a strong hint of self-mockery here, implying that finding the inn is about enjoying an uncomplicated heritage vision of 'Old England' rather than recovering a particular location from the novel (and there is certainly no hint of the Maypole's darker symbolism). Payn's story then proceeds, after detailing the complexities of buying a rail ticket to Epping, to the group hiring a grudging local cart driver and searching for the tavern, armed with a copy of the book. The driver, however, can only find 'the ugliest, commonest, newest, white-washedest railway beer-house' and knows nothing about Dickens or his story whatsoever. Epping Forest itself is equally disappointing

27

('Where are the deer, the trees, the "boundless contiguity of shade"?'). The article ultimately seems to mock the very idea of literary tourism, or at least to suggest that nothing can trump the experience of having read the novel.

Where, then, was the Maypole Inn? Forster, writing Dickens's biography, recorded the author proposing a ride to Chigwell, hinting at the inn's real-world inspiration:

> 'Chigwell, my dear fellow, is the greatest place in the world. Name your day for going. Such a delicious old inn opposite the churchyard – such a lovely ride – such beautiful forest scenery – such an out of the way, rural place – such a sexton! I say again, name your day.' The day was named at once . . . His promise was exceeded by our enjoyment; and his delight in the double recognition, of himself and of Barnaby, by the landlord of the nice old inn, far exceeded any pride he would have taken in what the world thinks the highest sort of honour.[35]

There was only one place in Chigwell which approximated Dickens's description in the novel: the King's Head. This old tavern lacked some key features – there was no porch, for instance – and it bore no resemblance to Cattermole's grandiose illustration. But this hardly mattered. George Cattermole's drawing, as noted above, barely resembled anything described in the actual book. The King's Head, therefore, swiftly established itself as *the* Maypole Inn.

I have not found any reference to this connection before the mid-1870s and, therefore, it seems likely that Forster's anecdote was itself the spur for the tavern becoming a destination for literary tourists.[36] Some would later contend that a different defunct local pub, actually called the Maypole, was the true original; others pointed out that 'the King's Head' in Dickens's day was actually situated next door to the established tourist destination.[37] An erstwhile neighbour of the great author, a certain Miss Powell, claimed that Dickens admitted to having created an amalgam of these different establishments: 'The fact is, I patched it.'[38] Regardless, the real-world King's Head looked the part and was roughly in the right location. The landlord, moreover, encouraged tourists, naming his old function room the 'Barnaby Rudge Room' or the 'Chester Room' (in honour of John Chester, a character in the novel who is accommodated at the Maypole).[39] Literary pilgrims soon began to appear. 'Luke Sharp' (punning pseudonym of one Robert Barr), a Canadian journalist writing for the *Detroit Free Press*, ventured to Chigwell, noting that Americans saw the English inn as a beau ideal of 'real homely comfort'.[40] The antique 'Chester Room' did not disappoint, as it was seemingly identical to the description in the novel.

The pub would also be much publicised by the actor Bransby Williams, who had made a career in music hall as a Dickensian quick-change artist. Williams performed on stage as different Dickens characters in a rapid succession of costumes, wigs, mannerisms and accents. He recounts in his autobiography how he cycled to the King's Head, a year or two after he had begun to find fame for his Dickens characters in the late 1890s. The landlord, one Walter Lewis, was also a fan of the great author. Lewis had once been a noted 'pedestrian' (the Victorian sport of distance speed-walking) and, in the manner of many a Victorian sportsman, had retired to run a public house.[41] Williams and Lewis, according to the actor, soon became firm friends. This friendship resulted in an innovative piece of theatrical Dickensiana in the spring of 1900. Williams decided to organise a charity event at the pub for the Daily Telegraph Soldier's Widows and Orphans Fund, where he would portray 'the very characters in the book [*Barnaby Rudge*] in the very place they were set by the novelist'.[42] This matinee charity fundraiser would take place in the 'Dickens Hall' adjoining the pub (a lumber room Lewis had revamped to hold public meetings). Bransby Williams was not alone, roping in other music hall luminaries, such as Herbert Campbell, Dan Leno and his daughter Georgina (who sang a ballad entitled

'Little Nell'). The afternoon of varied star turns culminated in Williams's characters from *Barnaby Rudge*, who, the programme informed the audience, 'have all lived and moved, and had their being on this spot' (as well as characters from *David Copperfield*, *A Tale of Two Cities* and *Oliver Twist*).[43] Costumes and scenery were provided gratis by a well-known theatrical supplier. To add to the immersive nature of the experience, a handful of old-fashioned stage coaches were chartered to convey select artists and audience members from Liverpool Street and Fenchurch Street stations.[44] Williams also offered a guided topographical tour – including showing off the 'Chester Room' – before the entertainments commenced.[45]

The event would be repeated a couple of times in subsequent years, in aid of the Music Hall Benevolent Fund (although never to such large audiences as upon the first occasion). Walter Lewis would even lend Williams furniture from the 'Chester Room' to accompany a performance based around *Rudge* characters at the Tivoli Music Hall in December 1900 (with Williams performing 'as Sir John Chester, as Maypole Hugh, the gipsy, as John Willet, the landlord of the Maypole Inn, and as Barnaby Rudge'). Williams also persuaded the *Royal Magazine* to put together a promotional photo shoot, featuring him made up as various characters around and about the King's Head and Chigwell.[46] The piece assures readers that the costumes are 'historically correct' and states that 'the spectator [seeing Williams] might easily imagine himself to be a witness of the actual episode', whilst offering brief summaries of various incidents from the book, symbolised by Williams's characters. The article's author adds that Dickens has lately fallen a little out of fashion, being too diffuse and lengthy for the short attention span of the modern generation. Nonetheless, we are informed that the great author – like Williams – will always be remembered for his delineation of *characters*.

The pub itself would continue to trade on its Dickens connection for some years. In 1912 the Mile End brewers, Mann, Crossman and Paulin, were promoting the King's Head as a Dickens-related heritage destination with its own guidebook.[47] The building would be listed by English Heritage in 1954, after plaster was stripped from the upper frontage to reveal its ancient wooden frame. The King's Head, therefore, has survived largely intact to the present day, albeit with some renovation and restoration. In recent years, however, the building has been occupied by a barbecue/kebab restaurant with extravagant selfie-friendly décor ('Don't be too shocked or surprised when you see enormous stuffed wild animals, colossal chandeliers, giant bronze statues and remarkable classic cars scattered all around this extraordinary 20,000 square foot property').[48] The connection with Dickens and his novel is reduced to a footnote on the company's website.

Bransby Williams's contribution to the pub's fame is perhaps the most interesting element of its Dickensian history. Many literary topographers promised readers that their books and articles describing real-world places – and visiting those places – would allow them to visualise Dickens's characters *in situ*, a sort of pleasant hallucination. Williams, working with the *Royal Magazine*, took realism to the next level, supplying not only the textual but also the photographic visual prompt, as if taking the literary tourist by the scruff of the neck and saying, 'Imagine *this!*' He was, after all, only taking the slightly topsy-turvy logic of literary tourism to its natural conclusion. For the literary topographer tacitly implies that the more one is presented with the *reality* of real-world place, the better one can *imagine* it, a very Victorian approach to fictional worlds akin to the historicism of, for example, W.H. Ainsworth's novels (replete with endless descriptions of histor-ical place and costume) or Charles Kean's revivals of Shakespeare (built around accurate costumes, sets and properties). Bransby Williams applied similar principles to the fictional world of *Barnaby Rudge* – the more one could *see* the place, buildings, furniture and so forth, the more one could *imagine* the novel.

Would Dickens himself have seen any merit in this sort of detailed historical recreation *in situ*? He certainly had a fascination with material antiquity and its potential for provoking memory, imagination and storytelling. But, equally, he often mocks those who fetishise historical objects (for example, the mounting block in *Barnaby Rudge*). Indeed, in one of the interpolated travellers' tales in *The Pickwick Papers*, 'The Bagman's Tale', Dickens actively parodies his own investment in the suggestive power of 'great rambling queer old places'. The story begins as the protagonist visits an ancient inn on the Marlborough Downs ('a strange old place, built of a kind of shingle, inlaid, as it were, with cross-beams, with gabled-topped windows projecting completely over the pathway'). He takes a room for the night which contains 'a strange, grim-looking, high backed chair, carved in the most fantastic manner'. The chair – perhaps in a dream, perhaps not – metamorphoses into an old man from the previous century with a rather lewd manner, who at one point gleefully remarks, 'hundreds of fine women have sat in my lap for hours together'. He/it then provides information which helps the hero to woo the tavern's landlady. This perverse comic ghost story, with its ancient setting and objects, seems to mock the whole idea of the past 'coming to life'. The chair, in particular, burlesques the notion that old objects 'speak to us' through the material traces left upon their surfaces, wear and tear, which prompts thoughts of how many other people have handled this thing or stood on this spot. What else would an old chair have to talk about, then, what else would it recollect, apart from bottoms? If nothing else, Dickens's willingness to mock his own literary effects shows remarkable confidence in his own abilities.

***

The King's Head, as the likely 'original' of the Maypole, arguably had a right to style itself as the definitive Dickensian inn. But another coaching inn, situated mere yards from the site of the White Hart in Southwark, one that possessed hardly any connection to Dickens or his work, would become considerably more famous. The George Inn was another ancient inn in the Borough, rebuilt after the Great Fire of Southwark in 1676.[49] The inn suffered from the same decline in prosperity that afflicted the White Hart, driven by the coming of the railway to London Bridge, but (partly) survived by a series of, as it were, fortunate amputations. Thus, in 1849, the building was sold to an expanding Guy's Hospital, which demolished the extensive yard and stables at the rear but had no use for the front part of the property. The surviving buildings were then sold to the Great Northern Railway (GNR) in 1874, who would go on to flatten and redevelop most of what remained. The galleried southern wing, however, was left intact as a public house and survives to this day, with the help of the National Trust, who took on the freehold of the property in 1937.[50]

The old tavern had long been well known to antiquaries but began attracting large numbers of Dickensian tourists from the 1880s. Alfred Rimmer popped into its courtyard in 1883, after visiting the White Hart, and found it 'scrupulously clean and always white-washed', albeit principally serving as a railway booking office. Fitzgerald, likewise, appreciated its 'bright and bustling air of business'. If one was looking for a Pickwickian atmosphere lingering in the Borough, the George was distinctly more pleasant and respectable than its tatty rival, the White Hart. This was the right sort of place, even if not mentioned by the great author (with the exception of a solitary sentence in *Little Dorrit*, where there is talk of a character having gone into 'the George' to write a letter). Joseph Ashby-Sterry would go much further, declaring it 'the most thoroughly Dickensian hostelry from cellar to roof-tree that you could now find in London' and claiming that to explore its interior was 'quite like reading a chapter of Dickens'.[51] His article on Dickensian sites in Southwark, written in 1888, summons up the ghost of Pickwick in a description where everything about the place is 'old fashioned', 'cosy', 'jovial' and 'convivial'. He even implausibly states that Dickens was secretly referring to *this* pub in *The Pickwick Papers*, not the White

Hart. Few have ever taken that claim very seriously, but it signifies how an association with Dickens was rapidly taking hold.

The George Inn, in fact, would become *the* Dickensian inn in the Borough, both by dint of outlasting its rivals and by design. By the 1890s, the George was effectively the last man standing. Mildred Roelker, writing in 1896, noted that the surrounding taverns had become 'so changed in name and appearance as to be unrecognizable'. But Roelker would find one tavern that looked the part:

> There are the stables and coach-houses opening off the yard, clean as wax and exactly answering your expectations. There, too, are the tap-room, the parlour filled with worthies smoking long clay-stemmed pipes around the table, coffee room, and finally the hostess presiding at her bar, the latter fragrant and agreeable, with oranges and lemons, and its rows of inviting looking bottles . . .[52]

This appealing vision of the coaching inn – kept 'clean as wax' – was no accident. The George had already become a carefully curated heritage experience, an 'olde worlde' pub preserved in aspic, much in favour with American tourists, who came to the inn 'for Dickens' sake'.[53] This canny cultivation of old-world charm and a connection with Dickens seems largely to have been the work of Amelia Murray, listed as 'manageress' on the 1881 census, and her daughter Agnes, who succeeded her mother to the role in 1903, managing the pub until her own death, aged eighty-one, in 1934.[54] Dickens enthusiasts were happy to play along. The pub might lack any noteworthy association with the author, but it could be described as part of a historic neighbourhood 'known to Dickens'; and the interior, likewise, was 'such as the Pickwickians and their ancestors revelled in'.[55] Such generalities sufficed for most tourists. The Murrays, however, went even further. Francis Hopkinson Smith, exploring literary shrines in 1912, found Agnes a 'cheery and comforting landlady' who assured him (somewhat implausibly) that Dickens himself had visited the pub regularly (she claimed that she had it on good authority from an acquaintance who knew the pub in the olden days). She even claimed that the author once had his own regular table by the window. She showed Smith the very room where Miss Wardle and Mr Jingle – the eloping couple in *Pickwick* – had stayed the night. The bedroom met his expectations of quaint antiquity and he was delighted that Miss Murray insisted that this was *the actual room* and pretended that these fictional events had literally taken place. This piece of drollery, played totally straight, was not unique. The Bull Inn in Rochester maintained the same pretence with Dickens tourists, showing them the very room where Mr Pickwick had *actually* stayed the night, as did the Great White Horse at Ipswich.[56] There are echoes here of Willet and the mounting block: the heritage object proves the legend. The bedrooms at the George, in fact, were kept deliberately antique, 'showplaces' for Dickens tourists, with four-posters, three-cornered washstands and even wooden steps for mounting into bed.[57]

Agnes Murray, indeed, had something of John Willet about her, keeping modernity at bay. Bertram Matz, an ardent Dickensian, writing in 1918, praised her for maintaining 'all the old traditions that such a place abounds in' and protecting the pub from 'the ravages of the modern builder'.[58] Her own 'cosy sitting-room' was filled with old photographs, pictures and ornaments, 'a spot quite out of the ruck of modern life'.[59] For the curious visitor, she would happily bring out 'the old pewter, post-boy's pistols and trade bills'.[60] In November 1926, Miss Murray let it be known – again, like some latter-day John Willet – that a gas fire had regrettably been installed in the coffee room and that she was 'quite sad about it' (that is, at seeing any change). She reported that her old customers 'don't like change, though the gas stove has not frightened them away'. This 'news' appeared in the *Daily News* but was also widely syndicated in the US local press – an example of the quaint, slightly backwards Britain beloved of the American tourist.[61] Dickens, unsurprisingly, was also sometimes summoned up for advertising purposes:

THE GEORGE INN – DICKENS knew the worth of real comfort and good fare: try them yourself at a DICKENS INN. Good bedrooms, excellent cooking, and English meat. Retired, quaint, old fashioned, yet close to modern business needs.[62]

There were other touches. The balconies were lined with rows of potted geraniums, Dickens's favourite flower.[63] Murray appears to have once claimed that the pub had not been 'consciously preserved' and that she only catered for 'travellers and the merchants of Southwark', as opposed to sightseers – but such talk was highly disingenuous.[64] Regardless, when Agnes Murray passed away in 1934, the *Dickensian* (the magazine of the Dickens Fellowship) remembered her as 'Miss Murray of "The George"', a 'genial proprietress' who had held sway over the tavern for decades.[65] She also received an obituary in the *Guardian*, an unusual honour for a pub landlady, redolent of how much she was a well-known London (Dickensian) character.[66] The next landlord of the pub was Leslie C. Staples, along with his brother Harold, who briefly ran the premises from 1935 to 1937, before the place was given over to the National Trust. Staples's tenancy put an even firmer stamp on the Dickens connection, for he was an active member of the Dickens Fellowship and would become editor of the *Dickensian* in 1944. The Fellowship had actually been approached by the owner, the London and North Eastern Railway, 'with a view to finding someone who would preserve the inn with its Dickensian traditions'.[67] I will talk more about the history of the Fellowship in Chapter 5, in relation to the founding of the Charles Dickens Museum. Suffice to say, established in 1902, the organisation was (and remains) a worldwide association of fans, devoted to the promotion and preservation of Dickens and his works. The Fellowship had long patronised the inn, even though it was slightly irritated by Miss Murray's exaggerated claims (not least when she remarked to Hopkinson Smith that they had verified that Dickens visited the inn and sat at a particular table).[68] Now there was an opportunity to take the reins. Staples undertook a heritage restoration project, stripping paint to reveal the original wood; uncovering a fireplace that had been hidden by a modern kitchen range; and, in a move unusual in any normal hotel, replacing modern beds with old ones. The 'Dickensian traditions' he was preserving, of course, were those invented by Miss Murray. He boasted that the pub attracted 'distinguished Dickensians, Shakespeareans, artists, authors, actors, travellers of every nationality'. Christmas featured an Elizabethan-themed 'Boar's Head Festival'. Staples even persuaded the BBC to celebrate Dickens's birthday and the Pickwick centennial with a brief outside broadcast from the George Inn in February 1936.[69] Actors were hired and the circus owner and coaching enthusiast Bertram Mills provided his coach and horses. The broadcast's script, preserved in the Charles Dickens Museum, takes its audience back in time to the 1830s, including a comic skit involving Sam Weller and a parrot, before returning to the present with the arrival of a wide-eyed American tourist. A surviving internal BBC memo, making arrangements at the inn, records the producer of the segment cheekily asking his manager: 'Possibly in an actuality programme like this real punch should be used?'[70]

Staples also readily continued the pre-existing tradition of the Tabard Players, an amateur theatre group, staging annual Dickens plays outdoors in the yard on the back of a lorry, raised above an audience of groundlings.[71] These annual shows began in 1925 and were put on in February on the Saturday nearest Dickens's birthday. They echoed the sixteenth-century use of inn yards as, in effect, theatres, and a parallel set of Shakespearean performances were given in April. The Dickens performances were usually held in conjunction with a small ceremony at the nearby Charles Dickens Primary School on Lant Street (which had been named after the author in 1894), when flowers were laid before a bust of Dickens in the school hall, officiated by the borough's mayor. Photographs featuring the Tabard Players in costume, in Dickensian settings, were a means of publicising the event. Hence assorted characters from *David Copperfield* haunt the interior of the pub in a publicity shot from 1930, taking a leaf from Bransby Williams's book ('Dickens's characters "waiting for something to turn up" at the George Inn, Southwark, London, an old Dickensian hostelry').[72] Exterior shots of fascinated crowds watching the outdoor performances were also widely publicised each year, adding to the building's visual fame as a Dickensian landmark. The shows continued until 1953, presumably adversely affected by the death of the company's founder and main-stay, Ross Barrington.

In 1943, the pub even acquired its own minor Dickens relic: the record of an 1838 insurance application by the great author to the Sun Life Company to insure his life for £1,000, which still hangs framed upon the wall (the label reads: 'presented to the George Inn by the Sun Life Assurance Society, 23–4–1943'). The application was not successful. Dickens kept a diary which recorded: 'Went to the Sun office to insure my life, where the "Board" seem disposed to think I work too much' (a highly accurate assessment).[73] Dickens had made Forster, and his doctor, a Mr Pickthorn, his referees, but their unrecorded responses – presumably that of Pickthorn, given Forster's well-known unquestioning devotion to his friend – prompted Sun Life to decline.[74] How many visitors have since come to the George specifically to see this obscure item is debatable; but its presence indicates how the tavern's connection with Dickens would become almost self-perpetuating. By the 1940s, a certifiable relic – if not an actual certificate of insurance – had accrued to the establishment.

In truth, however, the relic was not needed. The fact that so many visitors and tourists had already come to the George in search of Dickens during the previous half-century had already validated its connection to the great author. The National Trust has always tended to fudge the issue, with signs making vague statements such as 'Dickens knew the hospitality of this inn' (knew it personally? knew of it?). The Trust's website currently accepts Miss Murray's hearsay account that 'Charles Dickens visited the site when it was a coffee house' and notes that the building is mentioned in *Little Dorrit* (omitting to add that this amounts to a passing reference in a single obscure sentence). But the nature of the connection nowadays hardly matters. The George Inn has become a permanent fixture in touristic 'Dickens's London', demonstrating how custom and practice, and perhaps a little exaggeration and wishful thinking, can create literary shrines. Of course, the fact that the building managed to dodge demolition in the late nineteenth century, unlike the doomed White Hart, underpins everything. That was simply fortuitous, the various changes of ownership allowing for the retention of a profitable public house. But there is no doubt that the Murrays, in turn, successfully established and maintained the pub as a quaint, charming heritage site – a place that appeared old-fashioned rather than run-down, kept 'clean as wax', garlanded with literary associations, commercially viable – the perfect tourist destination.

Not every Dickensian site, however, would be so well preserved. In the next chapter, I consider a place of decay and desolation: the Russell Court burial ground, a memorable location in *Bleak House*, a criminally neglected graveyard in the heart of the metropolis. Such slumland localities would also interest literary tourists in the 1880s and 1890s, but few survived the turn of the twentieth century. Much of the darker side of 'Dickens's London' would be demolished to make way for a more modern city, succumbing to the 'rage for public improvement'.

3

THE BURIAL GROUND

With houses looking on, on every side, save where a reeking little tunnel of a court gives access to the iron gate – with every villainy of life in action close on death, and every poisonous element of death in action close on life – here they lower our dear brother down a foot or two, here sow him in corruption, to be raised in corruption: an avenging ghost at many a sick-bedside, a shameful testimony to future ages how civilization and barbarism walked this boastful island together.[1]

London had a problem with finding sufficient appropriate space for interments, long before Dickens depicted a neglected burial ground in *Bleak House* (published in serial form in 1852/3). During the eighteenth and early nineteenth centuries, burial sites in the most populous quarters were notoriously full to bursting. The bodies of paupers, in particular, received minimal protection from cheap coffins (known as 'shells') and their remains were liable to be exposed by incompetent gravediggers, passing dogs and vermin. One of the biggest obstacles to wholesale reform was that clergymen had a vested

40

interest in receiving payment for burial. Parishes ultimately made their own individual arrangements to address the question – often somewhat lax arrangements – from regular ad hoc exhumations (simply for the purpose of clearing some space) to acquiring overspill grounds.

The Russell Court burial ground, which inspired Dickens's noxious fictional locality, was originally one such auxiliary plot, purchased from the Duke of Bedford in 1723 by St Mary-le-Strand. The site, near the Theatre Royal Drury Lane, was conveniently close to the parish's magnificent newly built church upon the Strand. The place was doubtless hygienic enough when it first opened, but, with the passage of time, inevitably reached full capacity, becoming yet another plague spot. Moreover, by the end of the eighteenth century, the plot was surrounded by closely packed tenements. A certain Mr Groves, living in the vicinity, wrote a letter of complaint in the 1780s about a similar burial ground situated on Drury Lane, not far distant. The corpses of the poor were 'Tumbled into one Common Hole . . . [with] Dogs and Rats and Ducks gnawing at the half putri-fied flesh of the deceased poor who are buryed'.[2] Part of the problem was that the gravedigger used a wooden covering to spare himself the trouble of properly interring corpses of the poor until the grave shaft was completely full of bodies, a common practice.

The long-standing problem of unwholesome burial received fresh publicity during the 1830s, thanks to the ravages of cholera. This new contagious disease, hitherto unknown in Great Britain, was associated with slum districts and fostered a new sanitary awareness in the capital. In 1831, the government's Central Board of Health encouraged local Boards (groups of doctors, lawyers and other local worthies) to investigate and cleanse the capital's worst localities. These Boards went from house to house, arranging for limewashing, fumigation and whatever other steps seemed necessary. Such inter-ference in private property was politically contentious and it was abandoned immediately after the epidemic had passed. Nonetheless, it inspired the first widespread systematic examination of the housing of the poor and encouraged local protest campaigns, drawn from those dwelling amidst the worst public nuisances.[3] Residents in Russell Court and the adjoining streets formed one such local action group. They complained that their burial ground was both noxious and being farmed out to a neighbouring parish – St Clement Danes – for the disposal of cholera victims in shallow graves. This was deeply worrying in a period when the transmission method of cholera and other contagious diseases was essentially unknown, and many feared that so-called miasma (foul gas) from rotting matter carried the seeds of destruction. The windows of several properties literally abutted the ground, which was only thirty-six yards long and twelve wide. One resident's objections, passed on to the truculent church-warden of St Clement's, only produced a threat, 'to bury the very next person who died of cholera under his (complainant's) window'.[4]

Inhabitants of nearby Brydges Street also made a formal complaint to the Board of Health that 'every time the ground is opened, there is thrown up the half-decomposed remains of mortality, from which arise exhalations of the most noxious nature'.[5] By the late 1830s, it was claimed that foul-smelling miasma was 'continually steaming from the dead bodies'.[6] Locals despaired of the smell emanating from coffins broken up by heedless undertakers' men, desperate to make some room, and worried about the prevalence of fever in the district. The ground was visited by members of a government select committee in 1842, who received reports of its gases being fatal to a local gravedigger. A campaigning doctor, George Walker, noted that the ground was so full of corpses that the raised surface was now almost level with the first-floor window of the surrounding houses.[7] A particular *cause célèbre* was the death in a house adjoining the court of a certain Mary Ann Jagell, a poor needlewoman who sewed costumes for West End theatres, whose demise was widely attributed to 'the effluvia issuing from the burial ground'. A coroner's inquest recorded a natural death, but the jury asked that the official record show their 'strongest abhorrence of the condition of the burial-ground'.[8] Russell Court thus became a rather notorious spot, thanks in part to the complaints of nearby residents. The burial ground, however, was already familiar to Charles Dickens – something he later discussed in one of his letters.

***

We know that Russell Court was the real-world inspiration for the ground in *Bleak House* from a letter Dickens wrote to Sarah Hammond Palfrey (1823–1914), an American poet, novelist and philanthropist, whom he met en route to his reading tour of the United States in 1867. She must have quizzed him about its location, for Dickens would later oblige her by despatching a brief note with detailed directions, placing it near the Theatre Royal on Drury Lane. Dickens finishes his letter to Palfrey with the words: 'This important piece of information is in redemption of a pledge I gave you in Halifax Harbour walking the deck of the *Cuba* one bright cold morning in last November.'[9] This sentence is, unfortunately, all we know about this encounter. Did they discuss making tours of 'Dickens's London'? Dickens himself, according to James T. Fields, his American friend and publisher, occasionally explored his own literary territory with friends. He even sometimes playfully pretended that he 'saw' his characters in the street ('"Mr Micawber is coming; let us turn down this alley to get out of his way"').[10] The use of the word 'important' in the letter is clearly ironic, but is the author alluding to a shared joke about the unimportance of such matters, or is he gently chiding his correspondent for her interest? Regardless, this piece of correspondence makes clear that the ground in question was close to the Theatre Royal (although Dickens still does not explicitly name the spot). The directions in the letter, in truth, are slightly imperfect. Proximity to the theatre, however, narrows down the field to only two alternatives: the burial ground on Drury Lane which drew Mr Groves's complaints in the 1780s, and Russell Court.

But only the latter possessed a distinctive tunnel-like entrance – as described in the novel – and so we may safely assume that this was the 'original' which Dickens had in mind. Moreover, Percy Fitzgerald would later remark that Russell Court was well known to the novelist's acquaintances as the original of the ground in Bleak House.[11]

Dickens, however, reveals in the letter that he knew the spot as a youth ('when I was a boy, it was to be got at by a low covered passage under a house, and was guarded by a rusty iron gate'). This is intriguing in itself. The burial ground was hidden behind tenement housing, part of a maze of back alleys. It is tempting, therefore, to see this passing reference in the letter to Sarah Palfrey as early evidence of Dickens's desire to explore every nook and cranny of the great metropolis. One might think it curious that a teenage boy should have sought out such a wretched place, but it is important to understand that there was more to slum districts than disease and death. The street known as Russell Court, which the burial ground adjoined, was a winding passage paved with stone flags, part of a dense collection of narrow streets and alleys, close to the Theatre Royal. An 1848 report in the *Era*, London's principal theatrical paper, describes a meandering journey through this warren in some detail. There is the 'Dutch Sam' gin palace, its name etched into a magnificent gaslight that hangs above the doorway; the 'Shell Fish Warehouse', whose sign is a 'whistling oyster'; 'Mackrill's Noted and Original Baked Irish Fruit Depot', which displays a model steam engine to attract customers for its baked potatoes and ginger beer; and Mr Soloman's 'Masquerade Warehouse', which rented costumes to ball-goers. The article also describes a second-hand shoe shop, a bookstall, a pie shop, a second-hand clothes seller and a pawnbroker's.[12] The Kean's Head Tavern, on the Drury Lane end of the street, was a well-known public house for those who enjoyed Covent Garden night life. By the late 1830s, like many pubs in the district, it boasted a new concert room used for concerts, social clubs and 'harmonic meetings' – the precursor of music hall – as well as 'Judge and Jury shows' (risqué burlesques of judicial proceedings).[13] The Russell Court burial ground was a horror precisely because it stood in the middle of a densely occupied quarter of houses, shops and pubs. Thus it is not hard to imagine Dickens as a curious youth exploring this district (just as he wandered through the nearby slums of Seven Dials and St Giles, described in such detail in *Sketches by Boz*). Nor is it hard to see how Russell Court inspired the anonymous ground in *Bleak House*.

***

Dickens does not stint in describing the horror of the neglected graveyard in the novel. Rats scamper here and there amidst exposed bones. The very air is filled with poisonous miasma from rotting corpses. The burial ground, however, is not merely a grisly spectacle but also serves various purposes, not least as a metaphor for a neglected and mismanaged metropolis. The foul burial ground certainly speaks to a city plagued by what the Victorians dubbed 'the sanitary question' (the challenges posed by a rising tide of dirt and disease, including cholera), but it is also a place where legal, moral and social relations have fallen into dangerous disrepair. Thus we first learn about Russell Court through the pauper's funeral of a mysterious copy clerk dubbed 'Nemo'. His secret history is one of the ties that bind seemingly unconnected characters within the novel. The cruel truth which eventually emerges, involving an illicit liaison and an illegitimate child, hints that the graveyard represents a wider failure of the body politic. Dickens, in other words, implies that two related avenging spirits haunt this wretched locality: physical and moral miasma, the products of the corruption concealed beneath the surface of Victorian society. Both effect a grievous toll upon the living and play their part in the climactic death of Lady Dedlock – Nemo's erstwhile lover – upon the burial ground steps.

This admonitory aspect to Dickens's portrait of the burial ground becomes even more obvious if one looks at the text in close detail.

We first come across the place in chapter 11 of *Bleak House*, where it is described as 'a hemmed-in churchyard, pestiferous and obscene, whence malignant diseases are communicated to the bodies of our dear brothers and sisters who have not departed'. Dickens makes clear that this is a shameful object lesson in official neglect and turpitude. Thus, of the meagre gaslight which burns above the iron gate, he writes: 'It is well that you should call to every passerby, "Look here!"' The failure of authority to deal with the foul nuisance – and the wider ills it represents – are further highlighted by the efforts of Jo, a poor, uneducated crossing sweeper, who instinctively brushes clean the gateway in the absence of anything or anyone better.

The injunction to 'Look here!' carries over into chapter 16, where Dickens's characters themselves come to stare at the wretched locality. Lady Dedlock has begun to suspect that Nemo, the deceased copywriter interred in the burial ground, was her long-lost lover and the father of her illegitimate child. She prevails upon poor Jo to show her the spot where the mysterious man was buried. They follow a path through narrow back streets to eventually gaze at the 'beastly scrap of ground'. There is an accompanying illustration. We see the pair of them, depicted by Phiz, holding on to the bars of the gate, peering inside the ground, with Jo pointing out Nemo's wretched grave. The fact that Jo and Lady Dedlock themselves stop and stare, as illustrated, only strengthens the suggestion that there is something to see – *look here!* Phiz's visual depiction of the scene is also intended to be somewhat tantalising. We cannot see the actual spot to which Jo is pointing; we can only see them looking. To discover the full horror, we must turn to the text, where Jo guilelessly describes heaps of bones and a scuttling rat in the most matter-of-fact fashion. We must move from image to text, simultaneously layering Jo's description with our own moral and sanitary awareness. But there, in the text, we again come across an injunction to look: '"Look at the rat!" cries Jo, excited. "Hi! Look! There he goes! Ho! Into the ground!"' Jo's boyish glee at the sight of the rat is an indictment not only of the neglected ground but also of his own neglected (sanitary) education and how little this insanitary milieu perturbs him. But these repeated injunctions to *look*, of course, are also very much about the reader not looking away but paying attention to the urban horrors so easily ignored by the respectable middle class.

Dickens revisits the ground one last time in chapter 59. Lady Dedlock has fled her privileged existence, fearing exposure of her past. She is pursued by her illegitimate daughter, Esther, and the detective, Inspector Bucket, who hope to assure her that she is not in danger. Esther narrates the chapter, with the chase concluding at the burial ground. The place is now seen – looked at once again – through her fresh eyes ('heaps of dishonoured graves and stones, hemmed in by filthy houses with a few dull lights in their windows and on whose walls a thick humidity broke out like a disease'). Lady Dedlock has, indeed, come to this spot. She lies, disguised in the clothes of a poor woman, slumped at the gate – dead. There is an accompanying illustration of the burial ground gate, depicting this anonymous figure lying prostrated upon its steps (whose identity we only learn at the end of the chapter). The illustration is one of Phiz's 'dark plates', an innovative engraving method which used a machine to create a base layer of fine parallel lines, enabling him to produce a grim, shadowy mezzotint-like effect – a gloomy style suited to the scene and location. Again, the illustration is designed to emphasise Dickens's moral message. But the two illustrations and repeated injunctions to *look here!* also perform another function: framing the graveyard, inadvertently perhaps, as a sort of touristic spectacle. For just as Dickens's detailed portrayal of the Maypole Inn in *Barnaby Rudge*, alongside Cattermole's illustration, ultimately solicited the attention of literary tourists, so did these repeated evocative portraits of the blighted burial ground. Russell Court was thus fated to become a literary shrine.

***

It is sometimes said that *Bleak House* itself actually helped to bring about much-hoped-for reform in metropolitan interment. Certainly, Dickens was intent on publicising the problem. *Bleak House* was originally published as a serial between March 1852 and September 1853, a period when sanitary matters were being widely discussed and debated in the metropolis. George Walker, who lived close to Russell Court on Drury Lane, had already drawn particular attention to the problem of 'intramural interment' (that is, shoddy burials within the bounds of the city) in numerous pamphlets and public meetings. Burials were also one of the pressing topics which occupied civil servant Edwin Chadwick, who had spent most of the 1840s authoring government reports agitating for improved sanitation, sewerage and water supply. Chadwick had even recently tried (and failed) to turn burial into a centralised, government-run monopoly. Dickens was certainly keenly aware of these topical social questions. Indeed, it has been suggested that Little Nell's famous death (peacefully, in an idyllic rural church) was in dialogue with contemporary debate about burial reform and garden cemeteries.[14] On 10 May 1851, Dickens even gave a brief speech to a public dinner organised by the Metropolitan Sanitary Association, remarking:

> No man can estimate the amount of mischief grown in dirt, that no man can say the evil stops here or stops there, either in its moral or physical effects, or can deny that it begins in the cradle and is not at rest in the miserable grave.[15]

The burial ground in *Bleak House*, therefore, was Dickens's contribution to a particular sanitary campaign, a fictionalised example of the 'miserable grave' of the slums, an attempt to raise the profile of neglected and mismanaged ancient graveyards. There were obvious precedents. *Oliver Twist* had aimed a broadside at the Union Workhouse (the prison-like workhouses which had been introduced by none other than Edwin Chadwick in the early 1830s). *Nicholas*

Nickleby had highlighted child cruelty in Yorkshire boarding schools with its portrayal of the brutal and ignorant schoolmaster Wackford Squeers. *Bleak House*, amongst other things, would shine a particular light upon the horrors of slumland burial.

In fact, it is questionable whether the novel's contents materially affected the sanitary changes that came about in the 1850s. It is true that London's ancient, overcrowded burial grounds were finally closed by fiat of the Home Secretary, Lord Palmerston, in 1853. The burial ground in Russell Court, however, had already been closed in 1849 thanks to the efforts of local campaigners who had taken the matter to the Bishop of London. He had eventually issued a rather mealy-mouthed proclamation that the ground was 'inconveniently full' and that its closure was required to prevent 'serious mischief'.[16] Dickens, of course, was taking aim at *all* such grounds; that is one reason the place is left anonymous in the novel. Nonetheless, it is striking that the particular ground upon which he drew for inspiration was already closed. Moreover, reforming legislation – an act empowering the Treasury to loan money to parishes to build clean new cemeteries on the outskirts of the metropolis – initially came into force on 1 July 1852. The burial ground in *Bleak House* had only just featured in the book's fourth part, published the previous month (comprising chapters 11–13). Admittedly, the further amending legislation which enabled the Home Secretary to close the foulest graveyards was only passed in the following year, but there is little to suggest Dickens's supportive intervention was crucial – this sanitary work was already in train. The novel, however, did prompt late Victorian literary tourists to seek out Russell Court for themselves, to see some hint of the horrors he had described, to *look here!*

***

One difficulty, of course, for aspiring literary tourists in the 1870s and 1880s was finding the anonymous ground. Dickens's letter to Sarah Palfrey was then unknown to the general public. For the casual

reader, who had no access to Dickens's acquaintances or his correspondence, the location of the burial ground was initially something
of a mystery. There were a good number of such graveyards, closed in
the 1850s, which could have served as the original of that in *Bleak
House* (including ones nearer to the principal action of the book
in Chancery Lane and Lincoln's Inn). They had generally been
tarmacked over or laid out as gardens, with their crumbling grave-
stones relocated to line up along adjoining walls. Some sites were
in better condition than others, serving as public parks; others had
been left neglected, used for fly-tipping. Fortunately, the tunnel-like
entrance associated with Russell Court was distinctive. Pemberton
could not find the place in the first guidebook devoted to the great
author (*Dickens's London*, published 1876), but the American literary
editor of the *New York Tribune*, John Hassard, who wrote articles for
the paper describing his own Dickensian literary tour, identified the
spot in 1879.[17] Hassard's articles were widely serialised in various US
papers and then turned into a book in 1881, entitled *A Pickwickian
Pilgrimage*. He had been correctly informed that the graveyard
was near Drury Lane and successfully located Russell Court in the
network of narrow passages by the theatre. The district had changed
little since the *Era*'s survey from the 1840s. Hassard describes rag
and waste-paper shops, 'dreadful little greengrocers stalls' and a
pawnbroker's rubbing shoulders with a theatrical costumer's, dealers
in dancing shoes, stage props, stage armour and playbooks. Hassard
finds the tunnel, a 'stone paved passage about four feet wide, through
the ground floor of a tenement'. The graveyard itself, closed to burials
for thirty years, has become something of a dumping ground,
containing 'various rubbish, a woman's boot, a broken coal-scuttle,
the foot of a tin candlestick, fragments of paper, sticks, bones, straw
– unmentionable abominations'. He finally leaves the obscure locality,
satisfied with his discovery, surrounded by a 'dark and smoke-laden,
fog-dripped moisture' (thus conjuring up a suitably Dickensian
atmosphere for his readers).

Hassard's tour of 'Dickens's London' undoubtedly inspired other literary topographers, particularly those writing for an American audience. One such was Robert Barr, a Canadian journalist in London who wrote for the *Detroit Free Press* under the pseudonym 'Luke Sharp' ('look sharp!'). Barr would pen a surprisingly vivid literary account of discovering Russell Court, written a couple of years later, entitled 'A Movin' On' (referring to Jo's refrain in the book that he is always 'a-moving on' at the request of respectable society). The article begins with Barr noticing two watercolours showing scenes from *Bleak House* in a picture framer's window on nearby Wych Street. One is 'The Ghost's Walk', a terrace at the Dedlocks' country estate with an eerie history, as pictured in the novel. The other shows Jo and Lady Dedlock at the infamous burial ground, also as in the original illustration. The encounter with the paintings ultimately prompts him to explore the real-life Drury Lane, visit a shop which he thinks might be the 'original' Old Curiosity Shop, and finally visit Russell Court.

On one level, Barr simply describes how a typical literary tourist may discover quirky destinations by making diligent enquiries of the local population. He sketches the array of Dickensian scenes one may encounter, from frowsy shops to gin palaces and slums, and suitably Dickensian characters (for example the old shopkeeper on Drury Lane, and a 'ragged urchin' he meets in Russell Court, whom he playfully dubs 'Jo'). But Barr's account of this expedition is also highly self-referential. He repeatedly alludes to the fact that writing literary topography creates a form of spectacle for commercial consumption. The article thus begins with the two pictures in the picture framer's window. Barr makes clear that these are poor quality daubs, cheap commercial images; one is even stained with ink. These poor reproductions anticipate/critique his own efforts in the remainder of the article – his own ink-stained imagery. For, after all, what is literary tourism but an attempt to produce one's own inadequate picturesque representation of Dickens's fictional world? The subject matter of the pictures also has its own significance. For the practice of literary tourism might be described as a 'ghost's walk' (ghosts being a common metaphor in literary tourism for imagining dead authors and their characters *in situ*) and both the ghost and the graveyard hint at what has been dubbed the 'necromantic' origins of the literary pilgrimage (a sort of spiritual communion with the dead author). The 'ragged urchin' whom Barr dubs 'Jo' also informs him that he knows the grave-yard is of some interest, because a 'theater man he came and drawed a picture of the court and the gate', presumably as part of preparing a stage adaptation of Dickens's story. Barr's version of the burial ground thus seems to be constantly reproduced and re-experienced as part of some commercial display or another – sold and resold to the public by the 'picture-framer', the 'theater man' and Barr himself. Barr further emphasises the commercial character of his own work by offering to pay the 'ragged urchin' to pretend to be Jo, to complete a more immersive imagined scene ('I'll call you Jo for a penny'). The boy, meanwhile, acts like some showman of the place, a rather peculiar sort of tour guide (just as the original Jo guides Lady Dedlock in the novel). There is a strong hint of self-mockery in all this, or perhaps an author who thinks himself a little too clever to be writing about literary pilgrimage for the American tourist market.

The mention of a 'theater man', however, is noteworthy for another reason. One additional factor that turned Russell Court into a modest tourist attraction – including publicly identifying it as the original of the ground in *Bleak House* – was its famous representation on stage.

***

The first two dramatised versions of *Bleak House* appeared in East End theatres in the summer of 1853, before the serialisation of the novel was even complete. This was not unusual. Authors in this period had no intellectual property rights when it came to stage adaptations and, consequently, playwrights and theatre managers often attempted to exploit a book's current popularity, taking a much looser attitude to 'adaptation' than we generally would today (which included coming up with their own endings for the story). Both these versions, however, were staged shortly after the tragic death of Jo appeared in the serialisation, and that may well be important. Dramatists seem to have decided that, of all the elements in Dickens's complex plot, the poignant life and death of the neglected crossing sweeper would be the most pleasing to the theatre-going public.[18] Dickens, indeed, might well have agreed with them. Forster, in his biography, notes that the author had originally intended to make Jo more prominent in the story. A few more adaptations followed while the book was still fresh in the mind of the public. The part of Jo was often played by female actors, suited to a small, slender figure. A certain Marion Lacey played the part in *The Bleak House; or The Wandering Spirit of the Ghost's Walk* at the City of London Theatre in 1853, and Fanny Beaumont had the part in *Bleak House, or The Ghost's Walk* at the Strand Theatre in 1854. Interest in adaptations of the novel then diminished rapidly and none appeared in London in the 1860s. But there would be a striking revival of enthusiasm in the 1870s, largely thanks to the work of an actress known as Jennie Lee (*c.* 1849–1930) and a play written by her husband, John P. Burnett, simply entitled *Jo*.[19]

Lee was the daughter of Edwin George Lee, a Marylebone-based watercolourist and engraver. She took to the stage after her father's death in 1869. After a brief spell in London, she tried her luck in America, leaving behind her first husband and discovering a second in Burnett.[20] She took on the role of Jo in a version of *Bleak House* playing at the California Theatre in San Francisco, and her performance inspired Burnett to write his own version of the story that gave prominence to the crossing sweeper, providing a star vehicle for his wife.[21] They returned to Britain in 1875 (Burnett was a Scot by birth; Lee was half English, half Irish) and took the play to Liverpool and then London. The play was reportedly rejected by almost every London theatre manager, until it was finally given a short run at the

Globe Theatre on Newcastle Street (itself only a five-minute walk from the Russell Street burial ground). *Jo*, as it turned out, was the very definition of an overnight sensation. The plot was essentially a heavily reduced version of *Bleak House*, beginning at the Coroner's Inquest for Nemo and ending at Jo's death. The praise, however, was almost entirely for Lee's riveting performance as the crossing sweeper:

> a realism and a pathos difficult to surpass. A more striking revelation of talent has seldom been made. In get-up and in acting the character was thoroughly realised; and the hoarse voice, the slouching, dejected gait, and the movement as of some hunted animal, were admirably exhibited.[22]

The critics showered Jennie Lee with superlatives, and the greatest compliment was the half-dozen remarkably similar adaptations that rapidly appeared in London and the provinces (with very similar titles such as *Poor Jo*; *Jo, or, The Bleak House*; *Poor Little Jo*; and so forth), not to mention numerous music hall turns.[23] There was even a burlesque (comic spoof) entitled *Jo v Jo* which opened in October of the same year. This featured a chorus of ragamuffins and flower girls and played with the idea of a young actress taking on the role of a crossing sweeper on stage and proving to be more 'realistic' than the elderly real-life sweeper originally hired for the role (a feat she achieves by quoting touching passages from Dickens). Reviews make clear that the central performance was a direct parody of Jennie Lee's dialogue and mannerisms – again, something of a testimony to her success.

The general praise for the realism of Lee's performance was also reflected in her own publicity. Lee often told the story that, upon her first appearance in London, she had bought an 'authentic' second-hand broom for sixpence from a Charing Cross crossing sweeper. *Jo v Jo* naturally parodied this to the hilt, with the theatre manager within the spoof boasting of 'real rags, real brooms, and real mud'.[24]

The realism of the second-hand broom calls to mind Dickens's 'Meditations in Monmouth Street' in *Sketches by Boz*, where second-hand clothes reveal the life histories of their previous owners before magically coming to life before the author's very eyes. Dickens's sketch of Monmouth Street is a complex, multilayered piece of work, much commented upon by literary scholars. But, amongst other things, I would argue that it alludes to his contemporaries who produced books and plays which (over-)emphasised accurate historical costumery. Correct historical costume was something of an obsession for the historical novelists who followed Walter Scott in the 1830s and their literary critics; the same was true in the theatre.[25] Accurate detail in period clothing was considered a crucial prompt to imagination. 'Meditations in Monmouth Street' playfully takes this one step further: why should regular old clothing from the recent past not be equally or even more evocative, producing detailed personal histories of the owners? This was the power of Lee's broom, to silently invoke the real-world miserable history of its owner and thereby lay claim to a certain sort of realism, embodied in Lee's performance. Lee would go on to claim, somewhat implausibly, to have retained the same broom for all her stage performances, further emphasising its totemic authenticity. The public, in any case, were suitably impressed by Lee's pathetic rendering of the crossing sweeper. Dr Barnardo, the philanthropist famous for his founding of children's homes, considered the play 'wonderfully true to life'.[26]

What is interesting, however, is that the play also laid claim to *topographical* realism. The scene with Jo and Lady Dedlock at the graveyard featured as the climactic end of the first act. The 1876 programme boasted 'new scenery painted expressly for this production by Mr W. BRUCE SMITH realising the exact spots mentioned by CHARLES DICKENS in the novel of "Bleak House" and the original illustrations by Phiz'.[27] Moreover, the programme specifically described the location as 'Potter's Burial Ground, Russell-court, Drury-lane'. A 'potter's field' was a pauper's burial ground (a phrase with a biblical origin).[28] The name 'Potter's Burial Ground' was first used in the 1854 production at the Strand Theatre, and it is plausible that Burnett used a copy of the old play as source material.[29] But, more importantly, the 1876 production would explicitly draw attention to the real-world locality of Russell Court. This suggests that Bruce Smith was the 'theater man' who had come and 'drawed a picture', according to Barr's (real or invented) young urchin. Certainly none of the other contemporary productions made a virtue of topographical accuracy in their publicity material. A realistic version of the mysterious gateway was, therefore, placed before the public upon the stage, and it is safe to assume that this much-trumpeted reproduction prompted some to seek out the 'original' neglected ground. For the gate, like the broom, was a key part of Jo's iconography as a stage character. Lee's publicity photographs frequently show her mournful character seated next to the (theatrical prop) gate. There was even sheet music to accompany the smash hit at the Globe Theatre, a 'Galop for the Piano Forte upon Airs from the Celebrated Drama', whose cover features a drawing of Lee posing with her broom at the burial ground's gateway.[30]

***

Jennie Lee would go on to tour with the play for the next two decades, visiting not only the British provinces but also America, South Africa, India and Australia, to massive popular acclaim. The burial ground, meanwhile, would undergo a modest transformation, not many years after Lee's theatrical adaptation brought it wider notoriety. In 1886 the de facto rubbish dump in Russell Court ('the receptacle for dead cats and every other description of filth and refuse from the poverty-stricken houses') was cleared and topped with concrete and asphalt.[31] The ground had been purchased by the Metropolitan Public Gardens Association, which specialised in converting such places into modest children's playgrounds. Swings and slides were erected and an opening ceremony was planned. Russell Court was bedecked with flowers and bunting, and an invitation card was issued which referred to the ground being 'identical' with 'Tom-All-Alone's in Bleak House' (thus confusing the slum of that name in the novel with the graveyard). The festivities were superintended by Lady George Hamilton and Lord Dorchester, who opined that the Society's mission reflected 'the wholesome lesson inculcated by the writings of Charles Dickens of sympathy and interest in our poorer brethren'.[32] A drinking fountain dedicated to Dickens would also subsequently appear; but it was still possible, according to visitors, to imagine the ground, surrounded by houses, in its old incarnation. As one reporter mused, 'this little playground will inevitably become a memorial of Dickens'.[33] Indeed, it does not seem to have prospered as a playground. According to one report a few years later: 'The trees are faded, the rough children have broken the drinking fountain, the swings are out of order.'[34]

Purchase by the London County Council in 1893 meant that some repairs were made, but Russell Court was still 'dreary ... desolate ... funereal', as if stubbornly retaining its Dickensian squalor.[35] It acquired something of a new lease of life as a tourist attraction in 1894, when demolition work on nearby Catherine Street better exposed it to public view, allegedly attracting thousands of sightseers, including numerous American tourists.[36] The number sounds exaggerated – we have no way of knowing for certain – but the threat of imminent destruction was always a driver of tourism at heritage sites. That threat became real a couple of years later, when the Duke of Bedford proposed levelling the district for an extension of Tavistock Street. Complex negotiations followed with the London County Council, the parish of St Mary-le-Strand and the Duke of Bedford's management company, with the result that the ground was cleared of human remains. They were reinterred in the Brookwood Necropolis Cemetery in Surrey, a more successful giant overspill cemetery, opened in 1854, reached by the famous Necropolis Railway from Waterloo Station. By 1899, Russell Court and its surrounding streets had completely vanished. The ground was replaced by 'York Street' (the original name for the street extension, which was later renamed to become part of Tavistock Street in 1937) and Siddons Buildings, an early London County Council mansion block. There was, however, a last hurrah for this peculiar tourist destination. The iron gate to the burial ground was saved from destruction at the urging of John Hollingshead, the theatrical impresario who had also been one of the many promising young journalists whom Dickens had encouraged to contribute to his magazines *Household Words* and *All the Year Round*.[37] The gate was initially entrusted to the Rector of St Mary-le-Strand, who allowed it to be exhibited in the foyer of the Prince of Wales Theatre in 1899 as part of a benefit night for Jennie Lee, honouring her two decades of Dickensian theatricals.

Jennie Lee's career, in fact, was somewhat on the wane by this point – hence the benefit night. She complained that the success of *Jo* had 'killed her professionally'.[38] Theatre managers demanded novelty but refused to accept her in any other role. Since the mid-1890s, she had been touring with a cut-down version of the play that could fit into the bill of small suburban theatres and music halls. Thus, for example, she appeared at the Royal Holborn in February 1897 within a mixed variety bill, including Fred Zola, an 'eccentric comedian', known for his burlesque of a (female) ballet dancer and his comic song 'Bunki-doo'.[39] Part of the problem for Lee was that theatrical taste had changed. Her original portrayal of Jo was highly praised for its realism, in costume, speech and manner, but her performance now appeared rather dated. George Bernard Shaw, writing in the *Saturday Review*, decried the play itself as 'third-rate'. He gave Lee the grudging respect reserved for an old trouper but did not spare one of her co-stars:

Lady Dedlock . . . is quite worth seeing, especially on her visit to the graveyard where she combines a now ludicrously old fashioned sort of distressed heroine with a good deal of the Ghost in Hamlet, old style. How Miss Alma Stanley has contrived to recover the trick of a vanished stage mode so cleverly, and to keep her countenance meanwhile, I know not. But she does it with wonderful success, and I hope she will never do it again.[40]

There are echoes here of Mr Wopsle's amateur theatricals in *Great Expectations*, whose Hamlet 'died by inches from the ankles upward'.[41] A theatrical anecdote records that Lee herself was once asked by a limelight operator, in a hushed whisper, to 'Die quick, Miss Lee! Die quick!' on account of the block of lime being exhausted. From the beginning, some had criticised her performance as somewhat mannered, particularly the repetition of Jo's catchphrases ('the words "he was werry good to me, he was" repeated *ad nauseum* make one almost regret that the person in question was so very charitable').[42] By the 1890s, according to Shaw, the long-running play had itself become a sort of theatrical heritage experience, a glimpse into a lost dramatic world. Like the burial ground, the play itself had to yield to modernity.[43]

The Russell Court graveyard, however, was only one of a number of sites in 'Dickens's London' which would be demolished in the name of urban improvement at the turn of the twentieth century. The London County Council was particularly active in this regard, even though it simultaneously styled itself as preserver of the capital's history and heritage – a paradox I discuss in the next chapter.

4

KINGSGATE STREET TO
DICKENS AVENUE

L ouisa May Alcott, who would become famous as the author of
Little Women, toured Europe in 1865–6. She began the journey
as a nurse-companion to the daughter of an acquaintance, a 'nervous
invalid'. She was thrilled by her first visit to London and made a
point of returning to the capital towards the end of her tour, when
she had extricated herself from the role of nurse and helpmate. She
later remarked, 'I enjoyed myself there more than anywhere else
and felt at home'.[1] London, amongst other things, was somewhere
she could indulge her passion for literary tourism. Indeed, her diary
entry for the month of June 1866 provides us with the first recorded
instance of a tourist systematically seeking out sites in 'Dickens's
London'.[2]

This is not entirely surprising, since Alcott was a lifelong fan of
Dickens's work. Alcott and her sisters – just like her characters in
Little Women – once styled themselves as a 'Pickwick Club' in which
they each took the name of a principal (male) character.[3] Friends
recalled that she could recite large chunks of Dickens's books from
memory and was prone to dropping his characters and their catch-

phrases into conversation ('I remember that her assent always took the form of "Barkis is willin"').[4] Alcott twice saw Dickens himself give public readings, once in London and once on his second American tour. She enjoyed the performance but was displeased with the ageing author's dandyism ('Why will he wear two rivers of watch guards, meandering over his vest, a diamond ring on each hand, curl his gray hair and come upon the stage with a youthful skip? Oh, why?').[5] She did not, however, have any reservations about 'Dickens's London' and rejoiced in seeing the places the author had described in his novels. Thus, mixed up with visits to the Tower of London, St Paul's and Windsor Castle, Alcott's diary records pilgrimages to the Saracen's Head (a coaching inn featured in *Nicholas Nickleby*), Furnival's Inn (where Dickens had lodged at the start of his writing career) and 'Sairey's Gamp's'. The latter was Kingsgate Street, a modest little road in the heart of the capital, home to the bibulous nurse and midwife Sarah Gamp, a comic character from *Martin Chuzzlewit*.

Alcott lightly fictionalised her Dickens tour experience in an article entitled 'A Dickens Day', which appeared in print the following year. The piece describes fantasies of glimpsing Dickens's characters upon the streets and in the windows of buildings, and a visit to the slum of St Giles, accompanied by a policeman for safety.[6] The prime spot which her narrator wishes to see, however, above all others, is Kingsgate Street. She is not disappointed:

> Kingsgate Street, so like the description I am sure Dickens must have been there and taken notes. They knew the house in a moment: there were two dingy windows over the bird-shop; the checked curtains were drawn, but of course the bottomless band-boxes, the wooden pippins, green umbrella and a portrait of Mrs Harris were all behind them. It seemed so real that they quite expected to see a red, snuffy old face appear, and to hear a drowsy voice exclaim 'Drat that bell: I'm a coming.'[7]

Martin Chuzzlewit was a favourite of Alcott's and she reportedly delighted in giving impressions of the talkative Mrs Gamp to friends and family. She even dramatised Dickens's dialogue between Mrs Gamp and her confederate Betsy Prig as a two-hander for amateur theatricals, along with other Dickens scenes.[8] Naturally, therefore, Kingsgate Street was a desirable destination. Once again, we can also see the suggestive power of illustration when it comes to literary tourism, since the original novel contains a memorable drawing of Mrs Gamp's lodgings above a barbershop, as seen from the street, drawn by Phiz.[9]

Alcott's tour guide for the day – dubbed 'The Professor' in her fictional account – was a fellow American, Moses Coit Tyler, who was in London engaged in the unlikely task of promoting a music-based physical education system, which he credited with restoring his own health after a nervous breakdown. Tyler would become a highly respected academic, Cornell's first chair of American history. Nonetheless, in September 1866, he was obliged to serve as Louisa May Alcott's guide and chaperone. He wrote to his wife that he had been 'piloting Miss Alcott of Concord . . . a jolly Yankee girl, full of the old Nick and thoroughly posted on English literature'.[10] His letter outlines how, as a joke, he even asked after 'Mrs Gamp' in the real-world shop above which the fictional character was supposed to have had her apartments. Alcott's published account contains the same story. The proprietors earnestly took Tyler to be searching for a real-life nurse who lived round the corner, prompting a good deal of hilarity ('Miss Alcott had to continually turn her back to hide her laughing, and finally ran away to the end of the street to let off'). Alcott wrote to Tyler after 'A Dickens Day' was published, thanking him for putting up with 'an irrepressible spinster on the rampage'.[11] She reminded Tyler of some parts to their day she had omitted from the published story ('the professor tapping away at Milton's chimney for a bit of the original brick, and eating ginger-bread out of a paper bag in Smithfield') before swiftly reassuring him – a married man – that these fond memories belonged to 'a chronic spinster and [she] knew that the professor was already appropriated, so she could enjoy London with a free mind'. Alcott's letter finishes with an open invitation to visit her in Boston, at her own 'Gamp's Garret', mocking herself as akin to the gossipy old midwife – a fellow rampaging spinster – and perhaps obliquely alluding to her spell as nurse to the nervous invalid.[12]

Kingsgate Street would go on to become a destination for literary tourists, partly on the strength of Alcott's account. John Hassard also gives a detailed description of the street, which he found 'a short and shabby passage'.[13] There is a rag and bone dealer and a barber's (as in the novel) and he notes the presence of 'two young women, somewhat the worse for drink'. The inhabitants watch him closely and he feels a little out of place in what is plainly a poor neighbourhood. Nonetheless, the residents would become used to transatlantic visitors. By the end of the century, American gentlemen were said to be fond of visiting the barber's, which could be taken as the original of Poll Sweedlepipe's in the novel, and having a commemorative 'Dickens shave'.[14] Tourists were also drawn to the street because Mrs Gamp, the frequently drunken, incompetent, but nonetheless amusing nurse/midwife, was one of Dickens's best-known comic creations. She was famously always accompanied by her aged umbrella ('a species of gig umbrella; the latter article in colour like a faded leaf, except where a circular patch of a lively blue had been dexterously let in at the top'). 'Gamp', indeed, became popular slang for umbrella; and Dickens himself had included a performance entitled 'Mrs Gamp' in his public readings, with the action beginning on Kingsgate Street ('the lady lodged at a bird-fancier's, next door but one to the celebrated mutton-pie shop, and directly opposite to the original cat's-meat warehouse').[15] The little street in Holborn, however, was never *that* well known – at least, not until the late 1890s, when it came under threat.

At the turn of the twentieth century, London County Council finally began work on long-mooted street improvements which would cut a swathe through central London from Holborn to the Strand. The aim was to create a broad avenue, running north–south, linking the district east of Oxford Street and the Strand/Thames Embankment – which became the modern Kingsway and Aldwych. Kingsgate Street, unfortunately, was part of the area marked for demolition. Threatened 'historic' sites were of some interest to the late Victorian public and so headlines such as '"Sairy Gamp's" Home Goes' and 'Vanishing London: Sairey Gamp's House' began to appear in the press.[16] Editorials mused on the various Dickens-related locations which had been recently demolished (such as Russell Court) or were about to vanish under the new road scheme, including the home of Mrs Gamp. Few actually argued that Kingsgate Street should be preserved, but many waxed lyrical about what was being lost. Indeed, newspaper articles with titles such as 'Vanishing Dickens's London' or the more alliterative 'Disappearing Dickensland' were something of a staple for jobbing late Victorian journalists whenever they had a couple of column inches to fill. Most of these pieces struck a wistful but ultimately pragmatic note, such as an article in the *Pall Mall Gazette* that concluded, 'we have to sacrifice a good deal in sentimental associations for the benefits of national prosperity; but we must have more room to get about'.[17] Nonetheless, the modernising metropolis seemed to be in perpetual mourning for a lost Dickensian past – at least, going by what one read in the newspapers.

Indeed, this trope became so commonplace in the late 1890s that one publisher of Dickens's collected works even made use of it in their advertising. The headline of the advertisement in question (for the *Daily News*'s 'Memorial Edition of Charles Dickens Works') reads: 'DICKENS'S LONDON IS VANISHING'. The phrase is actually shown in quotation marks – as if quoting a press article – and the main body of the advert continues: 'Hardly a week passes in which the newspapers do not record the contemplated or actual demolition of some house, court, alley or even street, sacred to the students of the London portrayed by Dickens.' The text goes on to mournfully recapitulate various parts of London which have been 'remodelled almost out of recognition', while a vertical sidebar simultaneously proclaims: GOING! GOING!! GONE!!![18] The advertisement ultimately suggests that the only lasting monument to the author is his fiction – and so why not purchase Dickens's collected works? The advert amounts to a playful inversion of the traditional logic of literary tourism, where visiting the place normally follows from reading the book – as if to say, 'Can't visit the place? Well, you may as well read the books!'

Kingsgate Street would finally succumb to the London County Council's house-breakers in the closing weeks of 1902. But this chapter is less concerned with the demolition of Kingsgate Street itself than it is with the notion of a 'vanishing' or 'disappearing' metropolis to which it was closely linked in the press. This was a concept so familiar to late Victorian readers that it could be jauntily referenced in an advertisement. It reflected the rise of a preserva-tionist heritage sensibility, a sense that London was a metropolis brimming with neglected old buildings, threatened by redevelop-ment, worthy of documentation and/or preservation – a cultural phenomenon inextricably intertwined with the creation of Dickens's literary territory.

This nascent heritage vision of the metropolis often described its subject matter – the buildings to be documented and preserved – as 'Old London'. The term was something of a catch-all, a favourite of amateur historians, journalists and travel writers. One might compare 'Old London' to 'the Middle Ages', a similarly evocative but vaguely defined concept in the popular imagination, a period with obscure chronological boundaries and diverse romantic associations. 'Old London', indeed, could encompass buildings with specific historical links, from the Roman to the early Victorian periods; buildings possessed of a more general picturesque antiquity, representative of their type or era; and even places associated with fiction, including the works of Dickens. The suggestion was that 'Old London' lurked beneath the surface of the metropolis, in need of attention; it was a valuable, 'vanishing' or 'disappearing' cultural inheritance perennially teetering on the brink of destruction. 'Dickens's London' fitted well into this model of London's past, as yet another slice of neglected urban heritage.

The urge to document 'Old London' was, at least in part, a response to the improvement works of the Metropolitan Board of Works and its successor, the LCC, including the building of Kingsway and Aldwych. The charting of 'Old London', by both amateur antiquarians and official bodies, offered some slight compensation for the onslaught of modernity, as if to say, 'the streets you knew may be in ruins, but *something* historic and permanent remains' (even if only recorded or archived). Similar compensatory heritage-making happened elsewhere. Scholars have noted, for example, how the building of the Viennese *Ringstrasse* (a great circular boulevard enclosing the old city centre) was accompanied by a new-found fascination with 'Old Vienna'.[19] But the complex relationship between 'Old London' and 'Dickens's London' warrants more detailed investigation. Certainly, the two were often mentioned in the same breath by tourists and tour guides. A Miss Elwin, for example, working as a metropolitan guide and companion for visiting female tourists, promised that she would show them 'especially old London and the London described by Dickens'.[20] The relationship, in fact, was almost symbiotic. The notion that there was an 'Old London' waiting to be discovered beneath the surface of the metropolis helped to create the conditions in which 'Dickens's London' could thrive (as yet another imaginary layer to the city, accessible to the well-guided tourist). Simultaneously, Dickens's fiction was historicised, treated as a documentary of a vanished age, providing a lively and comprehensible vision of 'Old London'. Dickensian tourism exemplified and illuminated the sort of imaginative access to the past which buildings-as-heritage might offer to the public.

To tease out these connections between 'Dickens's London' and 'Old London', I look at two heritage projects from the late nineteenth century: the Royal Society of Arts blue plaques scheme and the work of the Society for Photographing Relics of Old London. I then turn my attention to the body that had the greatest influence in establishing a heritage metropolis, even as it simultaneously authorised swathes of demolition: the London County Council. The LCC certainly had some interest in 'Dickens's London' but only on its own terms, wary of being seen to cherish and commemorate the 'Dickensian' city exemplified by the likes of Russell Court and Kingsgate Street, the sort of slums which it had pledged to eradicate.

***

The late nineteenth-century interest in urban heritage and preservation evolved from the Victorians' obsession with history. The Victorians, by any measure, were fascinated with the past – learning about it, learning from it, recreating it. During the nineteenth century, an awareness of history, and a curious sense of discontinuity between past and present, became almost omnipresent. The Gothic Revival in architecture, the vogue for meticulously researched historical costumes on stage and the popularity of the historical novel have all been cited as indicators of this cultural shift; but others might be adduced. The number of antique shops in the metropolis, for example, rose from ten to two hundred in the early decades of the nineteenth century – a plethora of curiosity shops.[21] There had always been some antiquarian interest in the old buildings of London, but the notion that the capital had a whole collection of neglected 'historic' buildings, above and beyond its famous tourist landmarks, began to gain traction in the mid-nineteenth century. Books such as Charles Knight's popular historical and topographical compendium *London* (1841–4), first published in cheap serial instalments, did much to create this newly historic capital. Knight and his co-writers seemed to discover something 'ancient' or 'curious' on almost every street corner. One contributor was George Lillie Craik, who put the case for fully exploring London's historic built environment thus:

If any one of us were to come upon a great city, like that in the Arabian tale, not in ruins or decay, but presenting all the appearances of recent occupancy, yet with its streets silent and every house untouched, how should we be excited and thrilled by such a sight! Yet is not every old town even such a spectacle ... as perfect as that of Pompeii itself.[22]

The idea of the past as a sort of fantastical virtual world, accessed through discovering hitherto neglected buildings and material relics, was appealing. In particular, growing awareness of the immaculately preserved ruins of Pompeii, which seemed capable of conjuring up Roman life for even the dullest visitor, prompted thoughts about home-grown antiquity. London's own ancient buildings could surely provide similarly stimulating imaginative fodder. Tourists, naturally, had previously found certain old buildings evocative – for example the ruined monasteries, abbeys and castles of the English country-side, beloved of the Romantics. But books such as Knight's *London* fostered a growing interest in the history of more commonplace buildings, beyond the usual run of palaces, mansions and castles – a home-grown equivalent to the humble shops and houses recovered from the ash of Vesuvius. London's streets were thus increasingly seen through an antiquarian lens, as a historical spectacle, 'as perfect as that of Pompeii itself'. The idea that the past could be imaginatively summoned into life by seeking out London's neglected historic buildings was, of course, analogous to the idea that Dickens's characters could be visualised before one's eyes, if only one could find the George Inn, Russell Court or Kingsgate Street.

Victorian interest in the historicity of London's streets would ultimately find concrete expression in a number of programmatic heritage projects. One such project, which would also touch upon 'Dickens's London', was the brainchild of the Royal Society of Arts (RSA) – now widely known as the 'blue plaques' scheme. The RSA scheme established the first public memorial to Dickens in London, with the exception of his tomb at Westminster Abbey. This was a plaque at Wood's Hotel (formerly Furnival's Inn), erected in 1886, which simply read, 'CHARLES DICKENS. NOVELIST. LIVED HERE. B:1812. D:1870'. The memorial itself was then exploited by the hotel's proprietor, much in the same way that the Murrays exploited the supposed Dickens connection at the George Inn. The plaque thus became not merely informative, but the centre of a carefully crafted tourist experience.

The MP William Ewart first raised the idea of filling the capital with plaques to commemorate the residences of the great and the good in 1863. There followed occasional correspondence in the RSA's *Journal of the Society of Arts*, and an RSA committee was finally appointed in 1866. The first house to receive the honour was Lord Byron's erstwhile home on Holles Street, in 1867. Ewart's original parliamentary question, tabled in 1863, called upon the Metropolitan Board of Works (MBW) to address the question of plaques. This was because the MBW, established just eight years earlier, was the first ever local government authority with jurisdiction over the whole of London (albeit principally concerned with civil engineering projects, such as sewer-making and street-building). The proposal for plaques, in other words, belonged to an era when organising and systematising the chaotic metropolis looked increasingly feasible and desirable. Select houses in the streets were now to be systematically catalogued and labelled as de facto exhibits, monuments to the achievements of 'great men' who had lived in them, and, by implication, a great nation. The Great Exhibition of 1851 (instituted in large part by the RSA) had provided a national showcase for British industry, against a backdrop of rival products from around the world; and now the streets of London were to be in cultural competition with those of 'other nations in the habit of preserving memorials of their great men'.[23] The RSA's internal discussion paper on instituting this new form of commemoration would repeat this international comparison, drawing on a comment by the poet Samuel Rogers that similar plaques, observed on his travels abroad, were 'evidence of refinement and sensibility in the people'.[24] In truth, however, the aim was not merely to evidence but also to instil 'refinement and sensibility', bringing an extension of the controlled, catalogued world of the exhibition into the chaotic London streets.

Indeed, academics have identified how the organising principles of the Great Exhibition extended beyond its glass walls, an 'exhibitionary complex' which contained implicit rhetoric about the ordering of society, human progress and nationhood.[25] The RSA plaques fit this model, contextualising ordinary houses as orderly 'sights', making everyday buildings a historical spectacle for public consumption and telling a story of national greatness. The RSA plaques scheme, in short, was the logic and culture of the museum and exhibition applied to the city streets. This is not to say that the scheme lacked an imaginative component. The RSA project promised to make London, at least in a modest way, like Rome, a 'living museum and a virtual imaginary place'.[26] Historicising the streets of the capital, with reference to the homes of famous individuals, allowed one's imagination to conjure up these celebrated figures *in situ*, and perhaps even their historical milieu.[27] Naturally, Dickens would eventually be included.

The suggestion that Dickens's former homes should be memorialised in this fashion was made in a newspaper column as early as 1871.[28] The RSA's progress, however, was slow. The RSA was unable to secure permission from the relevant owners to erect a plaque upon any of Dickens's principal town house residences (in Doughty Street, Devonshire Terrace and Tavistock Place) and this refusal of house owners to cooperate with this heritagisation of their buildings was cited apologetically as one reason why the RSA, in general, only managed to erect roughly one plaque per year.[29] For some, the fear that one's home (or, in the case of landlords, one's valuable rental investment) might become a sort of public property, to be perpetually viewed by sightseers, outweighed any possible kudos of an association with the great and the good. The first plaque to Dickens in London, therefore, was ultimately sited in Furnival's Inn (which contained the modest apartment where he had begun *The Pickwick Papers* and featured as a location in *Martin Chuzzlewit* and *Edwin Drood*), erected in the spring of 1886.[30] The building's proprietor, John Whaley, was keen to memorialise Dickens because the site was a business concern, now known as Wood's Hotel. Literary tourists, who might eat and drink at the hotel, were positively welcomed. After the plaque had been erected, Whaley, who had only recently taken over the premises, began to highlight the Dickens connection in his advertisements, referring to the fact that 'Charles Dickens commenced writing the Pickwick Papers during his residence in Furnival's Inn'.[31] In 1888, adverts declared that 'The very rooms occupied by *the* master of fiction are reverentially preserved by the present proprietor ... who delights in showing them to his guests' and included the text of a press cutting from 1886 which praised Whaley for identifying the location of Dickens's chambers via an old rent book and helping to situate the RSA tablet in the correct spot.[32] Whaley also made known that the hotel once boasted an old waiter who avowed that he had served the young Dickens.[33] A guidebook from 1893 noted that Whaley had preserved 'the veritable rooms where many a time he [Dickens] dined', had put up watercolours of favourite scenes and characters, and that the place had become 'a kind of shrine to Americans, who far more keenly appreciate such literary memorials than do we'.[34] Again, one wonders if Miss Murray at the George Inn ever came and took notes, for both establishments offered Dickens fans a similar experience, not least the trip to a historic bedroom. The result, in any case, was a site that was constructed for tourists, a space that was both 'reverentially preserved' and yet, rather at odds with its supposedly timeless unchanging authenticity, simultaneously filled with Dickens-themed memorabilia. It survived until the building was purchased by the Prudential Assurance Company in 1894 and demolished to make way for their new offices, the ornate red-brick Gothic affair designed by Alfred Waterhouse which dominates Holborn to this day.[35]

***

While Mr Whaley used the RSA scheme to promote his hotel, others explored London's historic built environment from more disinterested motives, such as the Society for Photographing Relics of Old London (SPROL). The SPROL, an amateur heritage project devoted to recording historic buildings, was founded in 1875 by one Alfred Marks.[36] He had noted that an old coaching inn, the Oxford Arms in Warwick Lane, was up for auction, and he clubbed together with a few friends to pay for 'a set of photographic views' by professional photographers before it was demolished.[37] Marks invited any readers of *The Times* who were interested in London antiquities to contribute funds to the project, which might be expanded to other buildings.[38] This proved a success and annual books of similar photographs of old buildings, particularly those threatened with destruction, were then produced for subscribing members at cost price, with copies also taken by libraries of institutions such as the Society of Antiquaries and the Royal Academy. The scheme proved sufficiently popular that the SPROL published 120 high-quality photographs of various London buildings between 1875 and 1886, before finally running out of funds.[39] From 1881 onwards, the photographs were issued with accompanying letterpress (including text provided retrospectively for previously published photographs), which was typically a brief paragraph or two with some antiquarian and topographical detail. The SPROL, in other words, was an attempt by history lovers to visually capture and archive 'Old London' for posterity, at a time when photography was becoming 'the agent *par excellence* for listing, knowing and possessing, as it were, the things of the world'.[40] The project also, of course, offered a glimpse into the past – a form of time travel. To see examples of, as Marks put it, 'interesting specimens of street architecture of the beginning of the seventeenth century' that had survived relatively unscathed was itself, in effect, to glimpse the streets of olden times.[41]

The SPROL's portrait of 'Old London', however, geared to providing picturesque scenes of antiquity, was also undoubtedly somewhat influenced by Dickens. Marks's choice of subject matter is relevant here. Provincial amateur photographic surveys of historic buildings that took place in subsequent decades tended to reproduce certain scenes – 'the parish church, the rural village, the manor house, ancient cottages, traditional practice of agriculture and ritual observance' – creating and reinforcing a particular iconography of nationhood rooted in iconic rural landscapes.[42] Marks's choice of places to photograph was equally indicative of a particular way of seeing the world. The photographs do not, by and large, display the traditional tourist 'sights' of London. They depict a part of London's built environment hitherto rarely documented by the antiquarian: ordinary buildings.[43] Putting aside a handful of photographs of architectural fine details, the SPROL photographed fifty-eight different locations during the eleven years in which it flourished. Nineteen of these locations were old houses in public streets, two were public houses, two were shops and six were coaching inns. Half of the SPROL's subjects, in other words, were, in their heyday, commonplace domestic or service industry buildings. The SPROL's great contribution to documenting London's built environment was that it tacitly proposed that preservation-worthy heritage existed not only in the palace or church, or even the house associated with a famous individual, but in *ordinary places* (echoes of Pompeii, rather than Rome). One might compare Marks's set of photographs, for example, with Thomas Malton's similarly collectible set of London aquatints, *A Picturesque Tour Through the Cities of London and Westminster* (1792). For Malton, the 'picturesque' is predominantly to be found in neoclassical or Gothic grandeur – churches and government buildings – with even the most ancient structures that are included (e.g. the Temple Church) appearing perfect and pristine.

Many of Malton's plates have large expanses of open sky and a perspective that emphasises the width of principal streets, suggesting spaciousness and cleanliness. Crowded streets and shops only appear once, in the shadow of the Monument. London Wall, in reality a crowded City of London thoroughfare, looks positively rustic. In contrast, the SPROL's photographs present a different sort of 'picturesque' display. They are often rather gritty, highlighting ruin and decay. In other words, they show the sorts of peculiar old places depicted by Dickens – quaint shops, houses, coaching inns – and there are clear hints in Marks's letterpress, and the public response to the project, that 'Dickens's London' formed a sort of backdrop to the 'Old London' on display.[44]

Certainly, Marks was aware of a burgeoning body of literary topography in relation to 'Dickens's London', since he himself quotes from it. In the text which accompanies the SPROL's photograph of an old house in Lincoln's Inn Fields, Marks writes:

Mr B. E. Martin, in a series of most interesting papers on Dickens's London, has identified No. 58, the half of the house nearest to Lindsey House, as that of Tulkinghorn in *Bleak House, Scribner's Monthly Magazine*, March, 1881, Vol. XXI., p. 659.

Marks actually refers to Dickens and his work on half a dozen occasions. For example, he begins his paragraph on 'Old Houses in Holborn' (the Tudor frontage of Staple Inn) with a quote from *Edwin Drood* ("Behind the most ancient part of Holborn," says Dickens, "where certain gabled houses, some centuries of age, still stand looking on the public way, as if disconsolately looking for the Old Bourne that has long run dry"").[45] He concludes a paragraph on Barnard's Inn with: 'We must not forget that here Pip, of *Great Expectations*, at one time had his quarters in what Dickens rather harshly calls "the dingiest collection of shabby buildings ever squeezed together in a rank corner as a club for tom-cats." '[46] The entry for the White Hart Inn yard, after a couple of historical references and a quote from Shakespeare, reads: 'To come much nearer to our times, the reader will not forget that Dickens, in the *Pickwick Papers*, gives a picture of the Inn as it was in the coaching days. It was here that Pickwick met his future servant and companion, Sam Weller.'[47] The SPROL project also began with a threatened coaching inn. The Oxford Arms is not mentioned in Dickens's work, but, as noted in the previous chapter, Dickens himself rhapsodised about these 'great, rambling, queer old places' and his depiction of coaching was perceived as the definitive record of 'coaching days'.[48] It seems highly likely that a certain nostalgia for 'Dickensian' inns influenced the founding of Marks's scheme.[49] Dickens's fictional world, in short, illuminated the 'Old London' which Marks documented.[50]

One can also trace connections between 'Dickens's London' and the SPROL's 'Old London' in the contemporary reception of the SPROL's photographs. *The Times*'s review of the SPROL's published photographs for 1882 (which included 58 Lincoln's Inn Fields) explicitly links the project to Dickens. The reviewer remarks upon the rapid pace of change in London and says:

> Houses rich in interesting associations are no longer to be seen, and many of the crapulous-looking places haunted by Dickens, such as Field-lane and the network of streets to the south of Lincoln's-inn-fields have become parts of noble thoroughfares or sites of buildings intended to last for centuries. . . . No-one alive to the exigencies of a great city would desire to arrest the march of the destroying angel . . . blended with a feeling of regret when we find that something full of pleasant memories is either swept away or so altered as to become almost unrecognizable. The society in question helps to console the antiquary for his actual or impending losses.[51]

The review implies that the places photographed by the SPROL – old houses, coaching inns and so forth – are made legible through the medium of Dickens's work. The reader of *The Times* thus immediately knows the sort of place which is being discussed, a 'Dickensian' London of slums and alleys. The reference to Dickens also offers a vindication and explanation for the SPROL's unusual choice of 'crapulous-looking places' as heritage, worthy of photographic preservation. 'Dickens's London' provides a means for the public to comprehend and connect with a new heritage vision of the metropolis, which prizes decrepit, commonplace old buildings as much as churches and palaces.[52]

Equally, just as Dickens's work illuminated the 'Old London' of the heritage preservationist, 'Dickens's London' was itself historicised. I have already mentioned how Dickens was perceived as a sort of inadvertent historian of the coaching inn. In fact, by the 1890s, Dickens's early Victorian London had generally started to seem part of the distant past – another facet of 'Old London'. The author's own fascination with ancient buildings and antiquity undoubtedly helped this process along. There was a prevailing sentiment that 'Dickens's London' was 'bound up with the old places of London'.[53] Dickens's work, therefore, was framed as offering an historical spectacle to literary tourists in two ways: guiding them to sites which would have been considered as historic sites/sights in Dickens's own lifetime; and guiding them through the localities, manners and customs of an early nineteenth-century metropolis, now sufficiently distant to be deemed 'historic'. Bertram Wallace, writing of 'Dickens as an Antiquary' in 1901, describes his 'striking pictures of old London ... Inns of Court ... prisons ... coaching hostelries ... old burying grounds ... the mazes of relict streets lying away from the main thoroughfares ... spread before us in panorama through the works'.[54] 'Dickens's London' was now part of history, and to explore its nooks and corners was to step back in time – at least, if those obscure relics survived. For, as mentioned above, both 'Old London' and 'Dickens's

London' were said to be 'vanishing' thanks to the 'rage for public improvement and the encroachments of private speculation' which Dickens himself had identified half a century earlier in *The Pickwick Papers*.[55]

***

The curious thing about nineteenth-century London is that it was continuously 'vanishing' and 'disappearing' – hence Dickens's own comment about the survival of the Borough's coaching inns, as early as the 1830s. There certainly was a tide of newspaper reports on 'disappearing Dickensland' in the late nineteenth century, and reports about 'vanishing London' more generally. Nonetheless, the fin-de-siècle obsession with an evanescent metropolis did not necessarily reflect an increased rate of attrition. Indeed, many earlier destructive projects anticipated the redevelopment work of the London County Council, even if we put aside the more general upheavals caused by new bridges, canals and railways, new systems of paving and lighting, and the creation of endless new suburbs. The construction of Regent Street in the 1820s and New Oxford Street in the 1840s both involved major demolition projects. The 1850s and 1860s saw Bazalgette's massively ambitious and disruptive sewer-building project and the Thames Embankment. Dickens himself, writing in 1861, was astonished by the rapid building of the embankment at Millbank ('I had never seen it in any state of transition, though I suppose myself to know this rather large city as well as anyone in it').[56] Holborn Viaduct, Farringdon Road and Clerkenwell Road flattened central slums in the 1860s and 1870s. Shaftesbury Avenue and Charing Cross Road carved new routes through the West End in the 1880s.

The trope of a 'disappearing' metropolis, therefore, which became so prevalent at the turn of the twentieth century, reflected not so much a uniquely tumultuous period for the capital's old buildings as the Victorians' evolving perspective on history and heritage. Louisa

May Alcott actually provides us with another useful reference point, suggestive of how perceptions of such things were changing, as early as the 1860s. Her letter to Tyler notes that, on their travels, he chipped away a piece of 'Milton's chimney' as a souvenir. Such petty vandalism was actually a commonplace feature of literary tourism before the invention of the gift shop. But the 'Milton's House' in question was, in itself, symptomatic of a metropolis newly fascinated with its past and eyeing up its touristic potential as heritage. The property which Alcott and Tyler visited was at No. 17, Barbican (the date and the opportunity to take away a piece of the building make it almost certain this was the house, although other places had associations with the poet). The house was purchased by the Metropolitan Railway in 1865 and scheduled for demolition to assist with its works at Farringdon. The threatened demolition resulted in numerous short newspaper articles bemoaning the building's impending fate. An initial report appeared in the *Illustrated London News*, quoting from Knight's *London* and Symmons's *Life of John Milton* (1804), listing Milton's various lodgings in London, relating some biographical detail and providing readers with a sketch of the doomed property.[57] The story was kept alive by being allied to the contemporaneous redevelopment of Green Arbor Court adjoining the Old Bailey, including a house once inhabited by Oliver Goldsmith. Journalists in local papers across the country added their own gloss, emphasising destruction and disappearance ('One by one the landmarks of London are disappearing before the face of railway demolition . . .'; 'The insatiable genius of advancement is abroad; and if we do not take heed we shall not have a relic, sacred or secular, left for ourselves or our children').[58] The foreman working on the Barbican property wrote to *The Times* and promised admission to 'collectors of objects', giving the demolition further notoriety, resulting in a parade of acquisitive visitors who purchased a variety of supposedly Miltonian relics ('oaken joists, jewels, beading, window glass, doors, fanlights, iron palisadings, &c. at high prices').[59] Louisa

May Alcott was amongst them, her dutiful chaperone chipping away at the chimney breast.

The press articles mentioned above offered readers a dramatic narrative of present versus past; modernity versus tradition; destruction versus preservation. This was how such things would increasingly be framed and would become the tenor of similar articles about 'Dickens's London'. But Milton's House in the Barbican was not, in fact, a well-known landmark or an established historic monument prior to its demolition. Indeed, it was hardly known at all. The *Illustrated London News* article admitted that it had only been named 'Milton House' by its current owner, and an earlier *ILN* article from 1847 noted that 17 Barbican 'is pointed out [as Milton's residence] on questionable authority'.[60] It is, of course, hard to prove a negative, but I have been unable to find the house mentioned in any general London guidebook. It was certainly not a 'sight' on any standard tourist trail, since Milton, if mentioned at all, was generally linked to Bread Street, where he was born (although the actual house of his birth was destroyed in the Great Fire of London). He also had connections to a property in Petty France and there was his burial place in St Giles's Cripplegate, adjoining the Barbican.[61]

It is reasonable to assume, therefore, that for the vast majority of readers, reports in the newspapers of the house's destruction were the first they had heard of its existence. The Barbican house, in other words, only became a 'landmark' in the publicity that surrounded its imminent disappearance. The expectation of its imminent doom is what validated and valorised the house as a heritage site and attracted visitors. A narrative of heritage at risk itself *creates* heritage, lending new significance to what might otherwise be overlooked or ignored. The public visited the site and traded in relics precisely because the newspapers' narrative of loss and destruction authenticated its importance and imparted value to the souvenirs that could be purchased. A similar dynamic applied to Dickens's literary territory. The threat of a 'disappearing Dickensland' actually increased the perceived value of

what remained – a cycle which kept Dickensian literary sites continually in the papers. To put it another way, to frame a building as
threatened or 'vanishing' presupposed and emphasised that something of importance was there in the first place. This was also how the
'vanishing' trope functioned rhetorically in the numerous topographical and antiquarian press and magazine articles which employed it
(in relation to both 'Dickens's London' and 'Old London'). The notion
of 'vanishing' in the headline or introduction suggested a putative
absence or loss, for which the description of the place then compen-
sated. The reader was thus sold both problem and solution in a single
convenient package. The city was now a historical spectacle which
readers were informed might otherwise 'vanish' – but for them reading
all about it.

***

Some people, of course, actively wanted 'Old London' to disappear
– or at least make way for the new. Indeed, no one stepped forward
to barricade Kingsgate Street, to protect the home of Mrs Gamp
from the ravages of the London County Council. The LCC, however,
had its own curious relationship with metropolitan heritage. The
Council was keen to portray itself not merely as the creator of a new
vibrant metropolis but also as the custodian of 'Old London'. For a
start, it took over the RSA's struggling plaques scheme in 1900. The
inclusion of Dickens's home at 48 Doughty Street in the LCC
plaques scheme – the fourth plaque to be erected by the Council –
was probably influenced by the lobbying of Dickens enthusiasts. The
papers of Frederick Kitton, one of the founders of the Dickens
Fellowship, reveal that he was in correspondence with the relevant
LCC committee even before it had come to any conclusion on its
terms of reference, in early 1902.[62] The Council's pamphlet accompanying the plaque was written by Laurence Gomme, who, as the
Council's chief administrative officer, and a noted London historian,
was instrumental in persuading it to take an interest in heritage

matters.[63] The pamphlet testifies to the historical accuracy of Dickens's association with Doughty Street, citing Forster's *Life* and a contemporary postal directory, and provides a brief biographical sketch for the period 1837–9, quoting from Dickens's letters, particularly references to cheerful dinners at home. The plaque was erected on 16 December 1903. A second plaque was erected at Dickens's more substantial erstwhile home at Devonshire Terrace on 10 August 1904, since 'one tablet by no means represented the claims of Dickens to commemoration in London'.[64] A similar pamphlet was produced for Devonshire Terrace, largely chronicling Dickens's literary output during his time in the house. A further plaque would follow, erected at Dickens's childhood lodgings at 13 Johnson Street (formerly known as No. 29 when first occupied by Dickens's family) 'at the instigation of the Council of the Dickens Fellowship', on 23 August 1911.[65] This plaque was transferred to the Charles Dickens Museum upon Johnson Street's demolition in 1932, where it now sits in the museum's garden, with a further plaque below explaining its presence. ('Tablet from 29 Johnson Street, Somers Town, the Dickens family home from 1824 to 1829. The tablet was erected by the London County Council in 1911. The house was demolished in 1932.') Plaques themselves can thus become pieces of preservation-worthy history.

The fixing of plaques, however, was only one part of the LCC's wider engagement with the built environment and heritage. The LCC was a new local authority for London, with wide-ranging powers and responsibilities that extended far beyond those of its predecessor, the Metropolitan Board of Works (taking over the province of road-building and sewerage and expanding into areas such as entertainment, education, housing and public health). In its early years, from 1889 to 1907, it was dominated by social reformers, a coalition of progressives, religious and secular, liberals and socialists, who pledged to improve the mental, physical and moral condition of Londoners. The Council made known its interest in London's heritage in 1897 when it hosted a conference of public bodies about London's historic built environment and then agreed to print the register of historic buildings that was already being produced by the amateur antiquarian project of the Survey of London (founded by Charles Robert Ashbee three years earlier). In 1898, moreover, the LCC obtained legal powers to allow for the purchase of 'places of historical or architectural interest or works of art, or to undertake or contribute towards the cost of preserving, maintaining and managing any such buildings and places'.[66] The Council would go on to closely cooperate with the efforts of the Survey of London; create its own historical records section within its architecture department; and, from the early 1900s, produce its own documentation on heritage buildings and sites. This ranged from pamphlets about the 'houses of historical interest' marked by plaques to documentation about London's various idiosyncratic outdoor memorials.[67] In 1900, the Council used its powers to purchase 17 Fleet Street, restoring a Tudor frontage and allowing visitors access to the ancient fixtures and fittings of 'Prince Henry's Room' within.[68] The Council's progressives believed that preserving historical and literary sites of interest was culturally enriching for the citizens of the capital. As Ashbee noted in the first published volume of *The Survey of London* (1900), produced under the aegis of the LCC: 'We plead that the object of the work we have before us, is to make nobler and more humanly enjoyable the life of the great city.'[69]

The Council's early heritage work, however, was contemporaneous with its first great physical remaking of the capital: demolition and improvement works to build the new Haussmann-style boulevards of Kingsway and Aldwych (formally opened in 1905), as well as smaller projects dotted throughout the city.[70] Contemporaries saw a close link between the LCC's interest in heritage and its redevelopment work. The *Daily Mail* described the LCC as 'destroyer and conserver . . . doing its best to preserve interesting features' and noted that 'Mr Laurence Gomme, the Council clerk . . . zealously watches over threatened buildings'.[71] The *Saint Paul Globe*, an American newspaper, reporting on the Devonshire Terrace plaque, suggested that the LCC's memorial plaques were meant, in a sense, to compensate for the loss of 'buildings that link the present with the storied past' during the LCC's street improvement projects. American visitors, it was said, would doubtless appreciate the plaques, since they viewed London principally as 'a rich storehouse of literary and historic memories'.[72] The Council was forging, as another American journalist put it, a 'new, hygienic, well-ordered London' in contrast to the decrepit but much-loved 'old London of crooked streets and provincial ways'.[73]

The RSA plaques scheme, in fact, as I have already hinted, had always been a way of organising and displaying a certain vision of the past – a city and nation peopled by 'great men' – but, under the LCC, the scheme was now also intimately connected with the Council's plans for remaking the city as a great municipality. The retention of the 'best' of the old city, marked with a plaque, was, without doubt, a gesture, a symbolic compensation for the loss of historic property occasioned by LCC redevelopment. The Council's interest in curating historic elements of the built environment was also an attempt to portray the Council itself as both 'grounded in tradition and monumentally new'.[74] The LCC wished to make clear that its influence and interests extended into all spheres of public life, even organising and arranging the past. The Council was keen to present itself as authoritative when it came to deciding both past and future of London, emphasising its role as 'destroyer and conserver' – an authority upon virtually everything.

We can also see the Council's strategic use of history and historic place in the choice of 'Aldwych' and 'Kingsway' as names for their new grand avenues cutting through the centre of the city, which destroyed Kingsgate Street. The names were inspired by Gomme's antiquarian research, in which he had discovered a Danish self-governing community, granted land by Alfred the Great, in the 880s, in the very area through which the new roads were being built (both names originally appeared on ancient maps). This historic link was trumpeted in the accompanying publicity material when the roads were formally opened in 1905. *The Times* noted approvingly that the LCC, despite the destruction wreaked by its works, had thus 'preserved some vestige of the antiquity of the district'.[75] This was also significant in terms of the Council's ongoing strained relations with the quasi-autonomous City of London, the ancient 'square mile' that had come to be dominated by banking and finance. Gomme was laying claim to a (rather manufactured) ancient tradition of local government that existed beyond the City's boundaries.[76] More generally, these historic roots hinted that the Council's grand new streets were not wholly erasing the past but were part of a continuous evolutionary process: from simple Danish settlement to modern metropolis. The Council's dominant Progressive faction tended to see the new LCC as contributing to Whiggish progress from the petty factionalism of London's earlier parochial politics, and the historical intransigence of the overweening City of London, to a more rational and democratic system of urban government.[77] Gomme's preferred option of 'Aldwych' and 'Kingsway' bolstered this idea of progress, situating the Council and its work within a (fabricated) tradition; suggesting that the LCC was, in effect, the logical culmination of a thousand years of extramural metropolitan history; and linking it to the work of historians who believed Anglo-Saxon institutions, assemblies of individuals such as the folkmoot and witenagemot, were 'the cradle of English liberties'.[78]

It is interesting, however, that one name for the new streets which was considered, but not chosen, was 'Dickens Avenue'. Dickens featured in the final list of thirty-nine possible names for the two new streets which went before the Council's committee in 1903.[79] The list sounds long but the possibilities broadly fell into half a dozen categories. There were the blandly descriptive ('Broadway', 'The High', 'London's Avenue'), the regal ('King Alfred Street', 'The

King's Way', 'The Queen's Way', 'Victoria Avenue', 'King Edward Avenue'), the colonial/imperial ('Imperial Drive', 'Mafeking Avenue'), and memorials to the LCC ('The Council Broadway') and to two politicians ('Salisbury Drive', 'Gladstone Avenue'). The literary possibilities were 'Shakespeare Road', 'Shakespeare Street', 'Dickens Avenue' and 'Charles Dickens Avenue'. The Council's final report on the subject concluded, firstly, that one-word names (like, for example, the ancient names of Whitehall or Cheapside) were more memorable and distinctive, and secondly that they preferred 'to make use of some name which will recall and perpetuate the associations of the locality in which the street is situated'.[80]

This latter point, in fact, should surely have weighed heavily in Dickens's favour. Few, if any, Londoners associated the district with Anglo-Saxon London prior to Gomme's much-publicised research, whereas many were familiar with its Dickensian associations. A correspondent to *Literature*, a precursor to the *Times Literary Supplement*, noted that there were a dozen sites with biographical and literary connections to Dickens that might disappear thanks to the improvement works.[81] Joseph Ashby-Sterry – author of several pieces of Dickensian literary topography – had regularly proposed, from the beginning of the 1890s in fact, that one of the new avenues be named in Dickens's honour, using his weekly column in the *Graphic* to do so.[82] An article in the *Daily Mail* noted that the projected street would destroy Kingsgate Street, which American tourists regularly visited to see the home of Mrs Gamp, not to mention Sardinia Street, mentioned in Dickens's description of the Gordon Riots in *Barnaby Rudge*, as well as the (so-called) Old Curiosity Shop of Portsmouth Street (which, in fact, would survive). Others made similar points about the roads' destruction of Dickens-related sites and complained that 'Dickens' London has suffered so much already at the behest of the modern street improver'.[83] The *Daily Graphic*, in an article entitled 'The Last of Another Bit of Dickens Land', noted that the LCC works had also demolished the former office of *Household Words*, which had been incorporated some years previously into the buildings of the Gaiety Theatre.[84] Another press article remarked that the proposed demolition from the Strand to Holborn 'will run rough-shod through the haunts of Mr Pickwick, Jo, Mrs Gamp, Mrs Lirriper, and many other of Boz's merry immortals'.[85] Several papers noted that Dickens himself was only commemorated by a small road in Clapham, whereas somewhere more central and notable would surely be a more fitting choice.[86]

Why, then, was Dickens *not* chosen? Certainly, Gomme was immensely influential in his role as the Council's chief civil servant and clearly valued the idea of laying claim to a thousand years of progress, from the Danes to the LCC. The Council also described the choice of an ancient Danish name as a token of respect for the Danish-born wife of Edward VII, Queen Alexandra. The naming of actual streets after great men was also a continental tradition, and the Council doubtless had little desire to be seen as copying rival cities such as Paris.[87] 'Dickens's London', crucially, had also come to stand for precisely what the Council was trying to erase: the slum, the decrepit house, the narrow street.[88] As Percy Fitzgerald put it:

> DICKENS, indeed, is so bound up with the old places of London that it may be said that he has lent a peculiar flavour and charm to all town peregrination. He certainly must be considered to have been the best interpreter of the City to us. He supplied the tragic and comic grotesque meaning of the old courts, shops, alleys, 'all-alones,' 'rents,' etc.[89]

This back-alley vision of London was not something which the Council wished to memorialise, even if they respected Dickens's memory, since it had all the negative connotations of slumland. 'Dickens's London' was, at least for some, the polar opposite of a modern, improved city, with 'a perpetual air of squalor, dirt, bad beer, and general discomfort' (echoes of Albert Smith's brutal description of coaching inns).[90] As one anonymously authored newspaper piece put it, bemoaning the popularity of backwards-looking literary tourism, 'practically every month, arrive illustrated laments that the interesting London is passing, whereas there is no manner of doubt that the London, at any rate, of Dickens and Thackeray was not only dirtier but infinitely duller than ours'.[91] For some, the city of Dickens was rather primitive and filthy, whereas modern London promised a future of wide streets, embankments, green parks and squares, 'one of the brightest capitals in the world'.[92]

A contemporary cartoon from Frederick Kitton's scrapbooks throws some further light on the matter.[93] The cutting is marked as coming from *Scraps* (a penny magazine which flourished in the 1890s and early 1900s, composed of comic cartoons) and the text below the cartoon includes a quote from the *Daily Graphic*. The latter states that 'Charles Dickens Street' might have been a good choice of name for one of the new avenues, 'seeing that the author of *Pickwick* is so intimately associated with London and its streets'. The cartoon itself depicts a new street where the houses are not merely houses but bizarrely monumental sculptures – of Dickens himself, Bumble, Gamp, Sikes, Pickwick, Micawber, Mrs Gummidge and Sam Weller (with names such as 'Bumble House', 'Gamp Place', 'Sikes Court', 'Pickwick House' and so forth, reserving 'Sikes Court', 'Heep Court' and 'Bardell Court' for the more dubious entries leading to courtyards at the rear of the buildings). The small human figures standing in the street are also themselves Dickens characters. On the far right, the figure with a tailcoat and jaunty-angled hat is clearly Sam Weller, gazing in admiration at 'Samivel House', home to 'Weller & Co.', leading to 'Bardell Court'. Similarly, on the far left, Mr Bumble, distinguishable by his coat and hat, lurks in the doorway of his eponymous property. The text below concludes: 'Our Artist considers that the idea is excellent. By the exercise of a little ingenuity, Charles Dickens Street might be one of the features of the town' ('features', naturally, being a pun). Ostensibly, therefore, the humour of the cartoon is a simple *reductio ad absurdum* – why merely *name* the street after Dickens? Why not actually construct buildings that physically resemble Dickens and his famous characters? But this quirky cartoon actually critiques the idea of commemorating the author in a variety of subtle and interesting ways.

For a start, part of the cartoon's appeal is that it also parodies Dickens's own habit of reading human character from buildings and objects, and of giving buildings and objects human attributes. The *Scraps* cartoon takes this familiar Dickensian habit and makes it horribly literal, massive and concrete. The buildings in the cartoon thus resemble a sort of uncanny monumental sculpture, which offers none of the potential imaginative rewards to be found in Dickens's mingling of the animate and inanimate. Dickens, for example, reveals Squeers's character in *Nicholas Nickleby* by noting he possesses only one half-open eye, 'in shape resembling the fanlight of a street door'.[94] If the eyes are proverbially the windows to the soul, then sly Squeers pointedly has the bare minimum: a fanlight, half a window, through which nothing is visible, always guarded and secured. By contrast, in the *Scraps* cartoon windows are literally 'eyes', and vice versa. The cartoon renders Dickens's interplay between person and object ridiculous and empty. The implicit suggestion is that naming an imposing new thoroughfare 'Charles Dickens Street' is the equivalent of building a giant Pickwick sculpture – certainly monumental, but also hopelessly reductive, conveying nothing of Dickens's imaginative genius.

It is also worth noting that the cartoon's buildings – to the extent that they resemble buildings at all – are a somewhat ramshackle and ill-assorted collection. Bumble House is a sort of Alpine Gothic; Gamp Place is a squat building with cracked plaster; Sikes Court has a thatched roof; Pickwick House has rickety Tudor tiles; Micawber Buildings has an overhanging upper floor; Gummidge Place resembles a narrow late eighteenth- or early nineteenth-century town house. These are highly individual, quaint constructions, like Dickens's distinctive characters, with nothing to unify them visually. This is a chaotic, incoherent streetscape, with nods to antiquity – the exact opposite of the coming works of the LCC. The artist implies that the Council's modern improved street, even if named after Dickens, will be a far cry from the reality of 'Dickens's London'. Hence the inclusion of the unpromising 'Sikes Court' and 'Heep Court'. Districts containing alleys and courts (enclosed courtyard dwellings behind principal buildings on the street) were the proverbial slum parts of the metropolis, which the LCC was determined to remove.

Some, of course, valued the chaotic nature of 'Dickens's London'. A *Spectator* article from the previous decade, for example, decrying plans to 'Hausmannise London' along the lines of Paris or Vienna, contrasts plans for modernisation with the more 'romantic' London of Dickens and notes that the 'soulish, slavish regularity' of wholesale improvement may ruin the city.[95] For those who were opposed to wholesale change, 'Dickens's London' stood for an individuality and diversity in the built environment that was aesthetically and imaginatively rewarding. Dickens himself, who had been disquieted by the newness, linearity and regularity of American cities, would surely at the very least have understood such objections, whatever the broader merits of street improvements.

The cartoon, however, denies that a modern new street can bear any productive imaginative relation to Dickens's work; and one might even read its peculiar assembly of 'historic' structures as gentle mockery of heritage preservationism. The imagined world of 'Dickens's London' cannot be preserved or recreated without becoming ridiculous. The LCC, of course, might still have acknowledged Dickens as a great author and named a street after him, but the cartoon also hints at one further final argument against memorialisation. For Dickens himself appears as a building alongside his characters-as-buildings, in 'Author House', the entrance and chimneys being monumental spines of his books. As the accompanying quote from the *Daily Graphic* states, Dickens was an author 'so intimately associated with London and its streets'. To call a street 'Dickens Avenue' or 'Dickens Street' would inevitably call to mind not merely the great author but also the Dickensian streets of 'Old London' which the LCC was determined to erase.

That said, the LCC had some use for 'Dickens's London'. Dickens-related sites featured in its school 'reward cards'. Having taken on the functions of the London School Board in 1905, the LCC continued the Board's practice of utilising 'an elaborate system of reward cards, prizes, medal and certificates' to encourage punctuality and discipline.[96] Weekly good attendance earned 'tickets' which could be exchanged for a 'reward card' if the pupil was punctual for a full term, and then the King Edward VII Medal for Regular and Punctual Attendance for a complete year (and even a silver medal for seven years).[97] The reward cards typically reprinted existing images from sets of commercial postcards – famous places in London and further afield, birds, dogs, scenes from nursery rhymes – and replaced the normal blank reverse of the postcard with 'LONDON COUNTY COUNCIL REWARD CARD' and some instructive or explanatory text. The Dickens postcards given as rewards reproduced colour paintings of Dickens-related locations, included 'Charles Dickens' House, Gadshill', 'Gateway, Lincoln's Inn', 'Oliver Twist Arrives in London', 'Rochester from Strood Pier', 'The Bull Inn, Rochester', 'The Little Inn, Canterbury', 'The Old Curiosity Shop' and 'Mitre Court adjoining Serjeant's Inn'.[98] The images came from a much larger set of collectible commercial postcards issued in 1903–4, under the series title 'In Dickens Land' (which included drawings of scenes from the novels as well as topographical pictures).[99]

We do not know what dictated the Council's choice of cards and it would be unwise to assume a deeply considered rationale. There is no obvious logic to the cards selected and it is possible, for instance, that the LCC and the printers (Raphael Tuck & Sons) were utilising unsold stock from the earlier printing of 'In Dickens Land'. Indeed, to call them a coherent 'set' itself may be going too far. The text on

the reverse of three of the LCC cards is purely historical/topograph-
ical and makes no mention of Dickens or his work, even though
the images originally appeared in the 'In Dickens Land' series.[100] The
card 'Oliver Twist arrives in London' is particularly confusing.
The first sentence of the reverse reads: 'The spot depicted is in the
Minories, in the City of London, showing the quaint old hostelry,
the Fountain Inn, in the days of Oliver Twist.' Sure enough, the front
shows the Fountain Inn, with a nondescript boy walking past.[101] But
the tavern in question does not appear in *Oliver Twist* – the book
contains not even the slightest allusion – and was actually demolished in 1793. The reference seems to be derived from Francis
Miltoun's *Dickens' London* (1903), where the author mistakenly and
inexplicably claims the Fountain is 'referred to in "Oliver Twist"'.[102]
This erroneous attribution, however, highlights what *is* common
to all the cards: they all display a remarkably picturesque vision of
'quaint' and 'historic' buildings – a sanitised heritage vision of 'Old
London'. It is particularly striking that Oliver Twist's journey into
the metropolis which the novel describes as through little streets and
courts, ending in the foulest slums, is represented by the figure of a
boy passing the Fountain Inn, which resembles a well-kept heritage
attraction, complete with an attractive display of flowers laid out on
the pavement. The London County Council, in short, only wished to
put 'Dickens's London' before the general public when it formed part
of a neat and tidy, sanitised vision of the past – a blue plaque alluding
to a great man; a brochure describing hearty dinners at Doughty
Street; a colourful, cheery scene showing a historic inn – part of its
own orderly narrative of progress and urban improvement.

In the next chapter, I look at what became of two of Dickens's
former homes which the LCC graced with plaques: 48 Doughty
Street in Bloomsbury, and Dickens's childhood home in Johnson
Street, Camden. The former was purchased by the Dickens Fellowship
and opened as a museum in 1925. The latter underwent a more
peculiar transformation, briefly serving as a living memorial to the

great author, transformed into reading rooms for the poor children of Camden, the David Copperfield Library. The library's founder came up with the idea after noticing the LCC's plaque on the obscure North London street. Heritage sites/sights have a curious habit of producing more heritage.

5

A TALE OF TWO HOUSES

The houses of famous writers, posthumously maintained, restored or reimagined as a museums, have always fascinated literary tourists. Visitors, at the very least, may learn something of an author's domestic circumstances (for example, they might see the very desk where they sat down to write) and attempt to combine their impressions of the building with what they know of the author's life and work. There is a wistful sense that something of the author lingers in such places, a metaphysical *genius loci*, guarding the house where they once lived. Dickens himself visited one of the earliest and best-known 'house museums' during his 1838 tour of the Midlands: the historic property associated with Shakespeare's birth and childhood in Stratford-upon-Avon. He signed the visitor's book and perused the autographs of fellow tourists but found the elderly proprietress wanting. His laconic diary entry for 30 October 1838 reads: 'Stratford – Shakspeare – the birth-place, visitors, scribblers, old woman, – qy. whether she knows what Shakspeare did &c'.[1] Dickens knew his Shakespeare and doubtless somewhat resented being treated as one of the tourist herd.

Dickens's own fans began thinking about a Dickensian 'house museum' not long after the author's death. In fact, as early as September 1870, Barton Hill's 'A Pilgrimage', one of the first published pieces of Dickens tourism, included a guidebook-like floor plan of Gads Hill Place, anticipating the needs of prospective visitors.[2] Dickens's Kentish retreat certainly had the potential to become a literary shrine. Dickens had purchased Gads Hill Place in 1856 and it soon became his principal residence (and a convenient alternative to London after his rather scandalous and highly public separation from his blameless wife, Catherine, in 1858). He lived there until his death in the summer of 1870 and had everything arranged to suit his own habits and preferences. For example, he had a tunnel built to a part of his garden on the other side of the main road, a neat way to avoid mud, traffic and sightseers. The plot of ground in question, romantically dubbed 'The Wilderness', contained a wooden Swiss chalet, which Dickens used as an alternative to his indoor study.[3] Gads Hill Place even had its own unique mythology. Dickens's father had once pointed it out to him, when he was but a child, as the sort of desirable property that he might occupy in later life 'if he would only work hard enough'.[4] Moreover, Dickens liked the fact that Shakespeare's Falstaff was robbed at Gads Hill in *Henry IV, Part 1* (a literary association with the Bard of Avon which did not escape his future literary topographers). There was, arguably, no house more intimately connected with the great author.

Luke Fildes, the young illustrator of *The Mystery of Edwin Drood*, probably had this in mind when he began to sketch 'The Empty Chair' in the summer of 1870. He had stayed with the Dickens family at Gads Hill Place whilst they were in mourning and took the opportunity to begin work on a tribute to the dead author. His much-reproduced drawing, depicting Dickens's unoccupied desk and chair, was published as an engraving in the Christmas 1870 edition of the *Graphic* ('engraved in the most finished manner possible . . . suitable for framing').[5] Fildes's drawing poignantly alludes to Dickens's absence, with the author's chair positioned pulled back from his desk, as if he has just left the room. But there is also something of the 'house museum' about the depiction of the desk and Dickens's study. The room in the picture appears perfectly preserved, much as if it has been laid out for inspection by the literary tourist. Fildes's inspiration was, in all probability, a cartoon drawn by William Henry Boucher which appeared only a couple of weeks after Dickens's death in *Judy* (the conservative rival to *Punch*), likewise entitled 'The Empty Chair'.[6] A comparison between the two is instructive. Boucher's drawing has a smaller, more humble desk, at the foot of which is a heap of the author's novels with the pages tumbling open. Illustrations of Dickens's characters float around the edges of the cartoon, haunting the image, the ghostly immortal products of Dickens's imagination. Robert Buss's much-admired unfinished watercolour 'Dickens's Dream' (1875) (where the author sleeps at his desk, surrounded by 'dreams' of his characters) would develop the same theme on a grander scale.[7] In contrast, Fildes's picture has a stiff formality, a meticulous documentary rendering. The room, in other words, resembles an exhibit. Fildes added to this museum-like effect in the watercolour of 'The Empty Desk' which he displayed at the Royal Academy in 1871, diminishing the sentimental note by aligning the chair more neatly with the desk.

Gads Hill Place, however, would never become the literary shrine that many had anticipated. Unfortunately for the literary tourist, Dickens specified in his will that the property should be sold for the benefit of his dependants. The bulk of the contents were swiftly auctioned off soon after his death. The press described a carnival atmosphere, particularly around the nearby Sir John Falstaff public house:

> The sale drew together many of the elements of a fair. In front
> of the Sir John Falstaff, just 'over the way' a blind fiddler played
> 'Jack's the lad' while some farm lads danced; a conjuror drew

inexhaustible supplies of tin dishes from a cabman's hat, to the immense satisfaction of a gaping crowd; and opposite Dickens's yard-gate a ginger-bread dealer pitched his stall.[8]

Gads Hill Place itself would end up in the hands of Dickens's eldest son, Charles Jr (or Charley), a source of some acrimony. Charley Dickens outbid the reserve price set by the executors, John Forster and Dickens's sister-in-law Georgina Hogarth, but the latter suspected that Charley's presence in the auction room had dissuaded others from bidding, out of respect for the family connection. She believed, in other words, that, by accident or design, he had got the house cheap, and that a far better price might have been attained for the family if he had put his own interests aside.[9] There were also doubts whether Charley had the means to purchase and maintain such a property. These doubts proved well founded. He was obliged to sell up in 1879, a move which substantially diminished the chances of Gads Hill Place ever becoming a Dickens memorial.

The house's subsequent private owners would vary in their openness to literary pilgrims and one can hardly blame them. Walter T. Stephenson, for example, writing for *Vogue*, turned up unexpectedly one evening in 1907 whilst the family of the then owner, Frederick Law Latham, former Advocate General of Bombay, were at dinner. Finding the front gate locked, he effected an entrance via the stables and was then disappointed to be told the family were otherwise engaged:

> Whereupon I made bold to send in my card bearing a legend to the effect that I was the New York representative of a well-known English magazine, and had come 3,000 miles to see Gad's Hill. A few moments came back a courteous message from the Hon. Frederick that I might enjoy the freedom of the house, excepting the dining room. . . . I devoted half an hour wandering over the mansion, accompanied by the Argus-eyed maid.[10]

Gads Hill School, the owners since 1924, currently allow pre-booked tours, but only on a few weekends during the summer.

There were, of course, other biographical destinations that might become a Dickensian literary shrine, including his birthplace and his tomb. Indeed, a birthplace museum was opened in 1904 in Mile End Terrace, Portsmouth, which survives to this day. But the house has always struggled to lay claim to a deep association with the author, who only lived there for a few short months in his earliest infancy. Dickens's final resting place in Westminster Abbey, meanwhile, obviously attracts some visitors but forms one modest part of 'Poet's Corner' This hallowed ground, home to numerous other literary greats, has always been 'disconcertingly miscellaneous, noisy, even incoherent' in its impact.[11] In the early 1900s, therefore, Dickens's fans remained rather keen to see a 'Dickens house' established in the capital, and there was some precedent. Thomas Carlyle's house in Cheyne Walk had been opened to the public in 1895, and Dr Johnson's house in Gough Square would open in 1914 – so why not a house dedicated to their own beloved author?

This chapter tells the story of two London houses which were acquired to honour and preserve the name of Charles Dickens. One would become the modern-day Charles Dickens Museum, in Doughty Street, Bloomsbury (which every reader of this book should visit). But I begin with its long-lost rival – No. 13 Johnson Street, Camden, which briefly flourished as the David Copperfield Library – now all but forgotten.

***

Charles Dickens had no single much-loved childhood home in the metropolis. The family returned to London from Kent in 1822, when Charles was ten years old, after his father's employer, the Navy Pay Office, recalled him to Somerset House. John Dickens then rented a succession of rather downmarket properties to contain his growing household, perpetually teetering on the edge of respectability and plunging over the precipice when he was incarcerated in the Marshalsea Gaol (a debtor's prison). John, however, received a fortuitous inheritance with which he cleared his debts, and a few months later, towards the end of 1824, the family relocated to No. 29 Johnson Street in Somers Town, Camden (which was soon renumbered as No. 13, for reasons unknown to posterity).[12] This was another distinctly unassuming address, a narrow terraced house, some thirty years old, located on what was then the very edge of the capital.[13] Johnson Street, however, would prove to be the family's most enduring London tenancy. A childhood acquaintance of Dickens remembered the house as 'near rather a squalid part of Somers Town, but at that time an open situation, having at the back Rhodes's extensive cowfields, into which we made incursions over the garden wall'.[14] A contemporaneous advertisement for a local laundress, only a few doors down, alludes to her 'eligible situation adjoining the fields of Somers Town' (that is, away from the London smoke), but her very presence confirms that Johnson Street lacked social tone.[15] The Dickens family, in fact, may have left the street, after failing to pay the parish rates (local taxation), in the spring of 1827. But, if that was the case, then they soon returned: Dickens's youngest brother, Augustus, was born at Johnson Street on 10 November 1827.[16] They stayed at least until the spring of 1829, when John Dickens took out household contents insurance on his 'wearing apparel, printed books and plate'.[17]

The house – consisting of a ground floor, first floor, second floor and attic, with only two rooms on each – would have been relatively crowded. Dickens's older sister Fanny, a talented pianist, initially boarded at the Royal Academy of Music, but the house still accommodated Dickens and his parents, his sisters Letitia (b. 1816) and Harriet (b. 1819), and his younger brothers Frederick (b. 1820) and Alfred (b. 1822).[18] These were also the years when Charles received some formal schooling at the Wellington House Academy on the Hampstead Road (c. 1824–7). The school's irascible and violent headmaster, a Mr Jones, was described by one pupil as 'a thrasher'.

Dickens himself recalled him as 'by far the most ignorant man I have ever had the pleasure to know' but seems to have been treated less punitively than some of his fellows. Day pupils generally fared better in this regard, since, as another pupil recollected, 'there was a wholesome fear of tales being carried home to the parents' (a statement with perhaps all-too-neat echoes of Dotheboys Hall in *Nicholas Nickleby*).[19] Dickens would describe these schooldays in 'Our School', an article which appeared in *Household Words* in 1851, remembering, in particular, how the boys trapped and trained white mice.[20] His formal schooling, however, such as it was, ended when money grew tight, in the spring of 1827. The future author was then obliged to go to work as a lawyer's clerk at Ellis & Blackmore in Holborn. Forster later noted that Dickens 'had a surprising fondness for wandering about in poor neighbourhoods on Christmas-day, past the areas of shabby genteel houses in Somers or Kentish Towns, and watching the dinners preparing or coming in' – they doubtless reminded him of his childhood.[21]

The house in Johnson Street would become known to Dickens's fans after his death. Forster's biography had little influence in this regard, since it dwelt upon the family's earlier and much briefer residence in nearby Bayham Street (although Forster does quote a schoolfriend of Dickens who recalled 'a very small house in a street leading out of Seymour Street, north of Mr Judkin's chapel'). A correspondent to the *St. Pancras Gazette* wrote to the paper shortly after the publication of the biography, stating that his father had been a junior master at Wellington House who recollected that 'Mr Dickens, senr. lived in Johnson-street, Somers Town'.[22] The precise house number would be publicised in Frederick Kitton's *Charles Dickens: His Life, Writings and Personality* (1902). Kitton confirmed by reference to local rate books that No. 13 was the house in question.[23] Mary Ann Cooper (neé Mitton), the sister of Dickens's old friend Thomas Mitton, was another latter-day publicist of Johnson Street as a Dickensian site. The origins of Mitton and Dickens's friendship dated back to, at the very least, Dickens's time as a lawyer's clerk. Following his stint at Ellis & Blackmore, Dickens had briefly worked at the offices of Charles Molloy in Lincoln's Inn, where Mitton was an articled clerk. Mary Anne Cooper, however, would appear in the press in the early 1900s, claiming that the Mitton family had actually lived opposite the Dickens family in Johnson Street – and that she herself had been the 'original' of the character Little Dorrit. Mrs Cooper was ninety when this claim first appeared, in an interview with *Black & White* magazine, entitled '"Little Dorrit" as she is today'.[24] Her stories were vivid – memories of the teenage Dickens as her playfellow, or even childhood sweetheart, who aped the manners of the beadle at St Pancras New Church ('to the great indignation of this prototype of Bumble'), teased a haughty schoolmistress, and once disguised himself as a farm labourer for a lark. The young Dickens, she claimed, nicknamed her 'Little Dorrit', for reasons unknown – 'I was always "Dorrit" with Charles' – and later informed her at one point: 'The next book I write I shall put you in it, and I shall call it *Little Dorrit*.' Mrs Cooper enjoyed a minor celebrity on the strength of these recollections. Her story appeared and reappeared in numerous newspaper articles over a period of years and her death in 1913 was widely recorded. She was also, however, something of an eccentric. The local press noted that she had once trimmed her Sunday outfit with a set of small bells and had to be asked not to wear this melodious costume to church. Whether Dickens truly gave her the nickname 'Dorrit' – or even was a childhood friend – remains, therefore, a little uncertain. Regardless, her much-repeated story did something to increase awareness of Johnson Street as Dickens's childhood home.

The Dickens Fellowship persuaded the London County Council to affix a plaque to 13 Johnson Street in 1911. The Council was conscious that it already had two such plaques (at 48 Doughty Street and 1 Devonshire Terrace) but arguments that this was the author's only surviving boyhood home were persuasive.[25] The house remained only a minor site for the Dickens tourist until, a decade later, a plan emerged to use the old house as a novel yet apt tribute to the great author – a children's library.

***

The David Copperfield Library was the brainchild of John Brett Langstaff, a New York-born Episcopal priest who had served with the British army in the First World War and went on to run the Magdalen College Mission in Somers Town. The Magdalen College in question was the famous college at Oxford University. 'Missions' were a form of charitable outreach work, bringing together university students and working-class locals. Students would come to live in the mission house, experiencing the area first-hand and taking part in various projects. Langstaff, for example, set up a theatre group, which boasted of its community engagement ('The authors of the one-act piece are two twenty-year-old working men, Mr R.B. Smith who is in the shirt-making business, and Mr F.W. Stossner, who is in the leather trade').[26]

Langstaff – like many an American in London – interpreted the city through the medium of fiction, finding the inhabitants of Camden to be 'the counter-types of characters which one had suspected as the exaggerations of Charles Dickens'.[27] He was particularly struck by the sign placed upon Johnson Street by the LCC, and he had an inspirational idea – that the building, which was under threat of demolition, might be repurposed as a children's library (or, more accurately, reading rooms, since books would not be loaned).[28] The idea seemed very apt, for Dickens had always been closely associated with childhood. Both *David Copperfield* and *Great Expectations* famously begin with peerless evocations of a boy's early years. Many of his books also highlight those who would rob childhood of its innocence and joy: Fagin and Sikes in *Oliver Twist*; the stern capitalist, Dombey, in *Dombey and Son*; the cruel schoolmaster Squeers in *Nicholas Nickleby*; and the utilitarian businessman Gradgrind in *Hard Times*. Moreover, after the publication of Forster's biography, with its famous account of Dickens's traumatic childhood employment in a blacking factory, it was commonplace to suggest that 'the secret of Dickens's sympathy with neglected childhood is to be found in the story of his own early days'.[29] Dickens, in other words, had actually been the neglected child of his fiction, and so who better to associate with a library for working-class children? The LCC, in fact, had supported the erection of a Dickens plaque in Johnson Street partly because this was 'a poor and dingy part of London' – the plaque was intended to be a light in the darkness.[30] In modern times, the precise influence of the blacking factory experience on Dickens's character and fiction has been a subject of lively, often psychoanalytical debate; but, for Langstaff, it was enough that Dickens knew something of childhood misery.

Dickens himself, of course, was not a 'children's author' in the modern sense of the word, but many nonetheless considered his books ideal for children, particularly *The Pickwick Papers*. Indeed, the reputation of his early comic novel rode high in the early twentieth century, 'the novel which, above all others, is identified with the name of Dickens'.[31] Whether Dickens *was* especially popular with children in this period is harder to know. The youthful visitors to the 'junior rooms' of Croydon Public Libraries in 1926, for example, were asked to vote for their favourite authors. Dickens came fifth amongst the boys (after the adventuring/military stories of P.F. Westerman, Frederick Sadleir Brereton, G.A. Henty and R.M. Ballantyne) but did better among the girls, second only to the schoolgirl tales of Angela Brazil.[32] There were concerns, however, that 'a number of the girls put down Shakespeare, Dickens etc. from a feeling of superiority, because they were told at school that they should read and appreciate these authors'. A children's librarian at Stoke-on-Trent considered that *Oliver Twist* was the only one of Dickens's works which held perennial interest.[33]

Langstaff, regardless, milked the house's association with Dickens for all it was worth. In particular, he presented the building as the cradle of the great author's literary career, having been the erstwhile container of Dickens's own 'childhood library' of books. The implication was that this was the place where he first began to think about fiction and writing, despite the well-attested fact that Dickens became interested much earlier, at Chatham.[34] Within Langstaff's library, titles which Dickens had read as a child were even placed on a shrine-like shelf, proximate to his own fiction, thus representing 'the beginning and ending of Dickens's literary endeavour'.[35] This was also supposed to be a recreation of the very shelf known to Dickens as a boy, 'to stand exactly in the same position as in his day'.[36] This was the narrative Langstaff wove for publicity purposes, namely that, as the poet Alfred Noyes wryly summarised it, 'Dickens, in his own poor childhood, had discovered a few old books in a garret, and so entered upon the road that led him to a place in Westminster Abbey'.[37] Langstaff's own book about the library also conjures up an image of the young Dickens gazing out towards the Hampstead Road from his attic room and imagining the characters from his own 'library' of books – the characters of Smollett, Fielding and Defoe – riding into London. Somers Town itself, in other words, is tortuously framed as the 'classic ground' which inspired Dickens to produce fiction, the place where his imagination took flight. Langstaff also suggested, for good measure, that the house was not merely Dickens's childhood home but also the 'original' of the one occupied by the Micawbers and David Copperfield (located in the novel in Windsor Terrace, City Road). Dickens himself, in turn, was regularly invoked as the library's benign guardian angel, the project described as a 'manifestation of his happy personality'.[38]

The house was donated to Langstaff by local councillor Abraham Davis, who happened to own the freehold on the crumbling terrace – but considerable money was needed for repair and renovation. Langstaff's book describes the decay in some detail: rats and mice behind the woodwork; floorboards which, in places, were so rotten that one could put one's foot through them; blocked and overflowing drains; holes in the walls; windows falling away from the frame; and armies of insects. Langstaff took advice from the politician Cecil Harmsworth, who had bought Dr Johnson's house in Gough Square in 1911, paid for its restoration and presented it to the nation as a museum. Harmsworth urged that all original detail should be meticulously preserved. The few surviving period features, therefore, were carefully cleaned and repaired. The reconstructive efforts were supervised by Albert E. Richardson, Professor of Architecture at University College London, an expert in Georgian art and architecture, who, amongst other things, went to great lengths to find the correct marbled wallpaper. Fundraising and promotional events included a Dickens memorial dinner at the Lyceum Club and a seasonal reading of *A Christmas Carol* for cub scouts from the Magdalen College Mission ('around the very hearth where Charles Dickens sat as a boy, years ago, imagining faces in the coals of the basket grate'). There was also a 'Dickens Birthday Matinee' organised by the Shakespearean actor-manager Ben Greet at the Lyric Theatre, featuring, amongst others, the elderly Jennie Lee, briefly lured out of retirement (and received with rapturous applause). No opportunity was missed to extract money from the theatregoers. The turkey which featured in a scene from *A Christmas Carol* was not a prop but a real (deceased) bird, which was auctioned off to the audience at the curtain call.[39]

Most prominently, Langstaff organised a celebrity amateur production of Sir Edward Bulwer-Lytton's comedy *Not So Bad as We Seem*, staged at Devonshire House, Piccadilly. This was an echo of Dickens's own amateur staging of the play at the same address in 1851, for an audience which had included Queen Victoria.[40] There were efforts to include descendants of the original cast, and the play attracted the attention of the great and good. Various contemporary literary luminaries offered support, including George Bernard Shaw and H.G. Wells, with performers including Alfred Noyes, Rebecca West, A.A. Milne and William Pett Ridge, amongst others.[41] Ivor Novello even composed the overture. Margot Asquith, socialite spouse of the former prime minister, was given a non-speaking role, which seems to have irked her. Pett Ridge recalled of rehearsals that 'Mrs Asquith had a speechless part in the play, but atoned for this compulsory silence by giving her views with strange frankness'.[42] The play culminated with the cast members and programme sellers, all in period costume, taking part in quadrilles – a dance consigned to history – and then being joined by the audience for the more contemporary fox trot. The successful staging of the play was testimony to Langstaff's great talent at garnering support and publicity.[43] He himself quietly boasted of the highly visible press coverage, in what he humorously dubbed 'murder headlines' (meaning large print).[44] There were other attention-grabbing events. The placing of a wreath on Dickens's tomb on the anniversary of his death by 'Harry Adams, aged 9, of Somers Town, a cripple from birth' was also given much prominence in the press, a carefully orchestrated sentimental tribute paid by 'a real Tiny Tim'.[45]

News of the library first appeared in the media in 1920 and the building opened to its first readers on 3 May 1922.[46] Langstaff made a point of announcing that everything would be a suitable size and height for children, and that he would also include hygienic measures suitable for the poor. Thus, every child had to wash their hands upon entry and wear a blue or brown smock to cover dirty clothes ('I told the children that I planned to put them in brown covers in order that I might take the brown covers off the books', quipped Langstaff).[47] This was a uniform which also 'prepared the children for the business of reading'.[48] The work of attendants was to encourage reading above all else, and thus they were to 'tell the dragging part of the story, read the interesting part, leaving the children to read the thrilling parts'.[49] But, as the scheme progressed, twenty older children were themselves employed as staff, doubtless something of a cost-saving measure. They supervised various elements of the building. The 'Chief' monitored a wigwam on the first floor, dedicated to silent reading, and the 'Warder-of-the-Dungeon' was placed in charge of the 'Fairy Dungeon' in the basement (a toy-strewn crèche where older children could leave any babies they were minding for their parents). A Miss De Pollier, trained at New York Public Library, provided expertise on book selection and the library also received book donations from publishers and authors, and even from the French Embassy. These included books, and a letter, from Kate Douglas Wiggin, most famous as the author of *Rebecca of Sunnybrook Farm*, who herself, as a young woman, had started a free kindergarten in San Francisco. She was also the author of 'A Child's Journey with Dickens', which recounted her own chance childhood encounter with the great author during his American tour of 1868. ('"What book of mine do you like best?" Dickens asked, I remember; and I answered, "Oh, I like David Copperfield much the best. That is the one I have read six times."')[50]

Only a few months after it had opened, the library was presented as a gift to St Pancras Borough Council, with the hope that they might build upon Langstaff's work. There was a formal ceremony with congratulations from the great and the good, including a letter from Queen Alexandra, and a speech from the writer John Galsworthy. He recalled his own childhood reading of Dickens and worried that nowadays it might prove difficult to attract local children away from the cinema (an attraction he considered 'a cross between a thought-saving machine and a cocktail').[51] The following year, however, the Council grew cold about its potential new responsibilities. There was, after all, already a children's section in the nearby Camden Town Branch Library. The Council's Public Library committee concluded that this small back-street house was 'unsuitable for public library purposes' and they could not justify the estimated £400 per annum cost.[52] Langstaff, meanwhile, had already returned to the United States.[53] By the autumn of 1923, the library was under the care of an eclectic group of trustees, including Sir Sydney Lee (a leading Shakespearean scholar), Alderman Davis (the councillor who owned the freehold), Mary Tate (the American wife of Edwin Tate, son of the sugar magnate Henry Tate) and Elizabeth Ord Marshall, who served as the group's secretary. Ord Marshall was well known as the founder of the League of Empire, dedicated to promoting imperial sentiment in schools and international educational exchange projects within the British Empire.[54] Henry Dickens, the author's son and a respected lawyer, remained a supporter of the project; and William Pett Ridge served as treasurer (he would also hold the presidency of the Dickens Fellowship, 1924–6). Others lent their names to further monetary appeals and fundraising events, including Bransby Williams, the playwright Arthur Pinero and the actress Dame Madge Kendal.[55] In 1929, an unusual gift was installed – stained-glass windows created by John Winbolt, a member of the St Pancras branch of the Dickens Fellowship, showing some of Dickens's child characters (Paul and Florence Dombey, David Copperfield, Oliver Twist). A pair of windows showing Dickens himself, young and old, were similarly donated to the Dickens House museum on Doughty Street (which we will come to below).

William Pett Ridge, however, died in 1930, followed by Elizabeth Ord Marshall in 1931. The David Copperfield Library did not survive their loss. The project, which had started with such a burst of publicity and activity, starved of funds and support, ended with a whimper in 1931. The books were sold and the proceeds were reserved for charity. The carefully restored house was demolished the following year, part of street improvements that saw the road renamed as Cranleigh Street and a block of flats erected upon the site, named Cranleigh Buildings. This was, of course, not the first of Dickens's London homes to be destroyed. Furnival's Inn had been flattened in 1898 by the Prudential Assurance Company, to be replaced with a Gothic office block. Tavistock House, Dickens's home from 1851 to 1860, was likewise lost in 1901 (the site now forms part of the headquarters of the British Medical Association). The Dickens family's home in Bayham Street (from 1822 to 1823), another small house in Camden, made famous in Forster's biography, was demolished in

1910. Fans had scrambled to secure relics, including the attic window (the attic was believed to have been the author's bedroom) and an easily detached door knocker. A Camden estate agent acquired the attic door, front door and three stoves. But Johnson Street was different in that it had been specially remade as a sort of working memorial to the great author. The building, according to Langstaff, was simultaneously Dickens's childhood home and the 'original' of Windsor Terrace in David Copperfield (a claim, incidentally, also made for the house in Bayham Street); and, not only that, the house was intended to fulfil a moral purpose which chimed with both Dickens's lived experience (as a neglected child who discovered the joys of literature) and his views on the importance of both education and imagination in childhood. Langstaff had artfully loaded the site with a raft of Dickensian sentiment and persuaded others to do like-wise. Indeed, the house not only harboured its own crippled 'Tiny Tim' but, in an article which appeared in the *Not So Bad as We Seem* programme, was also transfigured by A.E. Richardson into two emblematic childhood characters: 'a child amongst houses, a regular Tiny Tim . . . the Peter Pan of Somers Town' (thus echoing Dickens's own habit of endowing inanimate objects and buildings with human character).[56] Richardson's article, in other words, both linked the small crooked slum house to Dickens's famous disabled child and simultaneously suggested that, by perpetually evoking Dickens's own childhood, it had the eternal youth of Peter Pan.

Nonetheless, despite such creative and fulsome sentiments at its inception, there seems to have been little notice paid to the David Copperfield Library's demise. There was a passing mention in the *Dickensian* and nothing in the press. This was, at least in part, because another house-as-monument – 48 Doughty Street, originally called 'Dickens House', nowadays known as the Charles Dickens Museum – could be found in nearby Bloomsbury.

***

Charles Dickens married Catherine Hogarth on 2 April 1836 while he was still living in a small apartment in Furnival's Inn. He was twenty-four years old and had already received critical acclaim for his lively collection of urban sketches, journalism and stories, *Sketches by Boz*. Catherine, four years his junior, was the daughter of a Scots journalist. The couple honeymooned in a cottage in Chalk in Kent, then returned to London, where Dickens had arranged to move from his original rooms in the building, costing £35 per annum, to a larger set costing £50. They thus acquired three rooms on the third floor, a lumber room above and a cellar.[57] The building itself was actually relatively modern, despite the quaint name. The original Furnival's Inn was an Inn of Chancery – an ancient college and place of accommodation for lawyer's clerks – whose medieval buildings had been demolished in 1818. The apartment, therefore, was not the thoroughly antiquated affair one might imagine. Nonetheless, it was still quite small, not least when Catherine's sixteen-year-old sister, Mary Hogarth, came to stay (Dickens records in a diary entry that she once kept house for the couple for several weeks). When Charles and Catherine's first child, Charley, was born on 6 January 1837, the need to find somewhere larger grew more pressing. Dickens, at least, felt relatively secure regarding his finances, having committed himself to several new writing projects. This included beginning work on the opening chapters of *Oliver Twist*, before he had even concluded *The Pickwick Papers*. He consulted 'a crew of house-agents and attorneys' and settled upon 48 Doughty Street in Bloomsbury, a town house in a late Georgian terrace, built to a similar design as 13 Johnson Street but considerably more spacious, located in a much more genteel neighbourhood.[58] Dickens's literary topographers would later record that the road had its own iron gates, manned by a gatekeeper in livery, but this barrier to through traffic seems only to have been erected in the 1850s.[59] Nonetheless, this was a respectable locality, suited to an up-and-coming young author.

Dickens, in fact, briefly mentions the neighbourhood in *Sketches by Boz*, describing Great Coram Street, only a few hundred yards distant. The district possesses a 'romantic dreariness', existing in a 'state of profound repose', only disturbed by the rumbling of a hackney coach and the occasional 'stray lawyer's clerk, on his way home to Somers-town', striking an iron boot heel on the metal cover of a coal hole.[60] It is tempting to speculate that Dickens himself was the 'stray lawyer's clerk' whose boots once clipped the coal-hole covers, disturbing the quietude of Bloomsbury. Certainly, the district was on the route of his walk from Somers Town to the chambers of his first employer in Gray's Inn.

The house proved to be an excellent choice, although Dickens's time there was marred by tragedy. The family moved in on 25 March 1837. On 7 May, Mary Hogarth, now living at Doughty Street with her sister and brother-in-law, died suddenly, aged only seventeen. Catherine Dickens, doubtless traumatised by the loss of her sister, suffered a miscarriage the following week. Dickens himself plunged into a paroxysm of grief and anguish, famously the only occasion on which he ever failed to meet his writing deadlines. Indeed, there was clearly a strong emotional attachment between Dickens and Mary Hogarth which, after her death, became something of a morbid obsession. He would dwell upon the thought that he should like to be buried close to her, buying a family plot in Kensal Green Cemetery in which Mary was interred. Dickens initially intended that the grave would be reserved for his mother-in-law and 'for us and our dear children' – they would all be together.[61] In the end, however, he gave the grave wholly to the Hogarth family, upon the premature death of Mary's brother, George Thomson Hogarth (1821–41). Many of Dickens's youthful, innocent female heroines undoubtedly owe something to Mary Hogarth's memory, most obviously Little Nell. Dickens would write in a letter to Forster that the finale of *The Old Curiosity Shop* – that is, Nell's untimely death – opened 'old wounds', such that 'Dear Mary died yesterday, when I think of this sad story'. The same letter also implies that he actively drew upon the memory of her death to place himself in the right frame of mind for writing the novel's ending ('I am afraid of disturbing the state I have been trying to get into, and having to fetch it all back again').[62]

Doughty Street, however, more than anything, was the home where Dickens came into his own as a famous young author, striking yet more publishing deals, wining and dining friends and acquaintances. But he did not remain there for long. Following the great success of *Oliver Twist*, along with the birth of two daughters (Mary, also known as 'Mamie', and Kate, known as 'Katey'), he desired a property more suited to his improved finances, social status and family circumstances. The family moved to No. 1 Devonshire Terrace in Marylebone in December 1839, which was to be rented for £160 (twice the cost of Doughty Street). Forster recalled it as 'a handsome house with a garden of considerable size, shut out from the New Road by a high brick wall facing the York Gate into Regent's Park'.[63]

There was little interest in the Bloomsbury house during Dickens's lifetime. Some recalled the Doughty Street address when they aired their recollections of the great author after his death, and, similarly, when Catherine Dickens died in 1879. Forster, of course, mentions it in his biography. The house became the family home of Montague Gossett, a solicitor, from 1856 until his death in 1882, but was then put up for sale by auction, with the suggestion that the building might serve as either a private residence or offices.[64] This reflected the shifting demographics of central London. Office space was in demand, but the middle classes increasingly preferred larger residential properties in the leafy suburbs to narrow Georgian town houses. The other alternative for a house in Doughty Street was multi-occupancy, with an owner letting out rooms to individual tenants, and this is what seems to have occurred. William R. Hughes, writing up his tour of 'Dickens-Land' in 1891, found a sign in the front window reading 'Apartments to let'.[65] There was, doubtless, a regular trickle of Dickensian tourists, thanks to the assorted works of literary topography which mentioned 48 Doughty Street in the 1880s and 1890s. An article in the *Daily Mail* in 1897 noted that 'The present occupier will tell you ... that the knocker on the front door is "the original one belonging to Dickens"'.[66]

From 1901, 48 Doughty Street became a women-only boarding house, managed by one Jane Lyons, receiving 'ladies, visiting or employed in London', the likes of clerks, teachers and typists.[67] The building now had a gold-lettered sign on the front door which read 'The Dickens House', under which Lyons 'modestly subscribed her own name in the same resplendent colour', and the door itself was now painted sage green, unlike the simple grained wood of Dickens's day.[68] Lyon's guests included Mary Richardson, a Canadian suffragette, released temporarily from Holloway Prison in October 1913 after going on a hunger strike (she was freed under the infamous 'Cat and Mouse Act', which recalled prisoners once they had recovered their health). On 10 March 1914, Richardson left the house, bought a small axe at a nearby hardware shop, then proceeded to the National Gallery and slashed the Rokeby Venus. She then released a statement which read: 'I have tried to destroy the picture of the most beautiful woman in mythological history as a protest against the Government for destroying Mrs Pankhurst.'[69] The combination of a boarding house which provided safe harbour for suffragettes and simultaneously served as a literary shrine for the fans of Charles Dickens was a curious one. Nonetheless, the 'Dickens cult' continued to pay homage.

Francis Hopkinson Smith recorded his visit, finding the elderly Miss Lyons to be a quaint Dickensian character, very much in the same vein as Agnes Murray, whom he had met at the George Inn. The interior seemed to belong to another era. The parlour was 'neat as a pin and as comfortable as a slipper' and the owner 'precisely the kind of landlady you would have expected ... with a soft comfortable English voice'. Hopkinson Smith, in fact, waxed lyrical about the old lady:

She might have stepped out of one of his books, for she unquestionably lived in them . . . . a certain done-up-in-lavender sort of an old lady, as if she had lived a good many years in one room and been folded up every night and laid away in a bureau drawer. There were ruffles, too, somewhere – I think about her throat, and some kind of fluting at the end of two long white cap strings that rested on her thin shoulders; and small shrivelled hands and a quaint bend of her back as she leaned forward to hear me better . . . Perhaps a woman of seventy, perhaps eighty, but very gentle and with a motherly touch about her . . .[70]

The principal Dickens relic on offer was the original door knocker, now screwed to an internal wall to prevent theft ('try a rap of your own on it, everybody does who comes'). Hopkinson was seemingly not allowed into guests' rooms, but the back bedrooms were pointed out from the gloomy back garden as being Dickens's study and the room in which Mary Hogarth had died. Jane Lyons's expertise on the subject of Dickens, however, was doubtful. Mary Richardson remembered her landlady boasting that Dickens had been a poor young lodger at Doughty Street who found fame there by writing *David Copperfield* (actually written at Devonshire Terrace, in 1849–50, at the height of his fame).[71] Lyons also claimed to have been Benjamin Disraeli's housekeeper, referring to a nearby plaque-marked house on the junction of Doughty Street and Theobald's Road, where Disraeli was born in 1804. Unfortunately, the Disraeli family left that property in 1816, when the future prime minister was only twelve years old. Jane Lyons, in any case, seems to have left the house in 1914.[72] The freehold happened to become available for purchase in 1922 and, thanks to the work of the Dickens Fellowship, Doughty Street became a museum in 1925.

***

Published calls for a 'Dickens museum' in London date back to the turn of the twentieth century. In 1901, Thomas Wright wrote a letter to the *Daily Chronicle* which argued for a museum 'in London, and preferably in one of the houses in which Dickens resided or with which he was connected'.[73] Wright was a schoolmaster and keen literary biographer who had just opened a similar house museum dedicated to William Cowper in his home town of Olney, Buckinghamshire. Wright was also acquainted with William R. Hughes, whose substantial collection of Dickensiana had been broken up and sold upon his death in 1899, and thought that a museum might prevent the future dispersal of similar collections. Wright is nowadays largely remembered by Dickensians for his *Life of Charles Dickens* (1935), which made explicit the affair between Dickens and the actress Ellen Ternan. Many at the time resented hearing about the author's secret sex life and considered Wright a scandalmonger. Some even insisted that the relationship remained absolutely platonic, despite the fact that Dickens had engineered a brutal public separation from his wife. Nonetheless, it was Wright who first actively proposed a Dickens museum, volunteering to set it up if there was sufficient support. Percy Fitzgerald, who had published a number of articles about what he dubbed 'Bozland', was asked to comment. He, however, rather preferred the idea of making Gads Hill Place a literary shrine and claimed that it might even attract more tourists than a house in London.[74]

It is surprising that Fitzgerald initially was not interested, because he was arguably Dickens's greatest and most active memorialist at the turn of the century. He was not only the author of numerous pieces of literary topography but also a prolific if not overly gifted sculptor: he donated busts of Dickens to the pump room in Bath (1905) and the Prudential Assurance building on the site of Furnival's Inn (1907), and he created a marble plaque with a curious relief of Dickens's face that he affixed to Dickens's honeymoon cottage in Chalk, Kent (1911). This was all done at his own expense. The statue of Dr Johnson by St Clement's Church on the Strand is another of his donations; and he proposed a similar statue of Dickens for Rochester, which was scuppered by objections from the Dickens family.[75] An uncharitable critic might suggest that the sheer number of donated pieces reflected their artistic worth. Fitzgerald also famously ran a 'Boz Club' at his gentlemen's club, the Athenaeum (which had been Dickens's own club), principally consisting of members who had known the great author personally.[76] In 1902, however, Fitzgerald also helped establish the more egalitarian Dickens Fellowship (the illustrator Harry Furniss tellingly compared the Boz Club to the House of Lords, the Fellowship to the Commons), taking on the responsibility of being its first president.[77] This was the body that eventually created a Dickens museum in Doughty Street.

The Dickens Fellowship – which survives to this day – was a club which anyone could join for a modest membership fee (one shilling per annum), with local branches in the United Kingdom and further afield, and regular meetings and lectures, devoted to all things Dickens. The intention was to keep the great author's flame burning, both nationally and internationally. The notion of setting up such a club was originally championed by the novelist and playwright Hall Caine. He had recently relaunched Dickens's journal *Household Words* – or, at least, borrowed the title – and the germ of the idea came from a reader's letter. Fitzgerald was swiftly roped in as a figurehead for the scheme. Bertram Matz, a retiring and unassuming employee at Dickens's erstwhile publishers, Chapman and Hall, and an enthusiastic collector of Dickensiana, was another important figure involved in the Fellowship's foundation. Indeed, he played a key role, including editing the Fellowship's magazine, the *Dickensian*, from its inception in 1905 up to his death in 1925. Arthur Waugh, managing director and later chairman of Chapman and Hall, fondly remembered Matz as a wise and diplomatic colleague of impeccable virtue:

a man of impregnable integrity, whose zeal for the house that published Dickens amounted almost to a religion. He had entered the firm as a small boy, and had made its service his first and only care.[78]

. . . the last of the Victorians, both in sentiment and conduct. He believed that literature should observe a decent reticence; that the best books were those which could be read without offence . . . that British fiction was all the better for fostering the belief that, somewhere or other in the end, the good does surely triumph and the evil get punished.[79]

It was the highly organised and methodical Matz who drafted the Fellowship's constitution, which included a moral component, a product of his 'Victorian optimism'.[80] He defined the organisation's objects as not only promoting Dickens and his work but also chari- table endeavours in the spirit of Dickens, 'to speed the love of humanity which is the keynote of all his work'. The Fellowship would, for example, regularly organise gifts of food and toys for poor children, and it founded a home for blind servicemen in 1919. But Matz also proposed that the Fellowship should 'assist in the preser- vation and purchase of buildings and objects associated with his name or mentioned in his [Dickens's] works'.[81]

The Fellowship, in other words, was always concerned, to some degree, with Dickensian place and places. Hall Caine thus promised at the inaugural meeting in October 1902 that 'pilgrimages' or 'tramps' would be made by members during the summer to 'those parts of the town and country known as "Dickens-land"'.[82] The following year, Bransby Williams pioneered the first Dickens Fellowship visit to Chigwell, and a trip was also made to Rochester and Chatham – the first of many (following the example of the Boz Club, who had made the same journey in 1901).[83] Branch meetings, likewise, often involved illustrated lectures on 'Dickens's London' and other Dickensian localities, given by both local members and professional touring lecturers.[84] The first modest exhibition of Dickensiana organised by the Fellowship in 1903 showed not only various collectible editions of the novels, and items associated with the great author, but also real-world relics: the much-loaned 'Chester Chair' from the King's

Head at Chigwell; the leather container which hung outside the Leather Bottle public house in Cobham (and the pub's wooden sign, showing Mr Pickwick); the well-known real-world original of the 'Wooden Midshipman' carved statuette which graced Sol Gills's shop in *Dombey and Son*; and the letter box belonging to the defunct offices of the *Monthly Magazine* (through which Dickens had posted his first published short story).[85] The Fellowship also made it known that it would advise foreign visitors on how and where to book Dickens tours of the capital; and, by the 1920s, the central London branch had its own topographical lantern slides and prepared lectures which could be loaned to branches.[86] But it was one thing to take a healthy interest in Dickensian topography, another to save buildings from destruction. The Fellowship's finances, in practice, did not permit the acquisition of Dickens-related properties, and much of its 'preservation' work ultimately amounted to raising plaques. Doughty Street, however, would prove to be the noteworthy exception.

Matz, in fact, had his eye on Doughty Street from the organisation's earliest days. He championed the somewhat contentious 'Dickens Stamp' scheme in 1910, in which fans were asked to buy penny 'stamps' which could be pasted into their Dickens books at home. The purpose was for the money raised to be given to Dickens's more penurious descendants during the centenary year of 1912 (some considered this to be meretricious money-grubbing). Matz, however, suggested that any spare cash might purchase 48 Doughty Street, to be preserved as an 'author's house', in similar fashion to Thomas Carlyle's house in Cheyne Row and Dr Johnson's house in Gough Square.[87]

The opportunity finally arose in 1921, when the Tichborne Estate in Bloomsbury decided to sell off land, including a block on 39–62 Doughty Street.[88] There was an initial plan to knock down these buildings and create a large hotel. The Fellowship scrambled to secure Dickens's erstwhile home, with the aim of creating, as Matz described it, a 'Dickens museum, library and picture gallery . . . [a] National Dickens Shrine'.[89] The house would also be the 'Dickens

Information Bureau, the Dickens University, where students shall gain all the knowledge they seek . . . topographical, historical, literary and bibliographical'.[90] On top of all this, the proposal was for the house to become the administrative home of the Dickens Fellowship and a place where members could meet, a sort of club house.[91] The proposal was quite ambitious, but Sir Frederick Macmillan, the Fellowship's president, declared that there could be no more suitable site since it was 'practically in the same state as in 1839'.[92] The only difficulty was that the freehold was initially purchased using the private funds of two of the Fellowship's committee members – Matz and one Lawrence Green – who needed to be reimbursed. There was also a legal obligation to buy the adjoining house, No. 49, which was initially let out as offices to recoup the cost (and only integrated into the museum in 2012). Finally, the Fellowship had to square things with the existing tenant, who had several years remaining on his lease. The initial cost for both houses was estimated to be £4,500.[93] Overall, £10,000 was required in order to cover the acquisition, create a charitable trust (which would include members from the City of London and London County Council), and pay for a caretaker and ongoing maintenance.

The Fellowship would, at least, not repeat the mistake of Brett Langstaff at Johnson Street. They both intended to hold onto the property for themselves and have a sufficient endowment fund that would guarantee its future, 'the *sine qua non* of permanence'.[94] By April 1923, Macmillan conceded that only £500 had been raised – a look at the initial subscription list shows that £100 of this was his own money – but he promised that the cause had not yet been thoroughly publicised and more money would soon appear.[95] The sum total, in fact, rose to £1,761 by July 1923, thanks to money from Fellowship branches in the United Kingdom, Canada and the United States; booksellers; publishers of Dickens's work; and even – one suspects thanks to an ingenious begging letter – 'firms who have used Dickens for advertisements'.[96] Coincidentally, Frederick Latham, the owner of Gads Hill, died in the autumn of 1923 and, had the Fellowship not already committed to Doughty Street, they may well have bought the property in Kent (for it failed to meet the initial reserve price at auction and overtures were made by Latham's estate). But there was no realistic possibility of buying and maintaining two Dickens houses. A year later, the Doughty Street fund amounted to around £3,000, including a remarkably generous $925 from a Frank B. Edmonds of Glen Cove, Long Island.[97] By the museum's opening on 9 June 1925 – the anniversary of Dickens's death – sufficient money had been acquired for the purchase, if not the endowment. Admission was one shilling.

Selections from Matz's own collection formed a good proportion of the initial museum offering. There was a good deal to draw upon. Matz's treasure trove included the reading desk Dickens used for his public readings; a baluster taken from the White Hart Inn; plus 1,200 separate books and 897 portraits of the author, 'mounted and arranged chronologically'.[98] Other objects in the initial assemblage of Dickensiana in the museum included a quill used by Dickens when editing *All the Year Round* and a model of the Maypole Inn owned by Bransby Williams. There were also a good number of curated commercial 'curios':

> china figures of characters from Dickens, plates, cups, saucers, with pictures, tea and biscuit canisters with scenes from Dickens; mugs and souvenirs from Dickens inns; a sardine tin with Pickwick's figure on the outside; a score or more of cigar boxes, tobacco tins, and match-boxes; and eight different packs of Dickens cards.[99]

The house itself, however, was not laid out as if still occupied by Dickens and his family. Rather, the rooms provided space for hanging Dickens-related pictures and paintings and glass-topped display tables for assorted manuscripts and letters; minor personal possessions such as 'a tortoise-shell card-case, an ivory note-tablet, and a pipe stop and knife'; and the obligatory lock of hair (cut from Dickens's head after his death by Georgina Hogarth).[100] These were not reconstructed period rooms and, indeed, modern gas fires were placed throughout, except in the basement.[101] Anyone familiar with the present-day museum would find the 1925 version remarkably bare. This was largely due to lack of funds, rather than an austere vision for the building; but some creative effort was, at least, expended in creating a 'Dickensian' atmosphere. Thus, early in 1925, members of the Fellowship dressed up in character and posed for photographs on the doorstep as Mr Pickwick, Arabella Wardle and the young Dickens, 'greeting' his own characters. This was essentially a promotional gimmick. The museum still wanted for funds, and the images appeared in an article in the *Graphic* published on Dickens's birthday in which Pett Ridge solicited donations, as well as being reproduced in other newspapers and magazines.[102] But there was also a more permanent fanciful display. The basement kitchen was fitted out as a Tudor parlour, complete with mock oak beams and latticed windows:

> something more like an inn-parlour of the past, with a tiled floor, and a great open fireplace, and settles, and pipes, and a kettle for hot brandy and water or pineapple rum: an old-fashioned cosy room where at any moment the sound of hoofs might be heard and the door might open and admit the burly figure of Mr Anthony Weller in his many capes . . .[103]

The kitchen, in fact, was ultimately designated not as an 'inn-parlour' but as a representation of the kitchen of Manor Farm, Dingley Dell, in *The Pickwick Papers*.[104] The conversion work was paid for by a J.K.O. Sherwood (another wealthy elderly resident of Glen Cove, Long Island) and a J.J. Price of New York, although it is not entirely clear if they had a say in planning the project or merely supplied a convenient donation.[105] Windsor chairs, a brass chestnut roaster, a copper warming pan and a pewter tankard were donated by sundry members of the Fellowship.[106] A 'Magicoal' electric fire containing fake coals glowed in the hearth.[107]

The Fellowship clearly wanted something in the house that would stimulate the imagination of visitors beyond mere relics, providing a more immersive experience. We can also see hints of this ambition in 'Under a Dickens Roof-tree' (1925), a publicity brochure published by John Wright & Co., the manufacturers of the museum's gas fires. This booklet was promotional literature: the fires are visible in many of the photographs; there is an advert for Wright & Co. at the back; and there is even a subtle reference to Dickens complaining about the price of coal (as if to say, 'if only he had gas fires!'). Nonetheless, the book was plainly authored under the aegis of the Fellowship and speaks to a desire to associate Doughty Street with the imaginative world of Dickens's books. The pamphlet ends by directing readers to a particular relic situated in the house's attic: a preserved window pane removed from Bayham Street. This becomes, we are told, a 'magic casement' through which visitors can conjure up an astonishing scene:

> Bit by bit, the immediate surroundings fade out of sight, and gradually a crowd of quaint people begins to gather . . . the procession of men, women and children created by the genius of Dickens comes thick and fast into our sight as we look through the Magic Casement . . . They all crowd round one stout, bald-headed gentleman of benevolent aspect . . . it is Mr Pickwick himself!

The writer of the brochure, in effect, promises visitors that imaginative visions of Dickens's characters may be had at Doughty Street and turns, in particular, to the spectre of Pickwick.[108]

The Pickwick Papers have rather fallen out of favour in recent decades, but, as I have already hinted, many people once considered Pickwick the first and finest product of Dickens's imagination. The choice of Pickwick (here and in the publicity photographs) was undoubtedly intended to suggest that the house contained something of the bonhomie, hospitality and good cheer found in Dickens's first novel. The kitchen, in turn, was the physical manifestation of this hoped-for Pickwickian mood, alluding to the fun and festivities that take place at Dingley Dell in the book. We should also perhaps remember that the balding, rotund figure of Pickwick was rather iconic in the early twentieth century, instantly recognisable to the general public. One can, for example, find him popping up in 1920s advertisements for the likes of whisky, mints, toffee, fish paste, baked beans, soap and even, rather counter-intuitively, motor cars ('. . . had Mr Pickwick lived to-day, his good taste and his keen appreciation of personal comfort would have induced him to pin his faith to the car which has come to be known as "the leader of its class" ').[109] To associate the museum with the well-known and popular character was simply good marketing. The vision of other Dickensian characters paying Pickwick homage in Wright & Co.'s brochure was also perhaps inspired by an illustration: Sol Etyinge's 'Mr Pickwick's Reception'. This drawing appeared as a bonus illustration in the first part of the serialisation of *Edwin Drood* published in the United States. Etyinge's unusual sketch shows Pickwick on a rustic seat atop a grassy knoll as a parade of dozens of Dickens's characters go past, acknowledging their great forefather (with Sam Weller standing at his side, pointing out the various individuals). The figure of Pickwick in Etyinge's illustration, presented as Dickens's ur-character, is also a proxy for Dickens himself, reviewing a triumphal procession of his life's work. The Fellowship were similarly keen to associate Dickens with the benign, hospitable Pickwick, promising a warm welcome at his house at Doughty Street. The primacy of Pickwick was also significant. Dickens only stayed in the house for two and a half years but surely Doughty Street gained special significance for its association with that important first book.

Interestingly, the *Sphere*, a rival publication to the *Graphic*, would provide its own twist on the doorstep publicity photographs of

Pickwick. A couple of weeks later, the paper's front page contained a drawing by Charles Buchel showing a cheerful Mr Pickwick welcoming the older Dickens to 48 Doughty Street (as opposed to the *Graphic*'s young Dickens welcoming Pickwick). The explanatory text below the image makes clear this is the present-day exterior of Doughty Street (the memorial plaque, in fact, is visible in the illustration) but with 'the novelist being greeted by Mr Pickwick, whilst his [Dickens's] young wife peers out from a ground-floor window'.[110] All in all, it is a very confusing scene and one wonders quite how the older Dickens, Mr Pickwick and the young Catherine are to be mentally or chronologically combined. There is a hint, perhaps, that the older Dickens is returning to his carefree youth – when, indeed, he still loved his young wife – and that visitors, likewise, will recapture their own youthful ebullience through visiting Doughty Street. The *Sphere* presented the drawing to the Fellowship, who included a reproduction of it in their guidebook to the museum, with the tag line 'Mr Dickens and Mr Pickwick meet on the door step of 48 Doughty Street'. This was pretty much the one element of outright 'fancy' in a booklet which otherwise stuck rigidly to the Gradgrindian facts, which would remain largely unchanged for many years.[111]

The pseudo-antique kitchen, of course, also represented a more generic nostalgic vision of oak beams and roaring fires, a quaint Tudor England particularly beloved of American tourists. As early as August 1925, it was noted that 'Americans, indeed, make up the bulk of callers'.[112] A visiting correspondent of the *Glasgow News* in 1927 checked the guestbook and found visitors from Rochester, NY; Minneapolis; Fort Wayne, IN; Haverford, PA; Worcester, MA; Syracuse, NY; Chicago; Boston; Duluth, MN; and Beverley Hills – he was the only visitor from London.[113] The Fellowship were well aware of this constituency and what they wanted from a visit to 'Old England'. Indeed, it is important to remember that Dickens, for foreign visitors, has always been part of a generalised pageant of English/British culture, framed to attract tourists. For example, an advertisement which ran in US papers in 1912, promoting travel to the United Kingdom, probably sponsored by Cunard (who feature prominently in the advertising copy), had the tag line 'Travel Britain – No country is Richer in Relics of Storied Past'. The text below touches upon every cliché of 'historic England' which might appeal to the American tourist:

> feudal castles, walled cities and grim battlefields . . . stately ancestral homes, slumberous old-world villages . . . panoramic changing scenery . . . the great Universities, the time-mellowed ivy-clad Cathedrals . . . Britain, land of bard and poet . . . the home of Shakespeare, of Dickens, Thackeray and Wordsworth . . . strewn with the tombs of kings and martyrs.[114]

The town house at 48 Doughty Street had to compete with these castles and cathedrals if it was to attract general visitors. There may also have been thoughts of a rival Dickensian attraction which could lay some claim to historical old-world charm, the so-called Old Curiosity Shop of Portsmouth Street, near Lincoln's Inn Fields. I will discuss its Dickensian history in Chapter 7, but it is sufficient to note here that this quirky old building looked like a perfect vision of Tudor England. The shop was a lopsided sixteenth-century cottage in the middle of London which, during the previous forty years or so, had managed to become *the* site for visiting Dickens-loving tourists. The Fellowship had always considered this building a rank impostor, and not without reason. Nonetheless, the Doughty Street kitchen – consciously or otherwise – may well have been an attempt to steal some of the shop's Tudor thunder.

Doughty Street, of course, endures to this day, fulfilling Matz's hopes for a museum, memorial and meeting place in the heart of London. There have been, naturally enough, considerable changes, not least the merger of No. 48 and its neighbour No. 49, creating space for an ever-changing roster of exhibitions, and the introduction of a gift shop. The trustees in the early years, according to the first curator, Doris Minards, puritanically refused even the sale of post-cards as 'not dignified'.[115] But this policy does not seem to have been applied very consistently or for very long. 'Seasonable gifts' were on sale for the Christmas period in 1927, located at various spots in the house, including Dickensian calendars with a daily Dickens quota-tion; playing cards featuring Mr Micawber; postcards featuring scenes from the novels; letter racks ('a model of the novelist seated in his chair'); Bardell and Pickwick nutcrackers; a Fat Boy corkscrew; and a range of toasting forks, ash trays and pokers.[116] The mock Tudor kitchen finally disappeared in the 1980s, when the museum decided to create a period drawing room (furnished exactly as it would have been in the 1830s) and began to extend this curatorial approach throughout the house, with great success. David Parker, the museum's then curator, acknowledged that some visitors and members of the Fellowship had fond memories of the old kitchen, but he suggested in the *Dickensian* that 'few will prefer an imaginary representation of a setting much better imagined between the covers of the novel to a scholarly reconstruction of Dickens's own milieu'.[117] One might argue, of course, that the recreation of period rooms is arguably as much about creating *imagined* spaces as it is about the recreation of places from Dickens's novels. The visitor who 'steps back in time' in such environments, however scholarly and detailed the reconstruction, still engages their imagination. Dickens himself suggests as much in 'The Bagman's Tale', with its peculiarly talkative 'strange, grim-looking, high backed chair' (as discussed in Chapter 2).

We cannot help but apply our imagination to historical real-world objects: they provoke and stimulate self-created visions of the past. Those visions are coloured by our own experience, not least our previous consumption of history and historical fiction. Dickens hints at this early on in *The Pickwick Papers* when the characters first come across the antiquity of Rochester Castle. Snodgrass, who is described as 'poetic', is filled with Romantic sentiment at the picturesque spectacle ('Magnificent ruin!'). Pickwick only has an interest in spotting antiquarian architectural detail ('"What a study for an anti-quarian!" were the very words which fell from Mr Pickwick's mouth, as he applied his telescope to his eye'). The theatrical charlatan Jingle, meanwhile, conjures up archetypal Romantic antiquarian imaginings about the castle and neighbouring cathedral ('frowning walls – tottering arches – dark nooks – crumbling staircases – old cathedral too – earthy smell – pilgrims' feet wore away the old step . . .'). Jingle's long stream of hyphenated staccato language – simultaneously brief and prolix – is typical of the playbills of the period, which advertised key scenic and plot elements in the same adumbrated style. Thus Jingle's ostensibly more imaginative visualisation of the past is, in fact, nonetheless derived from the Gothic imaginary of popular novels and theatre (just as Snodgrass's derivative response belongs to the picturesque tour, and Pickwick's the antiquarian guidebook). For all three men, Dickens suggests that their experi-ence when encountering this ancient place is actually somewhat clichéd and second-hand, framed by their own past experience of travelogues and fiction. We come to the past with our own imagina-tive baggage. Indeed, one might question to what degree (literary) tourists truly value scholarship and authenticity. For, as I will discuss in the following chapters, any true history of 'Dickens's London' – any history of Dickens tourism – must encompass the fake, the misplaced and the manufactured.

6

THE HAUNTED BRIDGE

Present-day London Bridge (built 1967–73) is a minimalist concrete affair, the epitome of mid-twentieth-century modernism, an unlikely place to find relics of 'Dickens's London'. Nonetheless, a narrow set of stone steps, leading down from the bridge to the vicinity of Southwark Cathedral, regularly receives visits from modern-day literary pilgrims. The blue plaque at the base of these stairs, underneath the bridge's supporting arch in Montague Close, explains their appeal:

Nancy's Steps
These steps and arch are surviving fragments of the 1831 London Bridge designed by John Rennie and built by his son Sir John Rennie. The steps were the scene of the murder of Nancy in Charles Dickens' novel Oliver Twist.

Many people, of course, simply come across these steps by accident, without consulting a tour guide or guidebook. The riverside walk hereabouts is dominated by groups of tourists seeking out Borough Market, Shakespeare's Globe and Tate Modern. Those who happen to notice the plaque are doubtless gratified to discover this 'surviving fragment' – a charming piece of Dickensian urban heritage. Indeed, these are precisely the sort of chance encounters with historic sites that make London so appealing to sightseers.

The plaque itself, however, is something of an oddity. The colour and design approximate the blue plaques produced by English Heritage, but no one seems willing to claim ownership of this wholly unofficial memorial. The contents are also rather questionable. It is true that Rennie's London Bridge was constructed between 1824 and 1831, alongside the famous medieval Old London Bridge (which was then finally demolished, *c.* 1831–3). The steps probably belong to that period. But the plaque's précis of the plot of *Oliver Twist* raises questions – at least, for anyone who knows Dickens's original novel. The text would certainly puzzle the Victorian literary tourists who first visited London Bridge in the late nineteenth century. They would know full well that, in the book, Nancy is killed in Sikes's lodgings, 'a mean and badly-furnished apartment, of very limited size ... abutting on a close and dirty lane'.[1] Nancy's death in the novel is a horrific moment of domestic violence, hidden away from prying eyes.

Dickens's original story, however, does feature a crucial scene located upon a flight of riverside stairs, a little earlier in the narrative. The stairs are the site of the meeting between Nancy, Rose and Mr Brownlow, where she reluctantly divulges secrets concerning Oliver's persecutors. Victorian literary tourists, therefore, would come to 'Nancy's Steps' to see where this encounter took place. Dickens describes the locality in some detail:

> These stairs are a part of the bridge; they consist of three flights. Just below the end of the second, going down, the stone wall on the left terminates in an ornamental pilaster facing towards the Thames. At this point the lower steps widen: so that a person

turning that angle of the wall, is necessarily unseen by any others
on the stairs who chance to be above him, if only a step.[2]

Unfortunately, these three broad flights of stairs, leading down to
the river, vanished when Rennie's bridge was demolished in the late
1960s. Compare Dickens's description with the modern reality and
it will quickly become clear that the present-day narrow Nancy's
Steps are merely a shortcut to Montague Close, and nothing like the
stairs in the novel. The modern blue plaque, in other words, marks
the site of neither the pivotal meeting (which ultimately leads to
Nancy's death, when news of her betrayal reaches Sikes) nor the
dreadful murder.

Nonetheless, Dickensian tourists have sought out Nancy's Steps
– in one form or another – for nigh on one hundred and fifty years.
In this chapter, I explore the significance of the steps in Dickens's
novel, their long history as a tourist destination and the reason for the
contemporary plaque's peculiar mistakes (not least, the popularity
and influence of Lionel Bart's 1960s musical *Oliver!*). The confusion,
in a sense, seems rather appropriate, for Dickens himself deliberately
obfuscates aspects of London Bridge in the original book. He
summons, to misquote a well-known phrase, the Ghost of Bridges
Past, merging the real and imagined, past and present, public and
personal. The London Bridge of *Oliver Twist* is actually a deeply
uncanny place, haunted by the gruesome shades of its medieval predecessor and Dickens's memories of his own childhood. Literary tourism
has itself been described as 'necromanticism' – a ghostly communion
with the dead author and their work – the real world haunted by the
ghosts of fiction.[3] Dickens's original description of London Bridge in
Oliver Twist, as a place between worlds, hints at this possibility of
bridging the gap between reality and fiction, rather anticipating the
coming of the literary tourist.

***

To understand Dickens's interest in London Bridge – and its place in *Oliver Twist* – we have to begin with his boyhood. As noted in the previous chapter, the Dickens family relocated to London from Chatham in Kent in the summer of 1822, when John Dickens was recalled to the Navy Pay Office's headquarters at Somerset House. In fact, for reasons unknown to posterity, the young Charles seems to have remained behind in Chatham for a short period. He belatedly followed his family to the capital, travelling unaccompanied in a coach. Later in life, he recalled the damp straw on the stage coach floor, imagining himself 'packed – like game – and forwarded, carriage-paid, to the Cross Keys, Wood-street, Cheapside, London'.[4] It was a miserable day, the city obscured by driving rain; and, although he happened to have the coach interior entirely to himself, he seems to have extracted little pleasure from the journey. The coach, romantically named the Blue-Eyed Maid, travelling from Kent to Cheapside, naturally would have taken him over the most easterly river crossing, namely Old London Bridge.[5] We do not know how frequently he returned to this part of London in the next couple of years, but in 1824, this imaginative boy could be found loitering on the bridge at the start of the day, watching the river traffic, dreaming of a better future.

I have already briefly alluded to this well-known period of Dickens's childhood in the previous chapter. Dickens's parents, struggling to pay off John Dickens's mounting debts, sent their eldest son out to work. This was bad enough for an intelligent boy who yearned for a good education and aspired to middle-class respectability. Worse still, he was to be employed in grubby manual labour, at a blacking factory close to Hungerford Stairs. He was obliged to stick labels onto pots of filthy shoe-black, along with uneducated working-class children (although he was originally kept separate from his co-workers, a short-lived token of deference to his superior social class). Throughout his life, he could still remember the miserable old building with complete clarity ('a crazy, tumble-down old house, abutting of course on the river, and literally overrun with rats').[6] Indeed, it is likely that this 'crazy, tumble-down old house' provided some inspiration for the decaying, sinister dens inhabited by the fictional Fagin in *Oliver Twist* (one clue being that a certain Bob Fagin was one of his fellow young workers). The young Dickens immediately longed for escape from this demeaning employment. When his impecunious father was arrested for debt and imprisoned in the Marshalsea debtor's gaol, any remaining hope seemed to vanish.

Charles was, at least, kept out of the Marshalsea itself and ultimately found accommodation in a nearby rented room, in Lant Street in the Borough. Nonetheless, he regularly visited the prison and would often wander the district, early in the morning, waiting for warders to open the Marshalsea's gates, so that he might breakfast with his incarcerated parents and younger siblings. His occasional companion on these meanderings was an orphan girl from the Chatham Workhouse, who had accompanied the Dickens family to London as their skivvy. The two of them would walk to Old London Bridge to watch the city awaken from its slumber. Dickens would later draw upon this memory in *David Copperfield*, taking inspiration from his own childhood experience:

> I was often up at six o'clock, and that my favourite lounging-place in the interval was old London Bridge, where I was wont to sit in one of the stone recesses, watching the people going by, or to look over the balustrades at the sun shining in the water, and lighting up the golden flame on the top of the Monument. The Orfling met me here sometimes, to be told some astonishing fictions respecting the wharves and the Tower; of which I can say no more than that I hope I believed them myself.[7]

Old London Bridge, in other words, was the place where Dickens began to fictionalise the capital, conjuring fantasies around the mysterious buildings that lined the riverside, recounting them to an anonymous orphaned child. It is, therefore, not altogether surprising that he should revert to this very familiar neighbourhood in *Oliver Twist*. But I suggest there is more to this particular choice of location than first meets the eye.

Dickens, after all, is not careless about locations in the novel. *Oliver Twist*, published in serial form between 1837 and 1839, is one of his most topographical works. The final leg of Oliver's journey into London, in the company of his new friend the Artful Dodger, is described so precisely that a reader might trace the orphan's progress on a street atlas. Likewise, the introduction to the concluding scenes in the riverside slum of Jacob's Island, where Bill Sikes deservedly comes to grief, reads like a perverse guided tour of the capital's hidden depths. Readers are regaled with an astonishingly elaborate and evocative description of the filthy, poverty-stricken district, introduced to them as if in a guidebook ('the visitor has to penetrate through a maze of close, narrow and muddy streets . . .').[8] The book is particularly fastidious about place. Yet there is no aspect of the plot which demands that the scene with Nancy, Brownlow and Rose Maylie take place on the bridge. Why are we brought to this spot for Nancy's revelatory meeting?

The choice ostensibly seems quite random. Nancy herself, in the narrative of the novel, has no particular ties to the district; and the thieves' final haunt, at Jacob's Island, although on the south bank of the Thames, is a good mile downstream. The meeting, in fact, *could* take place anywhere in London since, like all the underworld characters in the book, Nancy moves around the metropolis with remarkable ease, a symptom and symbol of the capital's endemic crime and poverty. We first meet her in Saffron Hill, a notoriously criminal district; but she is soon in disguise, dressed as a respectable servant, when she visits the Hatton Garden police court. Then we encounter Nancy at Bill Sikes's wretched East End lodgings, before she travels to the West End to meet the virtuous Rose (whom we ultimately discover is Oliver's maternal aunt). It is at this first meeting, fearing for Oliver's future well-being, that Nancy reveals the great secret of the story. The villainous Monks, a shady character who has flitted in and out of the narrative, has bribed Fagin to make Oliver a thief, to ensure that the boy cannot reclaim his lost inheritance. Rose wishes to talk further and involve Oliver's would-be patron, Mr Brownlow. Nancy is reluctant, but she makes Rose a rather peculiar promise: "'Every Sunday night, from eleven until the clock strikes twelve,' said the girl without hesitation, 'I will walk on London Bridge if I am alive.'"[9] This is to be their meeting place. Rose then conveys what she has learned to Brownlow, and, in due course, the pair proceed to the appointed location.

Certainly, Dickens suggests a symbolic contrast between the respectable West End and the proverbially vice-ridden East End in the initial meeting between Rose and Nancy. Southwark, then, south of the river, neither east nor west, perhaps serves as a sort of neutral territory. This is also the sort of public place where a meeting might seem to occur by chance. But there are other associations here, not least the fact that Dickens himself used to wait upon London Bridge, listening for the tolling of church bells, for the hour when he could enter the Marshalsea Gaol. The link to his own history cannot have escaped him as he wrote this passage. Nancy is bound to wait – just as the young Dickens waited – both haunted by their own criminal connections.

Dickens, however, also hints at the bridge's own history in his elaborate description of the meeting, specifically the history of its medieval precursor. For, when Dickens wrote *Oliver Twist*, it was not many years since the Old London Bridge had been demolished, in a manner which, I would argue, made a profound impression on the author.

***

The medieval bridge had long been a problem. Old London Bridge, connecting Southwark and the City of London, dated back to the early thirteenth century and was originally comprised of nineteen relatively small arches. Their modest proportions increasingly proved an obstacle to the ever-larger barges and boats that travelled the capital's 'silent highway'. The difficulty had been alleviated some-what by work carried out between 1758 and 1762, which knocked two arches into one, to create a wider central span for river traffic. This project also removed the last of the quaint houses which had been built on top of the bridge and its supporting piers, allowing more space for vehicles and pedestrians. Nonetheless, at the start of the nineteenth century, the bridge was still something of a throw-back, an obstruction to the increasingly frenetic back and forth of commercial shipping that dominated the great river. By the 1820s, proposals for a replacement had been circulating for decades and the City of London was finally in the process of sifting through archi-tects' submissions, including plans for new approach roads. The City worthies eventually settled on a fairly conservative design by John Rennie, who had died in 1821, to be built under the watchful eye of his son, John Rennie the Younger. Construction of cofferdams (enclosures within the stream of the river, pumped free of water) began in 1824 and a lavish ceremony marked the laying of the first stone in 1825. The interior of one of the cofferdams was divided into four tiers of galleries and covered with a great tent, topped with flags. Two thousand guests walked across a gantry from the old bridge and sat on rows of benches covered with scarlet cloth. The foundation stone, with a remarkably lengthy Latin inscription, was laid by the Lord Mayor 'amidst a discharge of cannon and shouts of God save the King'.[10]

Not everyone was impressed. To antiquarians, the new bridge seemed part of a threatening spirit of 'improvement' that was abroad in the capital, including 'alterations and modernisms ... pullings-down, and buildings-up; the turning of land into canals, and covering over old water-ways with new paved streets; erecting pert plaister fronts'.[11] It now seems rather curious to associate Georgian canals, paved streets and stucco with dazzling modernity. Nonetheless, Londoners in the 1820s were witnessing rapid urban development – including, for example, the creation of Regent Street and Regent's Park – and the emergence of a modern city that contained a curious mixture of old and new, cheek by jowl. This was particularly evident at London Bridge where, for several years, both the old and the new bridge (under construction) stood side by side, only a hundred feet apart. Demolition of the old bridge did not start in earnest until the new one was complete. Indeed, there seems to have been a brief period when both bridges were open – or perhaps partially open – to pedestrians. An 1831 print by Thomas Hosmer Shepherd shows fashionable promenaders on Rennie's uncompleted bridge, seemingly unconcerned by the absence of a finished parapet, looking down on its doomed medieval predecessor (the perspective is perhaps exaggerated in the print, but the height of the new bridge was almost twice that of the original).[12] Dickens himself, I propose, was struck by this contrast between old and new – this co-existence of past and present – for he puts his own literary spin on this weird conjunction in the pages of *Oliver Twist*.

For a start, there is something of the fairy tale about Nancy's promise that binds her to London Bridge every Sunday like some unbreakable spell; something of Cinderella in her departure at midnight; and there is a sense in Dickens's text that London Bridge itself undergoes a magical transformation as Rose and Brownlow approach. We find ourselves slipping back into a barbaric past as the bridge becomes a place of intense Gothic foreboding. Mist rises up from the river. The warehouses have 'lumbering shapes', like monsters lurking upon the bank beside impossibly dark waters. The old churches on opposite banks are 'giant-warders' (echoes of the giants Gog and Magog, said to be ancient tutelary deities of London). There is a hint that the bridge, perhaps even the city itself, is akin to a shadowy prison. Then the bell of St Paul's tolls 'for the death of another day'. The bridge, in other words, for a brief moment, becomes the nexus of a weird and deathly metropolis, a grim place of giants and monsters, and even a gloomy 'forest' of ship's masts in the background. Dickens goes even further – this is the witching hour:

> Midnight had come upon the crowded city. The palace, the night-cellar, the jail, the madhouse: the chambers of birth and death, of health and sickness, the rigid face of the corpse and the calm sleep of the child: midnight was upon them all.[13]

Perhaps the 'astonishing fictions' Dickens told to the 'Orfling' were along similar lines. Regardless, something uncanny is happening here. Is this still Rennie's bridge or is it something deeper and darker?

There is a sense in which it *must* be Rennie's bridge. Dickens often hints that his novels are set in the recent past, and he can be frustratingly vague and ambiguous about the precise period. To look for a definitive date can be 'to look for a precision alien to his spirit'.[14] But the set of stairs which Nancy bids Rose Maylie and Mr Brownlow to descend were a well-known *modern* feature of Rennie's new bridge. They lay at each end, on both the east and the wide sides, broad flights of granite steps, twenty-two feet wide, running down to the riverside, parallel with the parapet. We can see this width in the novel's accompanying illustration by Cruikshank, where, in the background, a waterman's skiff has been drawn up onto the steps, with plenty of room to spare. Dickens was generally rather fastidious about the work of his illustrators. There seems little doubt, therefore, that Dickens's characters *physically* find themselves on the recently built bridge, not its medieval predecessor. Nonetheless, Old London Bridge – the bridge of Dickens's childhood – haunts the scene in this uncanny midnight moment. Dickens often refers to the medieval past as a period of gross brutality (contrary to the prevailing Victorian interest in the romance of the Middle Ages), as I have already noted in Chapter 2. This is the spirit which he summons to the meeting place: barbarous antiquity haunting the present (with undertones, perhaps, of the 'barbaric' treatment he felt that he had received at the blacking factory). It is a very Gothic conceit – the eruption of ancient evil into contemporary life, the half-remembered past which is not quite buried – analogous to the submerged criminal underclass to which Nancy belongs, lurking beneath polite society. Thus, writing of the churches on opposing banks of the river, Dickens says, 'The tower of old Saint Saviour's Church, and the spire of Saint Magnus, so long the giant-warders of the ancient bridge, were visible in the gloom'.[15] The 'ancient bridge' here is the ghostly presence of Old London Bridge, evoked/invoked by the historic churches at the stroke of midnight. This is the tenor of the whole passage: the blurring of past and present.

The old bridge was also famously once the place for displaying traitors' heads on spikes, including those of the likes of Thomas More and Thomas Cromwell, generally at the stone gateway that once stood on the Southwark side. Dickens thus foreshadows Nancy's brutal punishment for her betrayal of Sikes. He also does this more bluntly in her own dialogue. Nancy tells Brownlow she has been imagining weird scenes of death, blood and fire. She has even been reading a book, which itself contains portents ("'I'll swear I saw 'coffin' written in every page of the book in large black letters, – aye, and they carried one close to me, in the streets to-night'").[16] The sort of fiction which the likes of Nancy might have read would indeed have been short, cheap and nasty – more penny dreadful than three-volume novel – containing a good deal of violence and death. But Dickens is being playful here in making Nancy a reader. Scholarly critics have noted how often Dickens likes to 'call attention to his own performance'.[17] Here we have a book within a book, both with grim portents in the text, for those who will see them. This is a self-referential nod to both his own Gothic effects and the horror of what is to come. It is as if he says to the reader: 'You may think I have gone too far here with all these grim touches – but I know exactly what I am doing.'

The stairs themselves also had their own ominous contemporary overtones in 1830s London. They would have reminded readers of pollution, both the stink of the sewage-laden Thames and something more besides. By the late 1840s, the managers of Rennie's new bridge had installed urinals on either side of the northern approach. Such facilities for men, increasingly common in the mid-Victorian era, were typically placed on public ground where there might be fewer nimby-ish complaints from local householders. Moreover, they were usually situated where objectional public urination was hitherto common-place. The riverside steps, in other words, were a place to step aside from the hustle and bustle, where a man (or a lower-class woman, willing to risk public shaming) might conveniently relieve themselves against a 'blank wall' (a darkened spot, not overlooked by windows). It is tempting to think that the northern side was chosen for new sanitary facilities because that was the more respectable side of the Thames. Regardless, descending the steps towards the river in *Oliver Twist*, upon the southern shore, is taking a step closer to London's filth. Nancy herself, talking to Rose, describes herself as a creature of 'the alley and gutter', and the idea of prostitutes as a kind of social pollutant was gaining ground in a century increasingly concerned with checking the spread and progress of contagious disease. The Southwark of medieval times, of course, was also infamous for its brothels. Nancy is leading Rose and Brownlow into the literal and metaphorical mire.

Rennie's London Bridge steps, highly accessible to the public, were also a notorious spot for suicides. A newspaper report from the 1840s records a policeman's conversation with a young woman standing anxiously on the stairs: 'He asked her where she was going, and she replied, while the tears ran down her face, "I am going to make a hole in the water".'[18] Nancy's decision to reveal the secrets of Fagin and his criminal associates is plainly suicidal. Bill Sikes has already made clear that to cross him means death (' "Well, then, keep quiet," rejoined Sikes, with a growl like that he was accustomed to use when addressing his dog, "or I'll quiet you for a good long time to come"").[19] Readers, moreover, have already heard Nancy contemplate the realistic possibility of dying at his hands.

London Bridge, therefore, is not a mere chance scenic location in the book. It is a place of pollution, treachery and death, but it is also a bridge at the heart of the capital, where good and evil, east and west, past and present can intersect and intermingle – a place simultaneously above ground and below – a place between worlds. Dickens, all in all, expends an immense amount of imaginative energy in setting the scene for Nancy's meeting with Rose Maylie and Brownlow, imbuing it with multiple layers of meaning and diverse associations. This, in turn, made it a memorable location for readers of the novel and suggested the real-world bridge as an apt location for literary tourism.

***

We can probably pinpoint the moment when Nancy's Steps became a tourist destination. For they were highlighted in an article written by the journalist Joseph Ashby-Sterry, one of the pioneering explorers of 'Dickens's London'. Ashby-Sterry was reportedly a self-effacing Edwardian bachelor of means, with an elegant suite of rooms overlooking Trafalgar Square, decorated with art and collectible antiques (including a prized set of claret glasses which once belonged to his literary hero). A pen and ink sketch in the National Portrait Gallery collection portrays him as a cheerful, balding gent with a monocle and a particularly extensive moustache, reading a newspaper propped up on a brandy bottle.[20] Beginning in the 1880s, he published multiple magazine articles charting places in 'Dickens's London'. He also used his long-running newspaper column in the *Graphic* (dubbed 'The Bystander') to campaign for a street named in Dickens's honour. He was credited with coining and popularising the adjective 'Dickensian' in preference to the more awkward 'Dickensonian'.[21] An author of what one obituarist tactfully dubbed 'light verse', he even poetically hymned the joys of exploring Dickens's Kent:

'Tis here, it may be truly said,
'Great Expectations' should be read!
Not only can you read the tale,
But live it in this peaceful vale![22]

Ashby-Sterry, in short, believed in the merits of experiencing Dickensian place for oneself. He also wrote a magazine article ('Charles Dickens in Southwark') and a poem ('The Haunted Steps') that both made a similar case for visiting a certain set of riverside stairs. He advised anyone possessing fond memories of *Oliver Twist* to make the journey to the edge of the Thames:

> descend the steps to the river, hard by the Bridge House Hotel, you will find yourself in the exact spot – with precisely the scenery of half a century ago – of the interview between Nancy, Rose Maylie and Mr Brownlow. If you go there about twelve o'clock on a dark night you will realize the picture to perfection . . .[23]

Ashby-Sterry, within a few sentences, suggests that literary pilgrimage to this spot will be a guided tour ('take my arm, trust in me, and I will personally conduct you . . .'); an informative antiquarian experience (a chance to see 'the scenery of half a century ago'); an opportunity to reimagine the scene from the book *in situ*; and a prompt for personal memories of Dickens the man and his work ('The last time I heard Charles Dickens read, he gave that most forcible and thrilling of all his readings – "Sikes and Nancy"').[24] He also suggests that the reader should 'lurk round the pilaster at the bottom of the flight and play at being Noah Claypole' (Fagin's spy, who is pictured in the foreground of the accompanying illustration to the article, looking up the vertiginous stairs) – at least, if one wishes to have a fully immersive experience.

The illustration, drawn by Alfred McCormick (1860–1943), helps emphasise the multiplicity of experiences and perspectives promised by Ashby-Sterry. The illustration shows Claypole's perspective on the encounter – looking up at the other characters – but also provides a vision of Claypole in the foreground, which stands for the reader-as-Claypole, 'seeing' the imagined scene. One might compare this foregrounding of Claypole with Cruikshank's original illustration, 'The Meeting', where the spy is concealed in the shadows, less prominent than the group that he is spying upon, more intent on listening than seeing. The illustration to Ashby-Sterry's article reverses Cruikshank's use of shadow, making Claypole central to the scene, more illuminated than those he observes, a proxy for the literary tourist. It is notable, too, that McCormick leaves all the faces essentially blank, with Claypole seen from behind with the merest hint of features, and Brownlow, Rose and Nancy totally distant, dark and indistinct. The literary tourist, it is implied, will fill in these blanks with their imagination. The picture as vignette, with its hard borders dissolving into the raggedly arranged wrapping of text – and vice versa – likewise suggests a dialogue between text and image, the real-world place and the world of the novel.

It seems unlikely that many tourists haunted London Bridge at the stroke of midnight (the hour of the meeting in the novel), as Ashby-Sterry recommended. Indeed, the article itself bids the nocturnal tourist to alert the nearest policeman to their presence on the steps lest they be mistaken for a potential suicide. This admonition was doubtless included in order to produce a certain frisson; but it hints at the potential insalubrity of the riverside location. The article, moreover, was published in late 1888, when the news was dominated by the 'Whitechapel Murders' and many an unwary individual was accused of being 'Jack the Ripper'. One has to suspect that Dickens-loving tourists largely confined their visits to daylight hours. Regardless, Ashby-Sterry's flight of fancy established the London Bridge steps as a destination for the literary pilgrim.

The fame of the steps, of course, was not wholly dependent on touristic articles and guidebooks (although a good number did follow). Theatrical adaptations continued to treat the famous scene on the steps as pivotal – and even featured it in their advertising. The 1905 stage adaptation starring Herbert Beerbohm Tree used a painting of the meeting on the steps as its advertising poster.[25] The production was proud of its elaborate set for London Bridge, 'of a particularly striking and massive character', with the river in the foreground and 'a huge section of the bridge [which] occupied the stage transversely, rising almost to the proscenium line'.[26] Some reviewers complained that the vast arch spanning the stage dwarfed and restricted the movements of the cast. But this meticulous and monumental recreation is rather suggestive of how familiar Nancy's Steps were to the theatre-going public, both as a scene within the novel and as a real-world location. Working on a very different scale, the amateur theatrical group of the Tabard Players, who annually produced a Dickens play on the anniversary of his birth, actually recreated the London Bridge scene *in situ* in publicity photographs for their 1936 production of *Oliver Twist* (although the play itself was performed in the yard of the galleried George Inn on Borough High Street). The steps remained a desirable location for Dickens tourists throughout subsequent decades. They were marked with a signboard in 1951, posted by the Borough of Southwark to inform visitors to the Festival of Britain of the district's local heritage. They would finally feature in *Mr Dickens of London* (1967), a one-hour made-for-TV literary tour, with the 'ghost' of Dickens played by Michael Redgrave, shortly before the bridge designed by Rennie was demolished to make way for its present incarnation (and shipped to Arizona and rebuilt at Lake Havasu as a giant tourist attraction).

***

The original Nancy's Steps, therefore, which first attracted Victorian tourists, were lost to posterity in the late 1960s – or, at least, buried. A contemporary plaque from the Southwark Heritage Association on Duke Street Hill, erected *c.* 2012, explaining the presence of two granite slabs left over from Rennie's bridge, notes in passing that 'two large stair chambers (including "Nancy's Steps")' were built into the fabric of the modern bridge.[27] Indeed, the lowest steps can still be seen when the river is at low tide, poking out from beneath a concealing wall of granite blocks. The original stairs, therefore, might still reappear, should London Bridge ever be rebuilt at some distant point in the future.

In the meantime, this leaves us with the faux blue plaque in Montague Close, which continues to reassure tourists that they have stumbled upon the real Nancy's Steps. The plaque, as already discussed, is wrong on two counts: these are not the steps featured in the novel, nor are the steps in the novel the scene of Nancy's murder. The explanation for the latter discrepancy, of course, lies in the influence of adaptations, namely the popularity of *Oliver!*, Lionel Bart's 1960s musical, particularly the cinematic version released in 1968 directed by Carol Reed. Bart's plot stitches together disparate elements of the original narrative into a fast-paced finale, beginning with Nancy's death, which now takes place by the river. One might argue, therefore, that the plaque, in this case, is not so much misleading as indicative. The film is doubtless much better known to a contemporary audience than the original book. This unofficial memorial reveals that, for many people familiar only with the cinematic adaptation, London Bridge *is* where Nancy is murdered. *Oliver Twist*, much like *A Christmas Carol*, is a novel which has transcended its literary beginnings, becoming a part of our collective imagination, recalled through the prism of adaptation. The current plaque, therefore, if nothing else, serves as an illustration of how literary shrines can become coloured by new associations and narratives which eclipse their literary origins.

Dickens himself, in fact, might even approve of such waywardness. There are, at least, several places in his work where he hints that stories and legends tied to place are preferable to dull, accurate facts. In *Little Dorrit*, for example, the slum inhabitants of Bleeding Heart

Yard prefer a fanciful explanation for the courtyard's name to the dry heraldic research of antiquaries. They relish competing tales of a grisly murder and an immured maiden pining for her true love. This is 'the one little golden grain of poetry' in their hard lives.[28] Dickens makes a similar case for the power of the imagination towards the end of *The Old Curiosity Shop*. Little Nell is comforted by exciting tales of knights and monks woven from the relics preserved in an ancient parish church. Some of these stories are veracious, some are far from accurate; but the 'old bachelor' who guards the church weaves his yarns with little regard to the facts. The relics are a starting point, but he is principally concerned with telling a good story with a sound moral. The 'old bachelor' is a proxy for Dickens and his own views on historical accuracy; that is, a good story – in both senses of the word – trumps everything. This love of a good story surely helps explains why Nancy's Steps continue to attract visitors in their current form, surviving their own annihilation. When the modern bridge was built, people were determined to find *something* that remained, to keep telling the story.

As for the plaque itself, no one seems keen to take responsibility for its erection, but it is rumoured to have been the work of a local business. We have already seen how heritage, tourism and commerce walk arm in arm. The plaque, however, is also a word-for-word replacement of a brown heritage plaque, branded 'Historic Southwark', that stood on the same spot for a couple of decades, erected by the local authority.[29] There seems to be some question as to whether this earlier article was stolen or removed on the grounds of belatedly acknowledged inaccuracy. Both these memorials, regardless, have served to entrench the surviving staircase as a tourist destination – as Nancy's Steps. Whether the plaque will remain in its present form is debatable. Some want to see it replaced and there is a distinct possibility that it will have vanished by the time this book is published. I do not hastily dismiss those Dickensians who would prefer greater accuracy in such matters. Nonetheless, as we have seen, in the original book Dickens himself transforms a then-modern bridge – the 1830s bridge, recently built by Rennie – into a place of Gothic nightmare. The original incident in the novel thus takes place in a fantastical limbo between the past and present – so how concerned should we be about accuracy? The present plaque's confusing rendering of the locality seems rather in keeping with Dickens's own warping of space and time.

Factual errors, in any case, are always enthusiastically embraced by tour guides, who simply make them part of a site's history, part of the 'whole story' which is only vouchsafed to the more discerning tourist. While the plaque's future may be questionable, the steps and the story, in one form or another, will likely endure. Most importantly, the surviving stone stairs rather look the part – narrow, steep, crooked and gloomy – evoking the mysterious and labyrinthine metropolis that Dickens created in his fiction, a vision of the Dickensian city which has subsequently been reinforced in innumerable cinema and television adaptations. They are, therefore, a visual link to the topographic distillation of Dickens's novels which lurks in all our heads, even if they bear little relation to the actual steps described and pictured in *Oliver Twist*. Indeed, it is a curious feature of 'Dickens's London' that there is a Dickensian city of the imagination, larger and more capacious than any particular site or memorial. That imagined city – our general sense of Dickensian place – can, in turn, produce new Dickensian localities. I refer not to the merely wilfully misplaced, such as Nancy's Steps, or exaggerations, such as the George Inn, but the wholly invented. For the biggest Dickens tourist attraction at the turn of the twentieth century was a complete invention, which can still be found to this day, situated in Portsmouth Street, Lincoln's Inn Fields: the so-called Old Curiosity Shop – the subject of the next chapter.

7

AN OLD CURIOSITY SHOP

On Christmas Day 1883, while the well-to-do feasted on their turkeys, geese and game, mince pies and plum puddings, a gang of labourers made their way to a crooked little road adjoining the historic square of Lincoln's Inn Fields. The task at hand was to erect timber scaffolding to shore up three rickety old houses at risk of collapse. The danger had only become apparent the previous day but the Metropolitan Board of Works had acted promptly and their surveyors were scheduled to carry out an inspection on Boxing Day. The Board, admittedly, were preoccupied with massive road-building schemes in the centre of the capital, cutting broad modern avenues through the slums. High Holborn had just been completed, and both Shaftesbury Avenue and Charing Cross Road were under construction. The fate of three old houses in an obscure side street was a minor question of public safety and nothing more. The surveyors, therefore, arriving at Portsmouth Street the next day, were surprised to find themselves pushing through an excited crowd of sightseers, including a number of American tourists. Thankfully, there had been no disaster overnight. The contractor's men had done their work and the houses remained intact. Nonetheless, all eyes were fixed upon one of the endangered properties, No. 14, a peculiar little shop, whose mundane trade was the accumulation and recycling of waste paper. The building itself was a squat, soot-blackened relic of Tudor London. There was a narrow little door opening onto a ground floor sunk below the level of the pavement, an overhanging timbered upper storey and a misshapen tiled roof. The reason why the crowd were interested in the building's fate, however, was explained by the giant inscription painted on the first-floor plaster in elaborate Gothic lettering:

THE OLD CURIOSITY SHOP
IMMORTALIZED BY CHARLES DICKENS

The surveyors openly discussed demolition and, shortly afterwards, news of the shop's imminent demise reached the press. The *Birmingham Mail* noted, a little tongue-in-cheek, that '"Little Nell" will now be more homeless than ever' (Nell, in the novel, flees the shop with her grandfather and the pair wander the highways and byways of England). Others reported on the peculiar phenomenon of throngs of literary tourists flocking to this little corner of London:

> Here and there among them was an artist, busy with pencil and note-book taking sketches of the tumble-down old place; and one could not fail to distinguish the noisy demonstration of the American traveller, as he demanded to know, with nasal eagerness, 'if that really was the home of Little Nell.' It was nothing new for the house to be stared at. For a year or two past, at any rate, it had been one of the stock visiting places of American tourists. 'They went there to worship,' a neighbouring shop-keeper said, 'took off their hats when they got through the doorway, and asked questions about Quilp and the Grandfather as if they had been actual persons. The ladies were worst. I have known them get down on their knees and burst out crying about Little Nell.'[1]

The publicity, naturally enough, only garnered the building more attention. Indeed, the shop on Portsmouth Street soon became so well known that the promoters of a stage version of *The Old Curiosity Shop* at the Opera Comique Theatre belatedly announced in the press that they were introducing a reproduction of its exterior as an authentic backdrop 'specially painted from the original house' (the work of W. Bruce Smith, who had likewise recreated Russell Court for Jennie Lee).[2] American tourists were particularly taken with its old-world charm, prompting rumours that the shop had been purchased by P.T. Barnum and was about to be taken down, brick by brick, and rebuilt in the United States. He had, after all, once despatched an agent to Stratford-upon-Avon, 'armed with the cash and full powers to buy the Shakespeare House, if possible, and to have it carefully taken down, packed in boxes, and shipped to New York'.[3] In fact, as it turned out, the Portsmouth Street building was sufficiently sound to survive *in situ* (albeit somewhat shored up, reportedly, strangely enough, under the guidance of Bruce Smith).[4] The shop would also, some twenty years later, survive the building of Kingsway, unlike nearby Kingsgate Street.

The groups of tourists, meanwhile, kept coming, first on foot and then in 'waggonnette' horse-drawn coach tours, 'constantly arriving to see the curious little house'.[5] Indeed, the Old Curiosity Shop soon became *the* Dickens literary shrine in London, perhaps even more popular than the author's tomb in Westminster Abbey. For tourists visiting from the United States, in particular, it became a familiar icon of 'Old England', reproduced as novelty gifts, represented in paintings, photographs, films, and, in the 1930s, recreated full-scale at international exhibitions. The shop, for example, formed part of the 'Merrie England' zone at the Chicago Century of Progress Exposition of 1934. It jostled for attention alongside simulacra of Anne Hathaway's cottage, Stoke Poges Church (renowned thanks to Gray's Elegy) and a gateway to the Tower of London.

This all now seems a little implausible. True, the building itself survives to this day, with the same Gothic inscription (although it has been repainted, in different variations of the script, at least twice over), overshadowed by the modern campus buildings of the London School of Economics and Political Science (the current owner). Nonetheless, there can be no doubt that its importance as a tourist destination has much diminished. There are fashions in tourism, as much as anything else; and the Charles Dickens Museum is now the prime destination in modern-day 'Dickens's London'. The real curiosity, however, is how this little shop achieved such worldwide notoriety in the first place. For the Old Curiosity Shop of Portsmouth Street, although undoubtedly a remarkably well-preserved (and repeatedly refurbished) Tudor relic, has never had any connection to Charles Dickens or his work – except in the imagination of the literary tourist. In this chapter, I attempt to explain how it achieved such remarkable prominence.

***

Shops and shop windows were a distinctive feature of the early nineteenth-century urban scene. The introduction of plate glass and gaslight, in particular, allowed for increasingly extravagant display. Dickens's description of Nicholas Nickleby's return to London by coach captures the astonishing show of wealth and plenty along major thoroughfares such as Piccadilly and the Strand:

> They rattled on through the noisy, bustling, crowded street of London, now displaying long double rows of brightly-burning lamps, dotted here and there with the chemists' glaring lights, and illuminated besides with the brilliant flood that streamed from the windows of the shops ... it was curious to observe in what a strange procession they passed before the eye. Emporiums of splendid dresses, the materials brought from every quarter of the world; tempting stores of everything to stimulate and pamper

... vessels of burnished gold and silver, wrought into every exqui-
site form of vase, and dish, and goblet; guns, swords, pistols, and
patent engines of destruction; screws and irons for the crooked,
clothes for the newly-born, drugs for the sick, coffins for the dead,
and churchyards for the buried – all these jumbled each with the
other ...[6]

The increasingly macabre tone in the passage, culminating in coffins
and churchyards, gives the reader reason to pause. There is something obscene lurking behind the splendour; and Dickens's thoughts
turn to the poor, who can never penetrate these temples to Mammon,
'guarded by one thin sheet of brittle glass – an iron wall to them'.
Shops in Dickens's work, in fact, often say something about social
inequality. In *Sketches by Boz*, the 'little dark chandler's shop, with a
cracked bell' and 'shops for the purchase of rags, bones, old iron, and
kitchen-stuff' speak eloquently about the poverty of Seven Dials.[7]
Esther Summerson in *Bleak House* gazes at 'the setting forth of shop
windows and the sweeping out of shops, and the extraordinary crea-
tures in rags secretly groping among the swept-out rubbish for pins
and other refuse'.[8] The shops of Saffron Hill in *Oliver Twist* are
seemingly largely devoted to the sale of pickpocketed handkerchiefs
and thus collectively form an 'emporium of petty larceny', emblematic of the district's endemic corruption.[9]

Dickens, however, is particularly fascinated with shops beyond
the principal thoroughfares, in hidden nooks and corners of the
metropolis. We see this in *Sketches by Boz*, where one sketch charts
the progress of a struggling premises in Lambeth ('Shops and Their
Tenants'). Dickens describes how the building, an untenanted private
house, becomes a linen drapers seemingly overnight, then a 'fancy
stationer's', and then is subdivided into a bonnet-shape maker's and
a tobacconist's. The maker of frameworks for bonnets yields to a
greengrocer, the tobacconist to a hairdresser and then a tailor. Finally,
the site reaches its lowest ebb, converted into rented rooms with a

dairy installed in the basement, complete with a small flock of 'melancholy-looking fowls'. This sketch evokes the impermanence and volatility of London life, not least as the building shifts abruptly from a private home to a shop and then back to rented accommodation. This is seemingly a place where the best laid plans count for naught, where ambitions repeatedly turn to dust. There is even a submerged hint of Dickens's own chaotic family history. For the final business endeavour, before the appearance of the dairy, is a 'Ladies School', whose brass plate echoes that of the abortive 'Mrs Dickens Establishment'. This putative school for young women was to have been superintended by Dickens's mother in Gower Street North, part of a desperate bid to keep creditors at bay. The young Dickens distributed circulars testifying to its merits, but the project failed to save the family from bankruptcy and the Marshalsea Gaol, since 'nobody ever came to school, nor do I recollect that anybody ever proposed to come, or that the least preparation was made to receive anybody'.[10]

The most well-known shops in Dickens's novels are similarly rather obscure places and often rather hopeless endeavours. Sol Gills in *Dombey and Son*, for example, keeps a ship's instruments shop, bursting with old nautical devices which have become largely redundant. No one sets foot through the door except to ask for directions or change. Gills is a thoroughly decent man but clings to a vanished past ('Seven-eighths of my stock is old-fashioned. I am an old-fashioned man in an old-fashioned shop, in a street that is not the same as I remember it').[11] He is a maudlin figure who seems to have run aground, while the world sails on without him. Equally, Krook in *Bleak House* owns a junk shop in legal London, which buys up rags, bones, 'kitchen-stuff', old iron, waste paper and bottles, second-hand law texts and documents – a shop full of degraded, used-up things. Krook himself is a filthy, drunken eccentric, a miserly illiterate who vainly attempts to teach himself to read and write in order to search for profitable information amidst the heaps of legal papers he has hoarded over the years. He is mocked as 'Lord Chancellor of the rag and bottle shop', and the shop is 'a dirty hanger-on and disowned relation of the law'.[12] Dickens's target here, of course, is the legal system itself. He implies that the hideous shop, with its heaps of mouldering papers, is a mirror image of the court of chancery, with all its interminable, impenetrable, soul-destroying legal business.

And then we have the Old Curiosity Shop – an antiques shop:

one of those receptacles for old and curious things which seem to crouch in odd corners of this town and to hide their musty treasures from the public eye in jealousy and distrust. There were suits of mail standing like ghosts in armour here and there, fantastic carvings brought from monkish cloisters, rusty weapons of various kinds, distorted figures in china and wood and iron and ivory: tapestry and strange furniture that might have been designed in dreams.[13]

The occupants of this rather weird place – once again, we never see any actual customers – are an unworldly teenage girl, Little Nell, and her grandfather, Mr Trent, another of Dickens's secretive, miserly figures. We eventually learn that the old man has a gambling addiction, which has led to his financial ruin. Debts are called in by Daniel Quilp, a money-obsessed, violent, lascivious monster, 'an elderly man of remarkably hard features and forbidding aspect' who is a 'dwarf' in stature, but with an oversized head, an ill-assorted set of teeth that resemble 'fangs' and long, crooked, yellow fingernails.[14] Quilp gleefully evicts Nell and her grandfather from their home and his malevolent goblin-like presence haunts the novel. But the principal subject matter is Nell and her grandfather's epic and wearying travels through England, homeless and desperate, which eventually bring them to an ancient rustic church where they find a measure of peace – or, at least, Nell finds a peaceful death.

1. Sam Weller (left) and Mr Pickwick (right) meet for the first time in the yard of the White Hart coaching inn, as drawn by Phiz (Hablot K. Browne). This famous illustrated scene from *The Pickwick Papers* suggested the real-world inn as a possible site of literary pilgrimage.

2. The final days of the White Hart coaching inn, taken for the Society for Photographing Relics of Old London, *c.* 1881. One side of the inn building had been converted into a restaurant and the remainder of the ground floor given over to a bacon curer (see the sign that reads 'H. Spencer, Bacon Dryer'). The galleries had been turned into cheap slum apartments for the poor. This was not the cheerful scene depicted in *The Pickwick Papers*, a disappointment for literary tourists. The inn was demolished in 1889.

3. American visitors gather for a photograph outside the George coaching inn in May 1910. The George, located mere yards from the site of the White Hart, was kept in pristine condition by landlady Amelia Murray (who tenanted the pub from *c.* 1869 until her death in 1903), and then her daughter Agnes (d. 1934), both of whom cultivated a connection with Dickens and catered to heritage tourism.

4. The Maypole Inn, as depicted by George Cattermole at the start of *Barnaby Rudge*. This highly embellished baronial mansion does not tally with the description in the novel, nor with the King's Head, the pub in Chigwell which inspired the fictional establishment (see next picture). Nonetheless, Dickens declared himself very pleased with Cattermole's elaborate and fanciful rendering of the building.

5. A photograph of the King's Head in Chigwell from 1947. The King's Head provided inspiration for the Maypole Inn in *Barnaby Rudge*. The site first became of interest to literary tourists when John Forster, writing his biography of Dickens, recalled the author taking him on a day trip to the village of Chigwell and the 'delicious old inn opposite the churchyard'.

6. The music hall star Bransby Williams made his living as a quick-change artist, portraying a range of Dickensian characters. He also became friends with the landlord of the King's Head in Chigwell (see above). He helped to make the pub a famous destination for literary tourists, giving performances on the premises, arranging a magazine photo shoot (where he posed as characters from *Barnaby Rudge* at various locations in and around the old tavern), even borrowing its furniture for 'authentic' backdrops to his stage shows. Pictured here, clockwise from top left: Sidney Carton from *A Tale of Two Cities*, Barnaby Rudge, Serjeant Buzfuz from *The Pickwick Papers* and Fagin from *Oliver Twist*.

7. In this sketch by Phiz, Lady Dedlock and Jo the crossing sweeper, characters in *Bleak House*, stare into the foul burial ground where the mysterious 'Nemo' has been interred. The neglected graveyard in the novel is a metaphor for the state of the metropolis. The pestiferous state of the ground, overrun by rats and leaking toxic miasma, speaks to a city that is not only insanitary, but one where legal, moral and social relations have fallen into dangerous disrepair. Dickens based his description on a real-world cemetery off Russell Court, near Drury Lane Theatre, which was closed after a long protest campaign by residents.

8. The actress Jennie Lee built a career playing Jo, the crossing sweeper in *Bleak House*, in a play simply entitled *Jo*, which was given its first run at the Globe Theatre, London, in 1876. The first act culminated in Lady Dedlock and Jo at the burial ground gate (see above). Advertisements placed great stress on the topographical realism of the play, boasting 'new scenery painted expressly for this production by Mr W. BRUCE SMITH realising the exact spots mentioned by CHARLES DICKENS in the novel of "Bleak House" and the original illustrations by Phiz'.

PERFORMED EVERY EVENING WITH GREAT SUCCESS AT THE GLOBE THEATRE.

DEDICATED TO EDGAR BRUCE ESQRE

"JO"

GALOP,
FOR THE PIANOFORTE,
UPON AIRS FROM THE CELEBRATED DRAMA,
BY
EDWARD SOLOMON.

LONDON,
ENOCH & SONS, 19, HOLLES ST CAVENDISH SQRE W.
PARIS: ENOCH PERE & FILS. NEW YORK, EDWARD SCHUBERTH & CO

9. Kingsgate Street, home to Poll Sweedlepipe's barber shop and the drunken nurse, Mrs Gamp, as drawn by Phiz in *Martin Chuzzlewit*. Louisa May Alcott – amongst the earliest Dickensian literary tourists – visited the street in 1866, writing a lightly fictionalised account, entitled 'A Dickens Day', which was published the following year. Many other American visitors would follow in her footsteps. By the end of the century, gentlemen could even obtain a 'Dickens shave' at the 'original' barbers. The street was demolished in 1902 as part of the London County Council's road-building schemes.

10. An image of Kingsway, taken from the Aldwych in 1909, looking north. London County Council demolished several sites in 'Dickens's London' as part of their modernisation of the capital. This photograph of Kingsway – which swallowed up Kingsgate Street (see previous image) – shows the orderly grand avenues which the LCC created. They were the antithesis of the narrow, crooked ways of 'Dickens's London'.

11. A cartoon from *Scraps* magazine, *c.* 1904, satirising the suggestion of naming the London County Council's new modern road (see image 10) as 'Dickens Avenue' (see Chapter 4). Other possibilities considered were blandly descriptive ('Broadway', 'The High', 'London's Avenue'), regal ('King Alfred Street', 'The King's Way', 'The Queen's Way', 'Victoria Avenue', 'King Edward Avenue'), colonial ('Imperial Drive', 'Mafeking Avenue'), and memorials to the LCC ('The Council Broadway') and politicians ('Salisbury Drive', 'Gladstone Avenue'). The name 'Kingsway' was eventually selected.

12. Dickens lived in an apartment at Furnival's Inn from 1834–37, a period which included his marriage to Catherine Hogarth and the birth of his first son, Charley. Despite the quaint name harking back to an ancient inn of Chancery, the building was relatively modern, having only opened in 1818. Later known as Wood's Hotel, the site was the first place in London to have a plaque dedicated to the memory of the author, erected in 1886. However, within a decade, the hotel was demolished and replaced by the striking red brick Gothic offices of the Prudential Assurance Company, which survive to this day, where the plaque was relocated.

13. The artist Luke Fildes, illustrator of *The Mystery of Edwin Drood*, began work on *The Empty Chair*, depicting Dickens's desk and study, in the weeks after the author's death. An engraving appeared in the Christmas 1870 edition of *The Graphic* and then a watercolour was exhibited the following year at the Royal Academy. There is something museum-like in the picture's meticulous documentary rendering of the desk and many expected that Dickens's home at Gads Hill in Kent – where he died – would be preserved as a memorial to the great man. The house, in fact, was sold to raise funds for his dependants.

14. In this illustration by George Cruikshank from *Oliver Twist*, Rose Maylie and Mr Brownlow meet Nancy at London Bridge, covertly observed by Fagin's spy, Noah Claypole. The scene is a turning-point in the book, where Nancy discloses secrets regarding Oliver's persecutors, which ultimately leads to her murder at the hands of Bill Sikes. Literary tourists visited these riverside stairs from the late nineteenth century onwards.

15. An 1831 illustration by Thomas Hosmer Shepherd showing the construction of a new London Bridge, designed by John Rennie, nearing its conclusion. Old London Bridge can also be seen, situated mere yards to the east (demolished once the new bridge was completed). This curious juxtaposition of the old and new would be reflected in Dickens's own use of London Bridge as a location in *Oliver Twist*, a place where past and present collide and combine in an uncanny and threatening fashion.

16. A page from 'Charles Dickens in Southwark', written by Joseph Ashby-Sterry, illustrated by Alfred McCormick, published in the *English Illustrated Magazine* in 1888. Ashby-Sterry suggests that his readers visit London Bridge's riverside stairs and, situated in the very spot described in the book, reimagine the key scene in *Oliver Twist* where Nancy betrays Fagin.

17. The Tabard Players, a Southwark-based amateur theatrical group specialising in annual performances of Dickens's work, recreate the London Bridge scene from *Oliver Twist* on the riverside steps described in the novel. This was a publicity photograph for their 1936 production of *Oliver Twist*, although the play itself was performed in the galleried yard of the George coaching inn on Borough High Street.

18. Two postcards showing the façade of the so-called Old Curiosity Shop in Portsmouth Street, near Lincoln's Inn Fields. The site began to attract visitors in the 1880s. The unlikely claim to a Dickensian connection was made so boldly, and the building looked so historical and distinctive, that the shop soon became a popular tourist destination, particularly with visiting Americans. The top postcard shows the exterior in the early 1900s, with the original inscription; the lower postcard shows the shop in the 1930s, after renovation, with a new inscription (note the change in style of lettering, and the spelling of 'immortalised').

19. A recreation of the Old Curiosity Shop (see previous image) at the Chicago World's Fair, held 1933–34, part of the 'Merrie England' zone, along with other historic buildings (such as a recreated Globe Theatre, and a gateway to the Tower of London). The inclusion of this small Dickensian shop amongst more ancient and established heritage sites reflects its remarkable popularity with American tourists in the early years of the twentieth century, notwithstanding the lack of any substantiated connection to the author and his work.

20. The 'Old London Street' was a zone of recreated medieval buildings, constructed for the International Health Exhibition, held in Kensington in 1884. The designs were based on research by the architect George H. Birch, representing long-lost individual buildings in the City of London. 'Old London' and 'Dickens's London' were strongly associated in the popular imagination, and it is no coincidence that Dickensian tourism began to flourish in the same decade as the 'Old London Street'. Both were responses to the late Victorian fascination with encountering and reimagining the (urban) past.

21. The ambitious set constructed for Thomas Bentley's film, *Barnaby Rudge* (1915), echoing the self-contained reconstructed world of the 'Old London Street' (see previous image). The set was created in a meadow at Walton-on-Thames and no expense was spared, with more than a thousand extras hired to recreate the Gordon Riots, shipped in daily by special train from Waterloo Station. Sadly, no footage survives.

22. A rooftop panorama from David Lean's *Oliver Twist* (1948), showing 'Fagin's Bridge' – an impressive combination of model and matte work. The scenery closely resembles 'St Paul's from the Brewery Bridge' in Gustave Doré's *London: A Pilgrimage* (1872), combined with the recursive quality of 'Over London – by Rail' from the same book (which likewise has rooftops and chimneys almost seeming to recede to infinity). Doré's book was a key visual source for the film's Oscar-winning production designer John Bryan.

23. Another award-winning recreation of 'Dickens's London' in the film musical *Oliver!* (1968), created by production designer John Box. This elaborate set for the song-and-dance number 'Consider Yourself' contained visual hints of Covent Garden, Smithfield Market and Ludgate Hill but was not mimicking any specific locality – a 'Dickensland' composed piecemeal from a range of references and sources.

24. A photograph of 'Dickens World', built in Chatham in Kent, which opened in 2007 and closed in 2016, having struggled to find sufficient visitors. Kevin Christie, the attraction's promoter, touted it as an alternative to traditional literary tourism, remarking 'People come to London expecting it to look like *Oliver Twist*, but it's not like that anymore, so we're recreating it'.

The Old Curiosity Shop is largely remembered nowadays – if it is remembered at all – for the saintly figure of Little Nell, whose demise touched the hearts of so many Victorian readers. Some, however, would come to see it as sentimental, manipulative and vulgar. Oscar Wilde's much-quoted tart comment that 'One must have a heart of stone to read the death of little Nell without laughing' is undoubtedly now much better known than the details of the novel. Dickens himself, of course, was not without a sense of humour; and, although in one letter he writes that he is 'breaking my heart over this story', in another he jokingly refers to committing 'Nellicide'.[15] His stated intention, however, was intensely serious: that Nell's demise should 'substitute a garland of fresh flowers for the sculptured horrors which disgrace the tomb' and offer consolation for those afflicted by the untimely death of loved ones.[16] The book, in fact, has strong allegorical elements – Dickens himself makes knowing reference to Bunyan's *A Pilgrim's Progress* in the text – and Nell, in a sense, is more a personification of hope and innocence than a rounded character. Likewise, the shop is less a particular struggling business than a symbol of all that is wrong with Victorian capitalism. Nell and her grandfather's flight to the ancient church represents, at least in part, a flight from the money-grubbing commerce of the nineteenth century, founded on avarice and speculation. Thus, early in the book, we see Nell pictured sleeping amidst the historic items in the shop – suits of armour and so forth – which are a mirror image of the historical relics at the old church where she eventually finds eternal rest. In the shop, these antiques are corrupted, reduced to consumer goods, divorced from their original context and meaning – they are ominous, threatening presences – whereas in the church, in their rightful situation, Dickens describes how they prompt engaging daydreams of the past, hinting at a peaceful transition to the hereafter. There is a strong hint, too, that Nell herself, in the brutal world of capital, is objectified – merely another item in the shop – a human trophy at the mercy of Quilp and other schemers.

It is no surprise, therefore, that Dickens does not provide a definitive location for the shop in the novel, which would surely detract
from its symbolic power. We cannot say for certain that there was
no 'original' of the Old Curiosity Shop – some have claimed that
Dickens once adverted to a shop located near Leicester Square – but
none has ever been definitively established. Indeed, there is a strong
suggestion within the novel that the shop is a place wholly of the
imagination. For, in Dickens's closing paragraphs, Kit Nubbles,
a friend of Nell, returns to the location of the shop some years
later. He finds that the building has been demolished during street
improvements. Furthermore, we are told that even Kit himself cannot
make out for certain precisely where it once stood. It is almost as if
Dickens erects a sign for the prospective literary pilgrim: DO NOT
LOOK FOR THE SHOP, YOU WILL NEVER FIND IT. And
yet, in the early 1880s, the real-world Old Curiosity Shop magically
appeared – thanks largely to American tourists.

***

As I have mentioned previously, one great difficulty for any Dickens-
loving tourist in the 1870s and early 1880s, before much in the way
of guidebooks had been written, was to locate 'Dickens's London'.
Yet, for some American visitors, there was almost a sense that merely
visiting the capital sufficed. Louisa May Alcott, readers may recall,
felt that being in London was 'as if I'd got into a novel' and conjured
up visions of Dickensian characters upon every street corner. For
American tourists, London was, to quote Nathaniel Hawthorne, a
'dream-city', a place first encountered and imagined through books
and stories, which thus felt rather fantastical when one arrived in
person.[17] The whole metropolis, therefore, could potentially figure as
part of a Dickensian daydream. This, in turn, presented something
of a commercial opportunity for the imaginative entrepreneur.
Indeed, by the early 1880s, it was said that every second-hand seller
of antiques and oddities claimed to be the original of the Old

Curiosity Shop. But it was a certain Mr Tesseyman (or Tessyman) of Portsmouth Street who first had the clever idea of literally dubbing his premises the Old Curiosity Shop – painted in extravagant Gothic letters above the entrance – 'for purely business purposes, as likely to attract custom to his shop, he being a dealer in books, paintings, old china, &c.'.[18] The actual contents were reportedly not particularly impressive, with one visitor remembering them as 'cheap relics of antiquarian interest, more especially the autograph letters of famous actors ... [the] whole store of books never worth five shillings altogether ... the shabbiest collection of insignificant odd volumes, in the raggedest and dirtiest condition'.[19]

The original subtitle to the sign read: 'Dealer in Works of Art', with no mention of Dickens. Tesseyman, however, died in 1877 and the premises fell into the hands of Henry Poole, a dealer in waste paper. The building then featured in an 1881 magazine article in the popular US publication *Scribner's Monthly Magazine*, one destination on a literary tour of 'Dickens's London'. The text of the article describes the connection with Dickens as fanciful, founded upon 'a pardonable, albeit misguided, desire on the part of the poverty-stricken neighbourhood to lift itself to an easy and inexpensive notoriety'.[20] But the accompanying picture clearly caught readers' imagination. American tourists began to appear regardless, prompting Poole to erase the sign's original subtitle and replace it with 'Immortalized by Charles Dickens'. This was the spectacle that greeted the surveyors of the Metropolitan Board of Works in 1883. Dickens, in fairness, *may* have visited at some point (there is no evidence one way or another). He certainly would have recognised the distinctive facade. John Forster's apartments in Lincoln's Inn Fields were a stone's throw away; and the shop was close to the parts of legal London which Dickens depicts in *Bleak House* and elsewhere in his work.[21] But that is all one can say on the subject. The shop's dubious notoriety was certainly not based on any actual resemblance to the shop described in Dickens's book, either in the text or as shown in the accompanying illustrations by Phiz and Cattermole. We only see a glimpse of the exterior in those drawings, but it is plainly an old terraced town house with a quaint projecting porch, nothing like No. 14 Portsmouth Street. Cattermole also depicts the interior as lofty rooms filled with antiques, matching the description in the text. The cramped, squat, real-world shop could never accommodate such riches – it is simply far too small. Charles Van Noorden of the Dickens Fellowship even produced a four-page pamphlet, written in 1902, marshalling the visual and textual evidence from the original novel to decry the shop's imposture. The Fellowship, indeed, have always tended to spurn the building as an outright fraud (describing it in 1911 as 'a piece of impudent deception which should long since have been put a stop to').[22] Nevertheless, examining the nature of the shop's appeal to literary tourists tells us something about the nature of Dickens's late nineteenth-century literary territory.

***

Some aspects of the shop's attraction are obvious. Most of all, to be blunt, it looks old. When American visitors came looking for 'Dickens's London', they also sought out 'Old London', a vaguely defined 'historic' capital with visibly antique features. 'Dickens's London', as we have seen, was increasingly being incorporated within a heritage vision of the 'old city' as a place of quaint historic survivals. The shop's archetypal Tudor features, not least its peculiar, crooked proportions, signified fascinating antiquity. Crookedness, in fact, was highly valued. Americans were said to yearn for the 'old London of crooked streets and provincial ways', the opposite of the typical American city.[23] Henry James, praising Chester for its antiquity, described the town's medieval city walls and streets as 'a perfect feast of crookedness' and suggested that it was childhood exposure to England's ancient, crooked buildings which had endowed Dickens with such a vigorous imagination.[24] Dickens himself might well have agreed. For, visiting Philadelphia in 1842, he declared that its 'regularity' was distracting and remarked that 'I would have given the world for a crooked street'.[25] Portsmouth Street was just such a street.

The so-called Old Curiosity Shop was also sufficiently obscure as regards its locality that it was not obvious to tourists until they were almost upon the building. The site was, in other words, somewhat 'hidden', not visible from major thoroughfares, a place that tourists had, in a small way, to seek out and discover. This relative inaccessibility made it a pleasing challenge to locate and hinted at the labyrinthine city familiar to readers of Dickens's novels. Moreover, while its exterior bore little relation to the novel's illustrations, it was considerably closer in appearance to Sol Gills's premises, as depicted by Phiz in *Dombey and Son* (not least in having an overhanging upper storey).[26] Put simply, it looked like it *might* belong in Dickens's world. The fact that the shop appeared quite distinct from its more modern surroundings only heightened its appeal. Buildings on either side of Shakespeare's birthplace in Stratford were demolished in the late 1850s, remaking a terrace into a standalone property, partly to highlight the house's visual impact. The Portsmouth Street Old Curiosity Shop was already strikingly different from its neighbours.

The quaint, compact and antique appearance of the building also lent itself very readily to reproduction, which did much to publicise this new tourist destination. Images of the shop were for sale to tourists from the beginning. During the first flush of publicity in 1883, pictures were sold for 2d. plain and 4d. coloured. The frontage was also much photographed, both commercially and by amateurs. One magazine article on Dickens's London in 1893 describes it as 'the only purely "Dickens scene" in London which the professional photographers have condescended to touch', and an astonishing number of postcards seem to have been produced. A search on eBay today finds dozens upon dozens of different images on commercial cards. The shop's owners, of course, played a major part in creating and distributing these images of the premises. While it was still dealing in waste paper, the shop also sold a variety of Dickensian mementoes, including postcards and prints depicting its facade. The shop's Edwardian owners, Messrs. Gill, Durrant & Dunning, 'Wholesale Stationers and Papermill Agents', who purchased it from Henry Poole *c.* 1906, sold a gift pack of three postcards in a printed envelope. The envelope itself had an old-fashioned woodcut image of the property, a stylistic nod to generalised 'Old English' antiquity. The postcards it contained included a drawing of Little Nell and her grandfather, a photograph of the contemporary shop, and a photograph of its cluttered interior showing the numerous Dickensian prints and knick-knacks for sale. Tourists, in other words, could take away a printed memento of the book, the building, and even the experience of being a literary tourist, showing the very room where they had stopped to purchase their postcards. This, in turn, might be shown or posted to friends and family, inspiring others to visit and experience Portsmouth Street first-hand. The shop also sold pictures depicting Little Nell and her grandfather in the doorway, visual representations of the Dickensian scenes that could be imagined *in situ*.

The Lewis family, who bought the shop *c.* 1925/6, continued to sell assorted reproductions of the exterior. The family were originally part of a tailoring firm called Sutton and Lewis, who seem to have bought the place as something of a novelty showroom, but they soon became involved in the business of tourism. Signs on the outside, visible in 1930s postcards, read: 'You are Welcome to Inspect this Bit of Old London, Built 1547, Admission Free' and 'When in Shakespeare Country, Visit our Depot, next Anne Hathaway's Cottage, Stratford Upon Avon'. The shop's Tudor appearance was, of course, akin to that of Shakespeare's Birthplace and Anne Hathaway's Cottage. A surviving undated bill on headed notepaper, listing 'H. Lewis' as proprietor, reveals the Stratford outlet was called 'Hathaway Acre' and dubs 'The Old Curiosity Shop' 'the First Antique and Gift Shop in England'. The printed advertisement copy on the side of the bill also reveals that, by the 1930s, the Old

Curiosity Shop dealt in general tourist memorabilia, not only post-cards but also prints, brasses, books and silverware themed around 'British landmarks', Dickens and Shakespeare. The bill itself is for a complete set of Dickens's novels to be shipped back to the United States. Each book, of course, would contain a bookplate testifying to its historic point of origin.

The fact that the building has often been reproduced in three-dimensional miniature, as an ornament – and other decorative items, such as door knockers, mustard pots, honeypots and money boxes – is also testament to its remarkably picturesque quality. The earliest mention of miniatures dates from 1888, when wooden blocks, with the facade of the shop painted upon the front, were said to be sold to American visitors for a highly profitable six shillings apiece. But I would also argue that there is a sense of the miniature about the real-world building. The shop feels like it is on a different scale to the world around it – as well as belonging, as it were, to a different time – which adds to its interest and gives it a slightly fantastical quality. Thus, miniature models of the shop, such as a Marutomo majolica honeypot produced in the 1930s, or even the version of the shop in the Lilliput Lane collectible pottery series of the 1980s, reflect not only the picturesque nature of the building but also some-thing miniature in its real-world appearance. The miniature, in turn, suggests the world of toys, 'a device for fantasy', associated with fantasies of ownership, wealth and display.[27] Lilliput Lane's model pottery series was actually advertised with the tag line 'Experience what it's like to own a majestic castle, a quaint, ivy-covered cottage, or a rambling English Tudor'.[28] It is also striking that the building was reportedly purchased by the Durrant family as a twenty-first birthday present for one Leonard Durrant, giving new meaning to the phrase 'gift shop'. Indeed, this *was* very much a Dickens-themed 'gift shop' and hence rather unusual for the period. For this sort of heritage retail establishment dedicated to a single author was some-thing of a novelty in the 1880s. Certainly, the museum gift shop had yet to flourish in London. To step inside this heritage site which served as a memorial to Dickens and his work, and to buy Dickens-themed goods, was a relatively unusual experience.

Finally, we should not underestimate the importance of the inscription on the building's facade. Wordsworth, in Book VII of *The Prelude*, describing London's overwhelming assembly of sights and signs, notes the names emblazoned on shops which act as a sort of 'title page' for the premises in question. In the case of the Old Curiosity Shop, the facade actually resembled the title page of a novel – with both author and title – making a bold claim to an association with the book, the fictional premises and Dickens himself. The very presence of the sign, in turn, authenticated the shop for many a visitor; and the arresting Gothic lettering laid claim to historical authenticity and importance. The facade, in fact, has always been the shop's most important feature. The cramped interior has never truly satisfied the visiting public. Occasionally, the tiny upstairs room would be opened for visitors curious to see the bedroom of Little Nell, as pictured in the novel. They rarely returned content:

> The American gentleman expressed himself as rather disappointed with the room from a spectacular point of view. He hinted to me that he had expected to find a Dickens manuscript or two, and possibly a relic of Little Nell here and there. But there wasn't so much as a hairpin.[29]

The shopfront, by contrast, became a reliable and increasingly familiar icon of 'Dickens's London'. Newspapers brought Dickens's descendants, such as Kathleen and Violet Dickens (his Australian granddaughters), to the doorstep for photo opportunities so that they might enjoy 'scenes immortalized in their grandfather's books'. They reportedly found London itself 'magnificent' but wondered if the spirit of Dickens was lost amidst the 'tubes, motor-buses and such like emblems of modern progress'.[30] Alfred Tennyson Dickens, one of the author's sons, who died on a Dickens lecture tour in America in 1912, relied on a publicity photograph which showed him emerging from the doorway and smiling at the camera – rather as if he had stepped out of one of his own father's books.

***

The Portsmouth Street shop, then, was always a fake, but an excellent one – the right building at the right time. It appealed to the Victorian fascination with 'Old London' and, in particular, the Tudor period, which was increasingly being framed as the formative age of Empire, 'when DRAKE and HAWKINS were sailing around the world and the English drama was rising into splendour'.[31] The shop looked suitably 'Dickensian' and one might also argue that a shop was an excellent symbol for a wider 'Dickens's London'. For Dickens himself was a famously commercially minded author, a tough negotiator of publishing deals, and highly conscious of his own image in the marketplace. He was also a master of visual description, from rapid-moving panoramas of urban life to almost microscopic examination of small household items. Dickens, as it were, put the nineteenth-century capital into his own shop window display.

8

DOWN NEWGATE LANE

I have focused thus far on real-world sites visited by literary tourists. But there have always been other ways for visitors to encounter 'Dickens's London' beyond the text of the novels – or perhaps I should say 'Dickensland'. The latter term, ripe with associations of the funfair and fantasy, seems appropriate. For this chapter examines representations and reproductions of Dickensian place, from topographically themed church bazaars to theme parks, early silent film to more recent cinema and television adaptations. What unites these diverse ersatz 'Dickenslands' is that they cater to our interest in exploration of his world – even if only 'virtual' exploration. Film and television adaptations, of course, have also profoundly influenced how the public perceives the 'Dickensian' metropolis in the first place, not least in establishing and reinforcing a particular set of visual 'Dickensian' tropes. Thus, whenever an establishing shot contains gaslights, cobbles, rooftop panoramas of smoking chimneys and so forth, there is a good chance the viewer mentally situates themselves in 'Dickens's London'. But I begin with a late nineteenth-century curiosity – the Dickens bazaar – a simple enough form of entertainment, one of the earliest Dickens-themed wonderlands.

***

From 27 to 29 June 1888, the principal function room at Holborn Town Hall became an immersive experience, a 'Dickens Bazaar':

> Mrs Squeers dispensed brimstone and treacle at so much per ladle, and Little Dorrit stood at the door of the Marshalsea ... Quilp was up to his pranks and Pegotty lounged idly against the post of his boat-house. The stall fronts were delightful reminders of the scenes in which our old friends have played a part. Mrs Corney presided over the Oliver Twist stall situated on old Saffron Hill, and outside it hung the handkerchiefs of Fagin's time. From the boathouse, dangling from a string, hung a row of fine shining mackerel ...[1]

The lofty galleried room could seat eight hundred guests for concerts and had its own stage and pipe organ, but the floor was cleared to make way for fifteen elaborately decorated stalls, designed to bear some resemblance to the likes of the White Hart Inn, the Old Curiosity Shop, Gabriel Varden's shop and Peggotty's Boathouse.[2] The event was a grand charity fundraiser for the internal refurbishment of a local church. The themed stalls sold various knick-knacks and the stallholders were dressed as representative characters appropriate to each location (for example Dolly Varden at the Locksmith's Shop). Some took their costumes very seriously, with one stallholder informing a journalist that she was wearing 'a careful copy' of a dress worn in the 1830s.[3] The refreshment stall at the end of the hall was even made up as the porch of the Maypole Inn, with a maypole planted in front and a 'village pump' to the side ('Fourpence given to the village damsel in attendance will secure a draught of its satisfying

nectar').[4] Some modest pieces of memorabilia were on display –
Baroness Burdett-Coutts, for example, lent portraits of the young
Charles and Catherine – and visitors could also buy engravings of
the author's famous characters. The evening entertainments featured
Dickensian recitations and amateur dramatics, including a reading
by the author's son, Henry Fielding Dickens. Other delights were
'Mrs Jarley's Animated Waxworks' (probably costumed volunteers
enacting historical tableaux); Punch and Judy; E.J. Dale, a comical
magician; and J. Williams Benn, who presented 'his popular Sketching
Entertainment, entitled "Some Characters from Charles Dickens"'.[5]
Benn was a 'lightning sketcher' who produced inoffensive amusements for church halls, schoolrooms and polytechnics (his other
routines included 'Notes on Noses, and the People who wear them'
and drawing whilst blindfolded). It is not clear how much was actually raised for restoration of the nearby St Peter's Church, Saffron
Hill – probably not the £400 that had been hoped for. The weather
was consistently bad and there was considerable disappointment that
Princess Beatrice could not attend the opening ceremony, as had
been promised. Nothing drew a crowd like the royal family, but the
Princess found herself unexpectedly in mourning after the death
of her brother-in-law, Frederick III of Germany. Nonetheless, the
Holborn Dickens Bazaar was the start of a trend.

Decorating the stalls at charitable bazaars as quaint historic buildings was actually something of a fad in the 1880s. The pioneer was
one George H. Bernasconi of Birmingham, who conjured up an 'old
street' – an Elizabethan street scene – for a bazaar in Birmingham in
1880. The 'old street' then toured and appeared as a novel backdrop
to bazaars in several other towns and cities, including Coventry,
Nottingham, Luton and London.[6] The buildings were actually
facades of wooden timber frames, with the detail largely on painted
canvas, said to amount to some 12,000 square feet. The biggest
financial success for Bernasconi was an event held at London's Albert
Hall in June 1881, managed by aristocratic society ladies, who

served at the stalls in period costume, in aid of the Chelsea Hospital for Women. It was a small step, therefore, from imagining a street of Elizabethan stall fronts to a Dickensian street a few years later. As already discussed, 'Dickens's London' and 'Old London' were remarkably proximate in the late Victorian imagination.

Indeed, at the first Bernasconi fair in Birmingham, a melodrama formed part of the amusements on offer (not, it must be admitted, within the Elizabethan stage set). This historical drama, *Gentle Gertrude of the Infamous Red Lyon Inn; or Drugged and Drowned in Digbeth*, was written by none other than T. Edgar Pemberton, author of *Dickens's London*. The Victorian tourists who were fascinated by the pageantry and historical immersion of the Elizabethan street were the same audience who delved into books of Dickens-related literary tourism. The stalls at the Dickens Bazaar in Holborn, however, did not belong to Bernasconi. They were the work of one Henry Bevis, who advertised himself in the programme as a 'Bazaar Designer and Builder'. The same advertisement lists his previous designs and thus provides an insight into the imaginary travels of the Victorians: 'Designer and maker of the Olde Englishe Fancie Fayre, the Alpine Village, the Russian Village, Baronial Castle, Japanese City, Oriental Palace, International Fair, Shakespearean Show . . .'. All these stall fronts, with accompanying props, could be swiftly erected in a church hall to suit the chosen theme. There was considerable demand for such things, and, like Bernasconi's sets, Bevis's 'Dickens Bazaar' would tour to other locations, while others would produce their own local versions. The 'Dickens Village' at the Alexandra Palace exhibition ground in 1899, for example, was a similar endeavour, claiming to be a 'graphically correct representation of the bygone days of Old London, of which the late Charles Dickens was so faithful an interpreter'.[7]

Dickens was chosen as a theme at Holborn partly because the nearby Saffron Hill slums – largely cleared by the 1880s – featured prominently in *Oliver Twist*. Who better, therefore, to serve as a figurehead for rejuvenating a church tending to the urban poor? But the bazaar's programme also makes clear that this was also a pragmatic decision, a novelty designed to attract a 'larger public' than might otherwise attend.[8] This choice reflected not merely the appeal of Dickens's novels, but also the contemporary fascination with Dickensian place. Here was a unique opportunity to see facets of 'Dickens's London' – and sites further afield – represented in three dimensions, albeit as elaborately designed pop-up shops. The Holborn Bazaar also hints at how closely Dickens's characters and buildings were linked in the public imagination, a connection between character and place which Dickens himself carefully forged. Readers have always struggled to think of Miss Havisham without conjuring images of Satis House; or the Peggotty family without their boat-house; or Little Nell without the Old Curiosity Shop – and vice versa. The bazaar admittedly only presented recreations of Dickensian place and people, but nonetheless it reflected the touristic interest in 'Dickens's London' that came to the fore in the 1880s.

***

The rise of historic bazaars was undoubtedly boosted by a similar, but far more ambitious, tourist attraction in West London: the replica of an 'Old London Street' at the International Health Exhibition, held in Kensington in 1884–5 (on the site of the present-day Science Museum).[9] Bernasconi's touring Elizabethan facades were seen by thousands, but the Health Exhibition was on a larger scale, an exhibition selling four million tickets over a period of six months. The exhibition's Old London Street, indeed, was so popular with visitors that it was retained for the subsequent two exhibitions held on the site. The buildings in question were from designs by George H. Birch, the noted antiquarian who later became the curator of Sir John Soane's Museum.[10] They represented a range of specific long-vanished buildings from the pre-1666 history of the City of London, based on historical illustrations. There was considerable stress on antiquarian authenticity in relation to particular buildings – 'faithful delineations from actual drawings derived from authentic sources'.[11] Some had famous associations, including 'The houses of Dick Whittington and Izaak Walton, the house where Guy Fawkes ... elaborated his gunpowder plot'.[12] The houses were built, unlike Bernasconi's mere facades, in three dimensions, almost full-sized, set around a street and modest market square, with artful ageing effects including crumbling plaster and real moss. The houses' ground-level space was filled with craftsmen at work on traditional handicrafts. The overall effect was rather picturesque, since no one was willing to incorporate the muck and dirt that would have actually rendered the Old Street a salutary lesson in public health (the original idea behind placing a recreated medieval street within the Health Exhibition). The *Telegraph* joked that Londoners would instead take the lesson that the modern metropolis was 'fifty degrees uglier nowadays' and yearn for a wholesale return to quaint gables.[13] *Punch* similarly joked that this was more like a 'charming group of houses that might with advantage be erected at Upham Road, Bedford Park' (Richard Norman Shaw's well-known Queen Anne housing development in Chiswick).[14] In the second year, a more realistic cobbled effect was applied to the ground (previously timbered flooring) and electric lights were introduced to accommodate longer opening hours. The craftsmen's displays were also replaced by modern shops, with attendants in quaint costumes and more Olde English (advertising goods such as 'Ye Patent Koffe Potte').[15]

The Old London Street, although recreating historic buildings, prompted some visitors to think about fiction. One newspaper reviewer remarked that it would allow visitors 'to try to realise the conditions and circumstances which surrounded our favourite heroes and heroines, as painted by Shakespeare and older writers'.[16] Another newspaper noted the spectacular aspect of this city-within-a-city by referencing Dickens:

Standing in this street one is irresistibly reminded of Mr Sam Weller's philosophic utterance whilst commiserating with a caged bird in the Fleet. Though it is not a 'prison within a prison' it may be termed 'wheels within wheels', for it is per se a busy little town within the confines of a building.[17]

It is significant that a journalist turned to Dickens in searching for a description of this *urbs in urbe*: another hint of how easily 'Old London' and 'Dickens's London' elided. Another newspaper article, discussing the workers on display in the shopfronts, noted that the men 'make one believe that the London apprentices of two hundred and fifty years ago must have been very fine-looking fellows, worthy of the admiration of the Dolly Vardens of their time'.[18] Varden is a character in *Barnaby Rudge* and it is striking that Dickens's novel, set in the late eighteenth century, readily served as an imaginative point of reference for a medieval street scene. Another newspaper columnist described the Old London Street as a response to 'Newness ... forcing itself in upon us almost everywhere' – that is, an antidote to redevelopment in London – and suggested that its quaint and picturesque Tudor buildings would remind visitors of ancient 'associations of the Christmas time ... that received a stimulus in recent days from the writings of DICKENS'.[19] Again, we see Dickens linked with a loosely defined vision of 'the olden days' and quaint antiquity.

Similar old streets were built in both Manchester and Edinburgh. But a curious postscript to the story of the Old London Street is that another version, designed by Birch, was built in New York at 728–730 Broadway in 1886. The project failed financially and was taken over by the London and Liverpool Clothing Company as a novelty sales room in 1888. Two years later, the property's owners were ready to make a new deal for the disposal of 'Old London': the site was to be leased for fifteen years to the actor and manager Katie Putnam. She was well known in the United States as a comedienne and interpreter of Dickens, having toured in the United States, Australia and the United Kingdom. She had won particular acclaim for playing the dual role of Little Nell and the Marchioness in a stage version of *The Old Curiosity Shop*, roles to which she returned repeatedly throughout her career.[20] In 1890, she planned to take over the 'Olde London Street' (the New York version was 'Olde' as opposed to 'Old') and remake it as a theatre, called 'The Old Curiosity Shop' or 'The House of Little Nell'. The theatre, it was proposed, would be used for 'exclusive production of Dickens' works' and would have 'scenes painted direct from the quarters from which the great novelist drew his characters', accurate representations of real-world London locations. The deal fell through and details are scant, amounting to only a handful of press reports.[21] We do not know if she planned to reuse or reopen the recreated medieval streets but there was clearly, at the very least, some publicity value in making a connection between an 'Olde London' attraction and 'The House of Little Nell'.

The 1880s, therefore, saw the advent of historical bazaars, the Dickens Bazaar and the Old London Street, not to mention the rise of the so-called Old Curiosity Shop in Portsmouth Street and literary topographers who charted sites such as Nancy's Steps, where it was suggested that one could immerse oneself in a three-dimensional Dickensian daydream. This was not mere coincidence. They all formed part of the same tourist-antiquarian phenomenon, a desire for intimate, imaginative encounters with 'Old London' through visits to historic (or pseudo-historic) localities. Indeed, one could argue that the 'Dickens's London' charted by literary topographers was itself not so far removed from the reproduction of quaint antiquity which could be experienced in the Old London Street. 'Dickens's London' was, after all, a similar sort of virtual experience, where one could stand amidst evocative buildings and conjure up visions of the past.

***

Modest recreations of Dickensian sites were also used to drum up interest in the Dickens Stamp scheme (designed to raise funds for his descendants, in anticipation of his centenary in 1912). These were fully three-dimensional versions of the Old Curiosity Shop at the 1911 Coronation Exhibition at White City (near the Shepherd's Bush entrance) and of 'Peggotty's House' (the boat-as-house in *David Copperfield*) at the contemporaneous Festival of Empire at Crystal Palace. Both were venues where visitors could inscribe their name for posterity in a 'Dickens Centenary Register' (and hopefully buy some stamps in the process), 'recognising the great services he rendered by his works to the whole English-speaking race ... in grateful testimony on the occasion of his centenary'.[22] The two sites were staffed by a winsome costumed 'Little Nell' and 'Little Emily' respectively. For those who could not attend, it was possible to submit a *pro forma* in the post, which would be pasted into this timeless register of affection for the great author – for the price of three stamps. The Old Curiosity Shop at White City, it must be admitted, was visually unimpressive, a clumsy 'Tudorbethan' affair which bore little relation to anything in the novel or even the famous shop on Portsmouth Street. The building's unconvincing half-timbered appearance merely offered a generic nod to 'Old English' antiquity.[23]

A simple replica of the White Hart Inn appeared at the British Empire Exhibition of 1924 at Wembley. This was a 'stand' of some kind, perhaps akin to a bazaar stall (no images, nor any thorough description, seem to have survived), which represented the coaching inn yard, complete with Sam Weller (probably a mannequin) and an interior 'old inn parlour' where visitors could browse through assorted Dickens relics and memorabilia. These were compiled by Matz, that leading light of the Dickens Fellowship and also a coaching enthusiast. The items included a piece of balustrade salvaged from the demolition of the original pub. The stand belonged to Day and Martin's Blacking, who had a particular affection for the White Hart, since Dickens had jokingly referred to their product in his original description of Sam Weller ('Mr Samuel brushed away with such hearty goodwill ... that would have struck envy to the soul of the amiable Mr Warren (for they used Day & Martin at the White Hart)').[24] Day and Martin had approached the Fellowship, and Matz had agreed to lend some items from his private collection. The stand itself was a rather quirky parting gesture on behalf of the firm since the old company, established in 1770, had recently sold off its remaining business interests and was in the process of winding up its affairs.

Undoubtedly, however, the Portsmouth Street Old Curiosity Shop stimulated the greatest number of reproductions (which is somewhat ironic, given the original building had no genuine connection to the author). Indeed, from the few pictures that survive, it seems likely that many of the stalls at Dickens bazaars described as 'The Old Curiosity Shop' were replicas of – or, at least, took inspiration from – the famous facade of the Portsmouth Street shop.[25] This is not surprising given the shop's wide-reaching fame and strong visual identity. Full-sized reproductions of the shop also appeared at exhibitions in the United States in the 1930s, beginning with Chicago's Century of Progress Exhibition in 1934. The recreated shop was contained within the 'Merrie England' zone of this world's fair, a 'village green', 'created by men who loved Old England deeply ... to give Americans who know England ... much of the charm, the rest, the assurance, that they get in visiting her, and to give those who have not yet been to England a foretaste of some of her delights'.[26] The zone included recreations of buildings from various parts of England (and also John Knox's house from Edinburgh) and from a variety of periods, both those still in existence and some long lost (for example the Globe Theatre, which was used to showcase performances of Shakespeare). The overall effect was very similar indeed to the Old London Street at the International Health Exhibition. The official guidebook, which was rather ill-informed, claimed that the exhibition's Old Curiosity Shop was 'designed from one of Boz's illustrations from the immortal story' and not based on the shop on Portsmouth Street (which, in fact, it closely resembled, including the famous inscription on the facade). The guidebook also misleadingly stated that the No. 14 Portsmouth Street shop had, in any case, been demolished. The text then hymned the 'shopping possibilities' within this recreation, which included 'first editions, curios, antiques, prints, post cards of the village'.[27]

It is striking, however, that in the process of three-dimensional reproduction, the Merrie England shop lost the very antique features which made Portsmouth Street such a rich site for imagining 'Dickens's London' and became merely a gift shop, retailing, amongst other things, images of itself. The loss was palpable: the tiled roof and frontage became more symmetrical; the building grew taller and larger; and the crooked corners, matching the crooked street layout of Portsmouth Street, vanished. The building was, in fact, peculiarly homogenised, as were subsequent rather third-rate versions at the Californian Exposition at San Diego in 1935, the Ohio Exposition in Cleveland in 1936 and the New York World's Fair in 1939. The shop became merely one 'olde worlde' attraction amongst a couple of dozen others. The brochure for the 1934 exhibition – breezily entitled 'So You're Going to Merrie England' – displays a giant cartoon transparency of Dickens himself stalking past the shop, one of several superimposed cartoon figures in the book which also include Christopher Wren, Shakespeare, Henry VIII and his wives' disembodied heads, and Dr Johnson, a lively visual representation of the 'ghosts' that may be summoned by a visit to 'Merrie England'. It seems unlikely, however, that many visitors felt a compelling Dickens presence amidst this clutter of competing heritage personalities and structures. Home movie footage from one family's visit captures it as the backdrop to predominantly 'Elizabethan' street entertainments, with halberd-carrying Beefeaters mustering the crowds and comic games of 'jousting' by actors mounted on hobby horses. The reproduction shop was merely one more manufactured 'historic' backdrop which formed part of Chicago's theme park 'Old England' (although cynics might suggest that much the same could be said of the building back in London).

***

The most fertile medium for recreations of 'Dickens's London' would, of course, increasingly be the cinema. Indeed, the advent of moving pictures in the late 1890s brought new adaptations of Dickens's work almost immediately, even when running time was no more than a few minutes and films were brief novelties, sandwiched between live entertainment on music hall bills or presented as side-show amusements. The earliest known surviving Dickens silent film is *The Death of Poor Joe* (1901), little more than a minute in length, showing the titular crossing sweeper waving to a passing policeman, or possibly 'cocking a snook', only to collapse pathetically in his arms and shuffle off his mortal coil.[28] We know it is Dickens's famous character partly because of the painted scenic backdrop showing a locked wrought iron gate, representing the gate to the Russell Court burial ground. The film, effectively a *Poor Jo* music hall act condensed into sixty seconds, would undoubtedly have reminded many viewers of Jennie Lee and her numerous imitators. Such depictions of individual scenes and characters, drawing upon a tradition of theatrical vignettes, were popular with early cinema audiences. Nonetheless, they were soon superseded by more ambitious and technically accomplished work. Indeed, the very same year, another British film, *Scrooge, or Marley's Ghost* (1901), attempted to compress the entire *A Christmas Carol* into twelve scenes, complete with special effects – seemingly transparent superimposed ghosts – lasting a total of six minutes. More elaborate adaptations of entire novels would follow within a decade (although, even today, film adaptations cannot accommodate Dickens's generous helpings of minor characters and associated subplots). Studio sets and scenery would become ever more expansive, and by the middle of the century, cinematic visions of the Dickensian

173

metropolis were enhanced by superimposed models and matte work. Yet there was another obvious scenic possibility explored by an early director of Dickens adaptations: simply filming in the real-world locations beloved of literary tourists.

Thus, Thomas Bentley (1884–1966) showed a realistic 'Dickensland' to the cinema-going public, releasing a series of Dickens adaptations between 1912 and 1921 which routinely used real-world localities associated with literary pilgrimage. Bentley had previously been a music hall artist, performing a one-man abbreviated version of *The Old Curiosity Shop* in which he portrayed all the characters.[29] He migrated into film thanks to a deal with Pathé, for whom he made *Leaves from the Books of Charles Dickens* (1912), in which he impersonated thirty Dickens characters, à la Bransby Williams. This was also a topographical film, with Bentley situated performing against a backdrop of 'still existing notable places and houses mentioned in the author's works' (and timed for release with the 1912 Dickens centenary).[30] Bentley then went on to direct a series of adaptations: *Oliver Twist* (1912), *David Copperfield* (1913), *The Old Curiosity Shop* (1913), *The Chimes* (also known as *Once Upon a Time*) (1914), *Barnaby Rudge* (1915), *Hard Times* (1915), *The Old Curiosity Shop* for a second time (1921) and *The Adventures of Mr Pickwick* (1921). The exploitation of real-world locations in Dickens's literary territory was touted as part of the films' appeal. The opening title card for *David Copperfield*, for example, stresses that the film shows 'actual scenes immortalised by Charles Dickens', and similar announcements were made in printed publicity. Promoting the 1921 *Old Curiosity Shop*, Bentley wrote of his own interest in Dickens-related topography:

> It used to be my delight . . . to hunt out the original spots described in the books, and to people them in my imagination . . . In later years, I revisited all my favourite haunts and photographed them for my private records, and this collection of several hundred

pictures is invaluable assistance to me when seeking to recreate the atmosphere of the period.[31]

Bentley's touristic approach to Dickens films was, in fact, an animated extension of Bransby Williams's photo shoot at the King's Head in Chigwell: here was the real place in all its detail, the very place Dickens knew, the very place he had recreated in his fiction (and Williams, as it happens, would feature as Gradgrind in Bentley's *Hard Times*). Williams's photographs had created static tableaux for the armchair tourist, simultaneously illustrating both the real-world place and the novel. Bentley's feature films, similarly, provided a virtual literary tour that, in effect, ran in parallel with the films' narratives. Bentley was also obsessed with other aspects of authentic detail, a stickler for historical accuracy in costume and props. He boasted, for example, that even the coins used in his films belonged to the right period. Publicity for his *David Copperfield*, when it was released in the United States, likewise assured the cinema-going public that scenes were filmed in the 'exact spot used in the original novel', with the costumes 'all faithful replicas of those of the Copperfield period'.[32]

Bentley's repeated emphasis on authenticity makes it somewhat odd that he also used the Portsmouth Street Old Curiosity Shop as a backdrop in his 1914 and 1921 adaptations of the book (both now lost to posterity). Cecil Hepworth, Bentley's producer on *Oliver Twist* through to *Barnaby Rudge*, was also a Dickens fan. Indeed, he recalled how his father had toured with lantern shows which included a fondly remembered set of topographical slides entitled 'The Footprints of Charles Dickens'.[33] Bentley and Hepworth would surely have known that the shop was inauthentic, but we can only assume that the site's fame and familiarity overcame any qualms. Both films had international distribution and many an erstwhile American tourist would have recognised the shop. Hepworth, in fairness, had less interest in topographical authenticity than his colleague (of whom he would later enigmatically remark, 'a rum chap, but I found him very pleasant to work with'). He records in his auto-biography that Bentley, while filming *David Copperfield*, returned from Dover and gleefully informed him that he had managed to secure a shot of the signboard proclaiming a particular house 'immor-talized by Dickens as the Home of Miss Betsy Trotwood'. Hepworth remarks tartly, 'I do not think he ever understood why I received this news with so little enthusiasm'.[34]

Not that Bentley baulked at creating his own Dickensian scenery. One of the most ambitious British films of the period was his *Barnaby Rudge* (1915), with a large outdoor set created in a meadow at Walton-on-Thames near Hepworth's studio: 'five full-size streets of Old London, with their cobble paving stones, quaint houses and gabled windows' – remarkably similar to the Old London Street of the International Health Exhibition.[35] Some of the bombastic publicity went further: – 'ENTIRE TOWN ERECTED TO OBTAIN REALISTIC EFFECTS'.[36] Sadly, all that remains of the film are still photographs. Advertisements and puff pieces in the press boasted of more than a thousand extras hired to recreate the Gordon Riots, shipped in daily by special train from Waterloo Station. Pictures were released of Bentley issuing orders through a megaphone to meticulously ordered contingents of actors, whilst standing atop a specially erected scaffold.[37] Nonetheless, even in this case, Bentley also made sure to use the King's Head at Chigwell, for both the interior and exterior of the Maypole Inn.

Bentley's highly touristic use of real-world locations, in short, offered topographical/historical accuracy and paraded real-world sites as the localities that had inspired Dickens. Literary tourists who wished to visit these real-world sites, therefore, were now not merely stepping into the world of Dickens's books but entering the world of films (much as those on Harry Potter tours of London do today). The film director's fascination with 'the exact spot', however, was not sustainable. There was little incentive for future filmmakers to limit themselves to a handful of real-world Dickensian locations as the years progressed. Relatively few parts of 'Dickens's London' survived wholly intact into the mid-twentieth century; and carefully designed sets could increasingly replicate or improve upon reality. Bentley himself would choose to use a studio set for the exterior of the titular building in his final remake of *The Old Curiosity Shop* in 1934, eschewing Portsmouth Street. The result was a pseudo-medieval street scene of half-timbered properties, plainly designed to evoke 'Old London' (although there is also a cast-iron boot scraper and Victorian street lamp to hint at the nineteenth century). The background images to the film's opening titles, likewise, suggest 'Old London': drawings of archetypal rambling Tudor buildings, with exposed timbers, projecting upper storeys and lattice windows. The film even starts at a rural coaching inn, with thatched roof and timber cladding, where a chance conversation provides an opportunity for a few sentences of exposition (whereas the novel itself begins with an anonymous old man pacing the streets of the capital by night). Bentley chooses a coaching inn, showing us the comings and goings of a change of horses; the blowing of a copper coach horn; the departure of a coach. This is 'Old London'/'Old England' during the age of the stagecoach, a nostalgic Pickwickian vision of the past. Bentley's 1934 film, in other words, would still deliver a dose of heritage tourism, if not actively worshipping at literary shrines.

***

David Lean would take a very different tack in the 1940s, exploring the possibility of using production design not only to represent 'Dickens's London' but also to suggest a distinctive – and rather dark – mood. The substantial sets depicting London street scenes in David Lean's *Great Expectations* (1946) and *Oliver Twist* (1948) thus have a very different aesthetic to Bentley's work. They are tinged with a gloomy, forbidding expressionism: sharp contrasts of light and shade and, particularly in *Oliver Twist*, angular, off-kilter geometry. Pip's first visit to London in Lean's *Great Expectations*, admittedly, sees him pictured atop a stagecoach in front of the real-world tourist attraction of St Paul's (shown at a steep upwards angle, conveniently hiding the surrounding bomb sites of post-war London).[38] St Paul's provides a neat introduction to the capital, an enduring London icon, as timeless as Dickens's fiction. But we swiftly move away from this familiar landmark when Pip climbs down from the coach into a custom-made simulacrum of 'Dickens's London' (created by Oscar-winning production designer John Bryan). The cathedral and the orderly, moral world it represents have vanished and we are thrown into the hubbub of the streets. Pip is searching for the office of Mr Jaggers, legal representative of his mysterious benefactor. We see him come across 'Newgate Lane' (according to a street sign) and hurry down a shadowy, crooked flight of stone steps, flanked by off-kilter iron railings. The name is a nod to the criminal lawyer's close association with Newgate Prison, hinting that we are on the borders of both legal London and its criminal underworld. The threshold of the office itself is brightly illuminated and seemingly offers the promise of a bright future. Nonetheless, Jaggers's prospective clients lurk ominously upon the steps, and walls and windows are heavily accented by shadow – could there be a catch? The exaggerated dimensions of a pair of gabled, half-timbered medieval buildings are also visible in the background. Their pinched, angular rooftops sit at odds with their more regular neighbours; they look slightly uncanny. This is 'Dickens's London' of a sort, but not based on the work of literary topographers, nor even any particular illustration in the novels. Indeed, there is no such place as Newgate Lane in the novel, nor can one find the name in a contemporary street atlas. Newgate Lane, rather, is archetypal, filled with generic signifiers of both the Victorian and the Dickensian city. Street furniture helps set the Victorian mood: projecting gaslights; iron railings and spikes; cast-iron bollards; even a rectangular wooden bunker-like dustbin. The crooked steps, meanwhile, speak to the twists and turns of

Dickens's labyrinthine metropolis; the exaggerated Tudor gables suggest menace rather than quaint touristic spectacle.

David Lean, of course, was not the first to associate the Victorians with their ironwork, nor Dickens with crooked antiquity; but he was influential. Many subsequent Dickens films, therefore, utilised the same visual cues, fixing them in the popular imagination as key elements of 'Dickens's London', untethered from any particular real-world location. Subsequent films also borrowed the panorama of rainswept rooftops and smoking chimneys, punctuated by church steeples, which appears later in the story. Lean's camera pans across the tiles from a distant silhouette of St Paul's, then pauses and zooms in upon one illuminated casement, Pip's chambers. Once again, none of this was entirely new. Bustling street scenes and rooftop panoramas appear in Dickens's fiction, and they had previously appeared both on stage and in film in other contexts. Nonetheless, Lean and Bryan's memorable and accomplished films helped to establish them as part of a Dickensian cinematic visual lexicon.

Lean and Bryan replicated and expanded upon some of these elements in their *Oliver Twist*. Playing with the chronology of the book, Lean has his hero enter London through a cacophonous Smithfield Market, seen at elbow level, from Oliver's point of view. We never see the entirety of the market, only a blur of people and animals, with the hint of shops in the background, and another glimpse of St Paul's. The Artful Dodger meets Oliver and persuades him to come and meet Fagin. The market dissolves to the next scene: a Dickensian underworld at dusk. We are looking at twin flights of irregular steps on either side of a roughly plastered, wedge-shaped building, seemingly on the point of collapse. Our view is from the bottom of the stairs, situated in a darkened gaslit street or alley. We can only look up at the distant upper world, represented, once again, by the cathedral, at the summit of the steepest flight. The cathedral, in fact, is the only part of the screen seemingly with natural light; the rest lies in darkness. Dodger and Oliver – with their backs turned to

St Paul's and the orderly, moral life it represents – stride into the foreground, hurrying down yet more stairs on our right, into the abandoned building which serves as Fagin's den.

This scene has the same generic physical signifiers of a Victorian or Dickensian city as its precursor in *Great Expectations* – gaslights, railings, crooked steps – but they are exaggerated into something bordering on nightmare. The wedge-shaped building and irregular stairs would not look much out of place in *The Cabinet of Dr. Caligari*. The darkness is pervasive in this underground world, and the illuminated shop windows at the bottom of the stairs seem to be almost swallowed by the gloom. When Oliver leaves Fagin's den the next day, there is a hint of daylight; but it comes in stark, brutal shafts, forcing its way through narrow gaps between the buildings. Later in the film, this same street – once again, at night – takes Sikes's pursuers to 'Fagin's Bridge', a rickety wooden crossing over the creek at Jacob's Island, an alternative route to Fagin's den. The bridge is an impressive combination of model and matte work, superimposed on live action, seen from a distance. It forms part of a nocturnal panorama of roof-tops and chimneys, like that in *Great Expectations*, overlooked by the great, darkened dome of St Paul's. But the panoramic perspective in *Oliver Twist* is strangely condensed and, again, nightmarish. The innumerable chimneys seem to crowd in upon each other and the bridge in the foreground is oddly mirrored by another further back. There is a strong suggestion of a surreal, endless, recursive loop – a limitless slum underneath the gloomy bulk of the cathedral – almost like something one might find in the contemporaneous work of M.C. Escher. Even the dome of the cathedral is a strangely bulky, menacing presence. 'Fagin's Bridge', in a sense, serves as pure spectacle, which could easily be omitted from the plot without any confusion. Nonetheless, it provides a visual suggestion of endless slums; and the rooftops, of course, subsequently figure in Sikes's ill-judged escape which leads to his death. Bryan famously took inspiration from Gustav Doré's engravings. 'Fagin's Bridge' closely resembles 'St Paul's from the Brewery Bridge' in *London: A Pilgrimage* (1872), combined with the recursive quality of 'Over London – by Rail' from the same book (which shows a similar, seemingly endlessly repeating series of rooftops and chimneys).

Lean does not completely duck out of depicting real-world places that might be visited by the literary pilgrim, but he recreates them to suit his purpose. London Bridge in the film actually seems to be a likeness of the lost medieval bridge, or, at least, how it looked having been remodelled in the eighteenth century (as made clear by the distinctive semicircular alcoves which line its pavements). The bridge's steps, however, resemble those of Rennie's bridge from the early 1830s. Such architectural intermingling was perhaps inevitable, given Dickens's treatment of this scene (as discussed in Chapter 6). But Lean and Bryan introduce their own uncanny element. When Nancy and Brownlow meet, they are dwarfed by the size of the darkened parapet, which lies behind them, above shoulder height. When they retire to the shadow-drenched steps, they likewise become shrunken figures, thanks to the bridge being composed of giant granite blocks, much larger than anything used in reality. London Bridge, in other words, looms dramatically over the characters, capturing the uncanny quality of Dickens's original description.

David Lean and John Bryan ultimately created a 'Dickens's London' divorced from Bentley's notion of authentic Dickensian place. Why go to the trouble of filming on the original Nancy's Steps when one could create a more evocative, monstrous studio set? As noted above, their visualisation of Dickens's dark metropolis would prove highly influential – the crooked steps, the ironwork, the shadows and so forth – but there were other ways to portray Oliver Twist's milieu once it was abstracted from real-world locations. Carol Reed's 1968 adaptation of Lionel Bart's stage musical *Oliver!* would liberally borrow scenes and visual elements from Lean's film and yet create an entirely different mood.

***

Oliver! contains only one scene shot on location, where our hero jumps on the back of a cart travelling to London.[39] The rest was all shot at Shepperton Studios in Surrey, even the remarkably convincing Georgian crescent containing Mr Brownlow's house, which forms the backdrop to the musical number 'Who Will Buy?' (so convincing that viewers still often mistake it for being shot somewhere in London or Bath).[40] Carol Reed and production designer John Box, much like Lean and Bryan, created their 'Dickens's London' from scratch, but no one comes away from the musical remembering darkness and shadows. As one critic put it, 'the horrors of Dickensian London have either been omitted or smoothly transformed', leaving viewers with a sense of 'all pervading jollity'.[41] The film is not merely upbeat – 'Food, Glorious Food' setting the tone, with its remarkably lively and tuneful gang of workhouse inmates – but an extravaganza. Bottle washers, milkmaids, policemen and prostitutes all break into choreographed dance numbers at the drop of a top hat. Oliver Reed, admittedly, provides a much-needed dose of genuine menace, but it is typical of the film that Fagin is largely a cheeky rogue who escapes his fate in the novel (public execution) to dance off into the sunset with the Artful Dodger. Some of the darkness is retained – not least, the death of Nancy – but it does not linger quite so vividly in the imagination. Broadly speaking, this is the mood of *The Pickwick Papers* – a book full of frivolity, good cheer and consequence-free fun – applied to *Oliver Twist*. The film, of course, largely took its cues from Lionel Bart's original stage musical, first produced in London in 1960. But Sean Kenny's innovative and original theatrical set – a multilevel wooden scaffold set around a rotating turntable – had a certain sparse bleakness, 'evocative of the decayed, ramshackle world of Dickensian London'.[42] The film musical would offer something much more expansive and superabundant.

How, then, does the 'Dickensland' of this film create its distinctive mood? The first glimpse of the city is actually in the opening credits, which are superimposed upon a nineteenth-century drawing of rooftops and smoking chimneys, once again in the shadow of St Paul's (another hint of Doré, to which Box, like Bryan, referred). The camera pans down and we discover there is more to this sepia image. We follow the trail of liquid from a woman emptying a chamber pot from a garret, revealing a narrow street filled with quaint overhanging buildings that seems to lead up to the cathedral. The foreground of the picture, although static and motionless, is a tableau of violent activity: two coach drivers fighting with whips as their vehicles clash; a man in danger of being knocked off a ladder; a woman leaping to the side to save herself; a street entertainer with tambourine and dancing dogs. The foreground figures, with the exception of a solitary policeman, are actually borrowed from Thomas Rowlandson's 'Miseries of London', a suitably busy and bustling comic cartoon from 1807. The film thus begins by parading its deference to authentic historical source material. Indeed, one of its selling points was its meticulous recreation of such detail, much like Bentley's films. But this static scene also provides a hint that *this* is the lively world we are about to inhabit. The London of the early nineteenth century will come to life before our very eyes, supplying what is missing from the current teasing image: movement and colour. Various other lively sepia-toned prints then appear under the credits, until finally there is a watercolour depicting boys in the workhouse working a treadmill, which dissolves into the moving image. The film proper begins.

The opening workhouse scenes, however, deliberately defer the pleasure of colour. They are grey and brown, dull as Oliver's existence, the only notable colour being Mr Bumble's navy and gold-trim coat, and brief snatched glimpses of the workhouse overseers' feast. Nor is there much colour in the scenes outside the workhouse, when Oliver becomes a 'boy for sale' in a snow-covered town, nor within Sowerberry's undertaker's shop. Lionel Bart and Carol Reed were in firm agreement that there should be 'no fun at all until he got to London'.[43] We finally see Oliver managing to sneak onto a cart heading to the metropolis. The screen fades to the cart's contents being unloaded, and Oliver's head emerges from a bright green basket of lettuce, like a child reborn. This is partly a visual reference to him being 'green', an innocent naïf ('My eyes, how green!' remarks Dodger in the novel, and in the film, when his new acquaintance doesn't recognise his street slang). He is also now seemingly drowning in 'food, glorious food'. But, most of all, those green lettuces are also the film's first big splash of colour, as if to say, 'Now the fun begins'.

Reed then tips his hat to Lean's *Great Expectations* with a steep-angled shot of the summit of the real-world St Paul's Cathedral (showing us Oliver's perspective from the basket), before Oliver clambers out and emerges, blinking, astonished, to stare at the spectacle of 'Dickens's London', as recreated at Shepperton – not least, a colourful passing steam engine. Precisely where we are in the capital is not quite clear. Reed's set, in fact, contains hints of Covent Garden (the baskets of produce; a church which bears resemblance to St Paul's Covent Garden); Smithfield Market (butchers and a meat store); and Ludgate Hill (which had a railway viaduct crossing the street from the mid-1860s, and again featured in an illustration by Doré).[44] The truth, however, is that we are everywhere and nowhere: this is a generic, albeit lovingly detailed, 'Dickensland', composed piecemeal from a range of references and sources.

Of course, part of the appeal of the scene that follows – containing the spectacular song-and-dance number 'Consider Yourself' – is the human population, the inhabitants of the metropolis. We encounter seemingly endless different groups of people: butchers, priests, policemen, washerwomen and many more. Reed's assemblage of these groups of anonymous characters, identifiable through their work-related costume, is redolent of the eighteenth- and nineteenth-century fashion for illustrations of urban 'types'. These collectible prints would show the typical beggar, cab driver, street acrobat, mudlark and so forth, and enthusiasts might purchase the entire set. Reed presents cinemagoers with his own all-singing all-dancing version of archetypal 'London characters'. But the background scenery is equally diverse and beguiling. There are many hand-painted signs and signboards ('Dr. R. McGillam Surgery, 2nd door on right', reads one sign behind our hero). There is also a sign for the *Illustrated London News*, an in-joke, since the journal's illustrations were one of the main visual sources used by Box (first published, to be pedantic, six years after *Oliver Twist*).[45] We see fly-posters for theatrical entertainments. There is the customary street furniture of railings, cast-iron street lamps and boot scrapers; a distant glimpse of a sewage 'stink pipe' (a staple of Victorian streets, to vent gas from the drains); and a green letter box (a rare object on the set that is a little before its time). The church colonnade on which the boys briefly rest even boasts convincingly eroded stone, fouled with white flecks of pigeon droppings. Many of the buildings are wooden or have wood cladding – perhaps a few too many, but realistic enough for an older part of London in the 1830s – and there are also half-timbered Tudor affairs. The overall effect is highly detailed and immersive. Reed's set, indeed, is much larger than those used in Lean's film. He constructed a small network of connected streets around a central church, with numerous corners and side turnings – again, a world much like the Old London Street of the International Health Exhibition.

Once the song and dance begin, we experience perpetual movement, swirling crowds and activity, our young heroes progressing through the metropolis, going left and right, finding something new at every junction. We are, in effect, taking a tour of these recreated London streets, and such is the sheer pace and overwhelming historical detail that it is easy to believe one never sees the same corner twice. This is, in fact, broadly true; and when the same spot is reused, some of the signboards, shopfronts and set dressing have changed. It would take a remarkably keen eye to spot this repetition at first viewing, amidst the parades of singing and dancing Victorians, strutting their stuff before the camera. Reed, for example, uses the same church twice. The first time it is adorned with a substantial-looking classical colonnade and porch; the second time it is stripped of this frontage, which is replaced with a couple of decorative miniature obelisks. We are meant to feel like we are exploring the nooks and corners of an entire city – and it works. Indeed, there is a passion for display and detail here that parallels Dickens's own fascination with describing people and locations down to the minutest aspect of their appearance.

Reed uses the same idea of showing us characteristic Victorian figures in the great production number 'Who Will Buy?' later in the film, when they form various groups and strut, dance and interact around the perfect recreation of a Georgian crescent. The fact that this scene begins with street sellers trilling the phrase 'Who Will Buy?' is itself also a nod to that same Victorian fascination with collectible sets of illustrated characters: a popular subcategory of such images was street vendors, showing their typical dress and describing their 'street cries'.[46] Curiously, the set of 'Who Will Buy?' seems to have been universally known as 'Bloomsbury Square' by the cast and crew, presumably because the real-world square was a visual reference point for Box's design. Bloomsbury Square, however, is not crescent-shaped and Bloomsbury is not mentioned in the original novel, with Mr Brownlow's house situated further away from the centre of town ('in a quiet shady street near Pentonville').[47] The curved terrace on display in the film has also drawn comparisons with the famous Royal Crescent in Bath and Cartwright Gardens, south of St Pancras Station (not quite Pentonville, but close enough). One might equally add the distinctive, albeit much more petite, Annette Crescent on Essex Road in Islington. But it hardly matters, since this is not really meant to be any particular square or crescent: it is an archetypal respectable street of the 1830s. Reed, in turn, fills the space with his archetypal groups of respectable figures: husbands departing for work, maidservants, window cleaners, delivery boys, schoolchildren and more. This is a veritable parade of Victorian costume and activity and we end with a literal parade: a marching band of guardsmen, who arrive in the street for no particular reason (apart from reminding any potential London tourists in the cinema audience of the Changing of the Guard at Buckingham Palace).

Yet while there are obvious similarities between the staging of 'Consider Yourself' and 'Who Will Buy?', in their parade of characters, there are also important differences. We begin, once again, with Oliver encountering a spectacular London vista, but only after he has woken from a restful slumber in Brownlow's town house. He thus gazes upon the street scene from a first-floor balcony (the first floor is not the typical place for a bedroom in a Georgian town house, but we can gloss over that). The gleaming white stucco-clad crescent, in other words, is introduced from above, a panorama, seen from on high (unlike the street scenes of 'Consider Yourself', where the camera is more confined). Ensconced in a secure, middle-class home, he can safely enjoy the hubbub at one remove. Indeed, during 'Who Will Buy?', the camera repeatedly pulls back to the balcony level to show us the generous expanse of curving terraced properties. Reed also makes a slightly different use of his groups of Victorian characters in this number. The choreography, by Onna White, now owes a little more to ballet than to the (equally carefully choreographed) Cockney knees-up in the earlier scene; and this dancing is rarely interrupted by other characters cutting across the foreground. The unimpaired balletic movements suit the more expansive open space but also hint at the orderly middle-class world laid out before us. Some of the groups of characters that appear are also lined up to mirror the repeating pattern of the terraced houses. Thus, identically dressed window cleaners and delivery men simultaneously perform comical interactions and dance moves with maidservants at each of the identical properties. John Box would comment that he himself came up with this idea, which makes perfect sense, as it seamlessly integrates action with design.[48] This visual repetition of buildings and people echoes the recursive rooftops of Lean's *Oliver Twist*, but it is spectacular rather than menacing – endless clockwork order (this is clearly the routine way in which the crescent begins each and every day) rather than endless chaos. The effect is enhanced by the fact that we cannot see where the crescent begins or ends. There is the peculiar sense, perhaps fortuitous, required by the set design, that it could go on forever.[49] Certainly, both 'Consider Yourself' and 'Who Will Buy?' are spectacular showstopping performances that feel strangely limitless. The viewer continually – joyfully – asks, 'Can there *really* be yet another group of characters appearing? Another corner to turn? Yet another chorus?' This suggestion of superabundance arguably echoes Dickens's own fulsome, descriptive prose. But it was also enabled by the expansive 'Dickensland' constructed for the production.

Oliver's introduction to both these astonishing spectacles is also remarkably akin to a tourist's introduction to the capital. His emergence through an archway into the overwhelming 'Consider Yourself' street scene – his uncertainty about quite where to go or what to do first – will chime with many recalling their own first visit to London (or, indeed, any big city). The opening of 'Who Will Buy?', likewise, when Oliver steps out onto the balcony, suggests something equally familiar to the tourist: waking up in a hotel, opening the curtains and checking out the panoramic view.

***

The stark gloom of David Lean's *Oliver Twist* and the extravagant technicolor world of *Oliver!* have undoubtedly both proved influential. Take, for example, another much-loved Dickens musical, Brian Henson's *A Muppet Christmas Carol* (1992), a film whose popularity has steadily increased since it first appeared thanks to repeated seasonal showings on television (as I write, a cinematic re-release testifies to its longevity). Henson's 'Dickens's London' amounts to a compact set of streets and alleys, much like in *Oliver!*. These streets, likewise, host a musical number ('Scrooge') which introduces us to the city and its denizens, albeit within a considerably smaller space and a cast composed largely of muppets. Instead of Reed's cast of washerwomen, policemen, butchers and so forth, we meet groups of talking vegetables, pigeons, cats, beggars, mice, horses and Christmas carollers.

We first see (Muppet) 'Dickens's London', however, via a panoramic view of rooftops and chimneys, which appears beneath the opening credits. This owes something to Lean's model rooftop panorama in *Great Expectations*, but simultaneously the vista is bright, the music jolly, with the rooftops pleasingly drizzled with snow. The half-timbered facades of many of the houses hark back to Bentley's era and the fascination with a quaint Tudor 'Old London'. But Henson also brings his own whimsical aesthetic. This townscape in the title sequence is overwhelmingly a rich brown and the buildings have a stylised, slightly primitive finish. This snow-capped panorama, in fact, looks very much like a vast collection of elaborate gingerbread houses, mouth-wateringly edible, dusted with icing sugar. One of the rooftops that appears as the camera pulls back over the vista even has festoons of beaded garlands, ostensibly part of the stonework but resembling the sort of looped festoon piping that used to be fashionable on wedding cakes. We are promised a veritable treat.

Likewise, when we get down to the streets, (Muppet) 'Dickens's London' contains a familiar checklist of Victorian/Dickensian signifiers – gaslights, damp cobbles, quaint mullioned glass in the windows, crooked steps, cast-iron bollards – but the overall scenic effect remains, very deliberately, a charming 'chocolate box' vision of the Victorian metropolis. That said, there are three exceptions. Most noticeably, there is the street outside Scrooge's house. We see it in the first half of the film, situated in a dark and gloomy corner, illuminated only by a narrow shaft of light that highlights the staircase which leads down to this miserable place (true enough to Dickens's own description of 'a gloomy suite of rooms, in a lowering pile of building up a yard').[50] Then there is the street where Bob Cratchit lives, whose tilting rickety Tudor houses have their own surreal (and comical) distorted geometry, redolent of a fairground funhouse. Both these places, in their own way, reference Lean's expressionist vision of 'Dickens's London': the darkness, the flight of stairs descending into darkness, the strange misshapen buildings (albeit the latter are now oddly cheerful). Finally, there is the dark future presented by the Ghost of Christmas Yet to Come, where the previously bright and cheerful sets are now all tinged ashen grey (much like the colourless workhouse world at the start of *Oliver!*).

Drabness, gloom and lack of colour, of course, have themselves become a visual clue that we are in 'Dickens's London' in film and television, echoing both the darkness in Lean's films and Reed's judicious withholding of colour in *Oliver!*. The 2005 BBC adaptation of *Bleak House*, for example, the first large-scale British drama to be filmed in high definition, specialised in extreme close-ups of faces emerging from shadow and had a thoroughly murky colour palette that 'captured the dark and grimy essence of Dickensian London', with the director, Justin Chadwick, praised for creating 'an appropriate visual language for Dickens – steeped in gloom'.[51] The muddy, miserable London exteriors were produced largely at a stable block on the Luton Hoo country estate in Bedfordshire, with set designers producing new facades and Victorian shopfronts but retaining the existing time-worn cobbles.[52] The immediate successor to *Bleak House* on the BBC was a 2007 version of *Oliver Twist*, directed by Coky Giedroyc, with its own generous portions of gloom and flickering candlelight. This version of the story also contained borrowings from Lean's work. For example, Oliver's entrance to London, where we suddenly find him in a bustling street teeming with people and carriages, is initially shot at child's height (like Lean's vision of Oliver at Smithfield Market). There is also a glimpse of the dome of St Paul's from below. But whereas Lean used a steep angle to conceal the devastation of surrounding post-war bomb sites, Giedroyc uses CGI to relocate a street scene filmed in a suitably antique-looking Middle Temple Lane to the shadow of the Cathedral. Middle Temple is one of the capital's historic lawyer's colleges, the Inns of Court. Dickens himself was very fond of the Inns as a quaint setting in his fiction, with, for example, Pip having rooms in the Temple in *Great Expectations*; Traddles having rooms at Gray's Inn in *David Copperfield*; and Mortimer Lightwood also having rooms in the Temple in *Our Mutual Friend*. For even in Dickens's day, the old Inns of Court seemed like a peculiar, fusty world, set apart from the bustling streets, with a curious atmosphere all their own. Nowadays, thanks to their well-preserved terraces and squares of Georgian and Victorian buildings, they regularly appear as not only 'Dickens's London' but also 'Old London'.[53]

Arguably, however, the real televisual successor to the BBC's *Bleak House* was *Dickensian* (2015), created by the *Eastenders* writer Tony Jordan. This series used the same short, half-hour episode format as *Bleak House* and was similarly marketed as likely to appeal to an audience of soap-opera fans (and, after all, asked the press releases, did not Dickens write much of his material for serial publication?). But Jordan took things further, with the series being a 'mash-up' which introduced multiple famous characters and locations from different Dickens novels into the same twenty-episode drama series (much like a dramatic counterpoint to the Dickens Bazaar at Holborn). Thus Satis House (Miss Havisham's decrepit home in *Great Expectations*) became a grand mansion within easy walking distance of the Old Curiosity Shop, not far from the Three Cripples public house (of *Oliver Twist*), Jaggers's office (*Great Expectations*) and the home of the Cratchits *(A Christmas Carol)*. The plot amounted to a prequel to *Great Expectations* (explaining the jilting of Miss Havisham), *Oliver Twist* (there is a good deal of Sikes, Nancy and Fagin) and *A Christmas Carol* (with the death of Jacob Marley as murder mystery, to be solved by Inspector Bucket of *Bleak House*). The set and production design were much publicised as a selling point for the programme, with the BBC even releasing a map of the main road, 'Market Street', and its surrounding alleyways. Michael

Ralph, the production designer, reportedly created not only the streets but also fifteen working fireplaces, used a thousand tonnes of sand and cement to make cobbles, and built a street wide enough to allow two horse-drawn carriages to comfortably pass at speed.[54] The series ended with the Artful Dodger discovering a solitary boy called Oliver, and the two children walking towards the Three Cripples, with its corner entrance framed to look distinctly like a similar entrance to the Old Vic public house at the heart of the *Eastenders* set (hinting at the Cockney soap opera as part of Dickens's cultural legacy).

Critical opinion about this programme was ultimately rather mixed. Many worried that *Dickensian* pleased neither Dickens fans, who found the mash-up too confounding and incoherent, nor soap-opera fans, for whom there was still too much allusion to or reliance upon Dickens's original fiction. The proximity of so many Dickensian people and places did seem, at times, a little uncanny. The programme also suffered from chaotic scheduling on either side of Christmas, making a regular appointment with the show, as with a soap opera, impossible. Many viewers enjoyed it nonetheless, and an accompanying exhibition at the Charles Dickens Museum proved very popular. *Dickensian*, in any case, borrowed the gloom of *Bleak House* and the visual lexicon of Dickensian place that Lean's films helped to entrench: the ironwork; the dark passages; the archways; the prevailing darkness, barely kept at bay by flickering gaslights. There was also a strong hint of fog (the BBC's *Bleak House* from 2005 had received some criticism for its lack of fog) and a good deal of remarkably pristine snow on the ground, a nod to innumerable film versions of *A Christmas Carol*. Most of all, again, muted, drab colours predominated, an 'appropriate visual language for Dickens'.

***

One obvious consequence of elaborate studio sets, and the ever-increasing use of CGI, is that the artificial 'Dickensland' of film rarely overlaps with the 'Dickens's London' of the literary topographer. Real-world places, such as Middle Temple Lane, generally stand for somewhere else, incorporated into a new cut-and-paste digital world of scenic effects. In 2007, however, a tourist attraction opened in Chatham which attempted to reproduce the sort of self-contained physical set produced for *Oliver!* and make it available to the public as a real-world visitor attraction: Dickens World.

There was some precedent for this development. There had long been plans to create a theme park version of 'Dickens's London'. Eric Morley, chairman of the Mecca Organisation, planned an 800-acre British Disneyland in the early 1970s, not far from the M6 motorway at Cannock, to be called 'Merrie England', whose scope was 'from Camelot to the present, emphasising imaginative but authentic period design'.[55] This was to include tours in sedan chairs running on a monorail; a recreation of the Globe Theatre; an olde-world Drury Lane; a recreation of Vauxhall Gardens; plus a Music Hall and 'Dickens's London'. Like at Chicago's 'Merrie England' zone, Dickens was to be merely one heritage asset amongst many. There were also plans to a recreate the Crystal Palace and a new Old London Bridge, which would be built across an artificial lake. One million pounds was allegedly spent on landscaping the site, but the money ran out – thanks in part to the mid-1970s economic crisis – and nothing more came of the project.

A more realistic prospect, perhaps, was the 'Disneyland-type entertainment, taking the London of Dickens as its theme' that was proposed for the Royal Agricultural Hall in Islington in 1979.[56] The hall was to house Dickensian streets and facades, and the developers would also make use of the existing theatre within the building as a sort of heritage music hall, devoted to Victorian song and dance. The plan was the proposal of Romm Doulton, an American businessman who hoped to work with the Whitbread business empire in developing the site, but he could not find sufficient backing beyond their tentative interest. Doulton's later claims to fame include patenting the 'Sensortron Geotechometer', a battery-powered GPS compass, and various other unrealised theme park ventures, including one based on the long-running *Archers* radio soap opera, which was reportedly to be entitled 'Forever Ambridge'.

Rochester, meanwhile, had the Charles Dickens Centre at Eastgate House, an Elizabethan town house, which itself features in *The Mystery of Edwin Drood*. This tribute to Dickens, owned by Medway Council, was opened in 1979 and closed in 2004, due to dwindling visitor numbers. The centre was a combination of museum and visitor experience ('It's fun – It's educational!' boasted an early flyer).[57] The public walked through a winding set of twenty-one small rooms whose contents variously referenced Dickens's biography (from Dickens's early years to 'Last Days in Rochester') and themes from the novels ('Crime and Punishment', 'Dickens and the Theatre' and so forth). Display cases showed model miniatures of Dickensian interiors and street scenes. There was, for example, a miniature slum scene, with houses seen from both the exterior and a cut-away sectional view of the buildings. Waxworks and marionettes also represented scenes from the novels, such as Lady Dedlock and Jo at the burial ground gates, or Miss Havisham in her bridal gown. Sound and lighting effects added to the experience. One supposed highlight was trumpeted in all the advertisements: 'Witness the wicked murder of Nancy'; 'Hear Nancy's Bloodcurdling Scream!'. This was an attempt to attract those who enjoyed the gory delights of attractions such as the London Dungeon, although there was little to actually see: a waxwork of Sikes with a raised cosh, and the hands of Nancy clutching at a curtain (with nothing more of her visible).

Dickens World at Chatham, however, was something different again: an immersive experience, recreating 'Dickens's London' with archetypal 'Old London' buildings, which could be explored at leisure. There were various individual attractions dotted throughout the site, including animatronic characters, a Victorian schoolroom with a 'strict' actor/headteacher, a Victorian gift shop (inevitably 'The Olde

Curiosity Shoppe'), a Gothic-looking town house ('The Haunted
House of 1859' – a reference to Dickens's story of that year – replete
with projected ghosts), a 3D theatre that showed an animated
film about Dickens's life and work, and a bevy of costumed actors
wandering the set to interact with the public. There was also a
single theme park ride, albeit a fairly gentle experience: the 'Great
Expectations Boat Ride' through the 'sewers' amidst the recreated
slums (with a good number of rickety, half-timbered Tudor buildings, tottering chimneys and missing tiles) overlooked by other
visitors criss-crossing the canal on wooden walkways. Apart from
animatronic rats frolicking in the water, which seem to have rarely
functioned, the boat trip also included a narration about Magwitch's
escape from London, during which the boat rose to the rooftops and
finished with a rapid drop, guaranteeing visitors a soaking. Part of the
hoped-for appeal of the ride was that it gave an excellent view of the
recreated Dickensian cityscape.

Indeed, the notion of stepping into a recreation of the city was key
to the entire project. Kevin Christie, the attraction's promoter and
majority shareholder, suggested that hc began the project precisely
because the reality of modern London did not live up to the 'Dickens's
London' of the popular imagination, bluntly stating: 'People come to
London expecting it to look like Oliver Twist, but it's not like that
anymore, so we're recreating it.'[58] He boasted of evoking 'a true sense
of Victorian landscape' and talked about reproducing authentic
period architecture.[59] Press reports dutifully recounted that this was
a 'painstakingly recreated Victorian London' (although some were
more cynical than others, with the *Guardian* describing the Victorian
streetscape as an exercise in tired nostalgia with its gaslights, cobbles
and artificially weathered buildings).[60] Dickens World, according to
Christie, provided a handy alternative to trawling the streets of the
capital seeking out the dwindling 'Dickens's London' of the literary
topographer. Here was something altogether more amusing and yet
simultaneously authentic in its recreation of period detail. Of course,

in practice, this was still very much a stylised theme park vision of the metropolis, the work of a consultancy based at Pinewood Film Studios, who had designed the Jorvik Viking Centre in York. Dickens World, indeed, was nothing like the physical reality of nineteenth-century London in innumerable ways, antiseptically clean (despite visual nods to London's filth) and located within a retail park in Chatham.

Being in the wrong place may have been part of the attraction's downfall. Earlier plans to locate the site in King's Cross had proved too costly due to the capital's rapidly rising property prices. The result was a London-related attraction that struggled to attract tourists who were visiting the capital. Ultimately, Dickens World failed to turn a profit. The public were also confused by the presence of a solitary water ride: was this a theme park or not? Christie regularly berated reporters that it was 'not a theme park, but a themed attraction', clearly wary that press publicity might create – forgive me – great expectations of Dickens-themed thrill rides. There were also various technical problems, from the dysfunctional animatronic rats to reneging on a promise to provide a 'dark, smoky, moody London, full of smells and mist' (the wholesale use of smell was soon abandoned as off-putting and liable to flood the entire hangar-like space).[61] The attraction, in short, never made sufficient money and was only kept afloat by the company renting out adjoining space to a cinema chain and restaurants. The Great Expectations boat ride closed in 2012, with reports of overall losses running from £500,000 to £1 million per annum. Prices were slashed and the venue was repurposed as a guided tour experience, with the theatre space let out as an unlikely concert venue. Dickens World finally succumbed to the inevitable and closed its doors for good in 2016.

Dickens World was, of course, thoroughly Victorian in its conception, comparable to the Old London Street or even, with its inclusion of a canal boat ride, Imre Kiralfy's remarkable 'Venice in London', a late Victorian walk-through recreation of Venice at Olympia, replete with (scaled-down) canals and gondolas.[62] Indeed, it embodied the ideal of the Victorian exhibition, providing a mix of instruction and amusement (although perhaps never to anyone's entire satisfaction on either account). This version of 'Dickens's London' also plainly owed a good deal to Lean's *Oliver Twist* and Carol Reed's *Oliver!* with its 'rickety backstreets, roped bridges, and miasmatic waterways' evoking the Jacob's Island slum, as depicted in both films.[63] Christie, who employed a member of the Dickens Fellowship as a consultant regarding Dickensian authenticity, also had an eye to the recent successful television adaptation of *Bleak House*, which had been publicised as a sort of neo-Victorian soap opera. The suggestion that his themed attraction was doing Dickens's novels a disservice – whatever its merits, the venture did little to expose visitors to Dickens's prose – was repeatedly met by the rejoinder that Dickens himself was a populist who today might have written for the soaps.[64] I take that argument with a pinch of salt, since Dickens – if he suddenly found himself in the twenty-first century and took a fancy to visual media – would surely have wanted to write blockbuster films or prestigious limited series that showcased his own genius, rather than collaborating on never-ending weekly serials. The latter existed in the Victorian period – Gothic penny dreadfuls such as G.W.M. Reynold's *The Mysteries of London*, which actually outsold Dickens – but such cheap sensational works were not part of the respectable middle-class world which Dickens wanted to inhabit.

Christie might, in fact, have done better appealing to the strong visuality of Dickens's fiction. Dickens's vivid and detailed descriptions have often drawn comparison with painting and the visual arts. Some even consider that he anticipated aspects of cinema. Vincent van Gogh reread *A Christmas Carol* on an annual basis and remarked to fellow artist Anthon van Rappard that there was no other writer 'as much a painter and draughtsman'.[65] Sergei Eisenstein argued that fellow film director D.W. Griffith discovered montage through his imitation of Dickens and, more generally, praised the 'optical quality' of the novels.[66] *Oliver Twist*, in fact, contains a prime example of that remarkable quality, when Dickens introduces the riverside slum of Jacob's Island:

> To reach this place, the visitor has to penetrate through a maze of close, narrow, and muddy streets, thronged by the roughest and poorest of waterside people . . . he makes his way with difficulty along, assailed by offensive sights and smells from the narrow alleys which branch off on the right and left, and deafened by the clash of ponderous waggons that bear great piles of merchandise from the stacks of warehouses that rise from every corner. Arriving, at length, in streets remoter and less-frequented than those through which he has passed, he walks beneath tottering house-fronts projecting over the pavement, dismantled walls that seem to totter as he passes, chimneys half crushed half hesitating to fall, windows guarded by rusty iron bars that time and dirt have almost eaten away, every imaginable sign of desolation and neglect.[67]

This could easily work as a scene in a film, a tracking shot progressing through the slums, because of the way Dickens handles point of view and movement. For a start, the reader is placed in the position of a 'visitor' to the decaying district. The 'visitor' (or 'traveller' or 'stranger') in nineteenth-century fiction often serves as a sort of avatar for the reader, an 'imaginary instantiation of an alternative self'.[68] The reader is asked to briefly imagine themselves 'there' in the form of this anonymous stranger and thus allow themselves to be drawn into the fictional universe that is depicted upon the page. Such figures are often positioned in a lofty panoramic position, taking an overview of the world. Dickens, however, does something different, throwing his 'visitor' into the neighbourhood's claustrophobic 'maze of close, narrow and muddy streets'. This anonymous visitor still offers us a sort of panoramic introduction to the district – in that it seems comprehensive – but we find ourselves at ground level, turning left and right, moving through the streets and alleys. In fact, everything seems to be moving and animated, including the 'visitor': the thronging crowds; the trundling wagons; even the decrepit houses, which are 'tottering' as we pass by, chimneys 'hesitating to fall', vibrating with a typically Dickensian malignant energy. There is also something distinctly microscopic in the way in which that last sentence shifts from the general to the particular, another form of movement, from streets to houses – house fronts – windows – iron bars – the rust and dirt upon those bars. Our attention is gradually focused upon the smallest visual detail – the rusty iron – which becomes metonymic for the work of 'time and dirt' upon the entirety of this much-neglected district (and, indeed, symbolises the corrosive relation which the neglected slum bears to the rest of the metropolis). We zoom in and zoom out.

Dickens, in other words, had the eye of a filmmaker and welcomed visitors – one might even say 'tourists' – into his own highly visual recreation of the nineteenth-century metropolis. The sets of David Lean, Carol Reed, *Dickensian* and Dickens World, even when there is no reference to real-world buildings, draw upon Dickens's own proto-cinematic gaze. They respond to the author's own carefully constructed world, his meticulous attention to the smallest detail, as much as they are simultaneously in a tradition of recreations of urban space dating back to nineteenth-century exhibitions. Dickens himself was the first and best Dickensian production designer – as those rusty iron bars attest.

9

SOMEBODY ELSE'S SIEVE

The most remarkable thing about touristic 'Dickens's London' is its endurance. More than one hundred and fifty years after the author's death, one can still purchase guidebooks and take guided tours. People still want to see something of the actual localities which Dickens described. Even the restrictions of the recent COVID-19 pandemic proved only a minor obstacle to the determined literary topographer. London tour guides soon produced 'virtual' walks, livestreaming their progress through the capital or broadcasting recordings, to 'enable participants to explore the streets of Dickens London from the comfort of their own homes'.[1] The constancy of 'Dickens's London' is particularly surprising given that so much has been destroyed. I have discussed how 'disappearing Dickens's London' was something of a lazy journalistic cliché in the late nineteenth-century press. Nonetheless, the 'rage for public improvement and the encroachments of private speculation' have undoubtedly laid waste to a good deal of the territory. Indeed, the gradual process of attrition began within a decade of Dickens first being published and has continued for nigh on two centuries. The Fleet Prison, for example, depicted in such detail in *The Pickwick Papers*, closed in 1842 and was soon demolished. The noxious tidal creeks of Jacob's Island, which feature so prominently at the conclusion of *Oliver Twist*, were much improved by sanitary reforms in the 1850s following the ravages of cholera. The local Medical Officer of Health for Bermondsey in 1856 boasted that Dickens would not recognise the area; and it became a commonplace for local charity workers to quote Dickens's description of the district as a yardstick for its sanitary and moral improvement ('where "the crazy wooden galleries" once hung over it, stands Peek, Frean and Co.'s splendid biscuit bakery').[2] Likewise, the construction of Holborn Viaduct in the 1860s, and related improvement works on nearby streets, saw the slums of Saffron Hill – the site of Fagin's den – yield to a modern carriageway and commercial buildings.

Slums, of course, were the perennial target of Victorian reformers, and none of the slum districts depicted by Dickens survived unchanged into the twentieth century. The notorious 'rookery' of St Giles/Seven Dials, featured in *Sketches by Boz*, which famously could not be entered safely at night without a police escort, was largely pacified by the 1880s. Thus, *Dickens's Dictionary of London*, an alphabetically arranged guidebook to life in London published by Dickens's son Charley, proclaimed in 1879 that 'the Dials are now traversed by omnibuses, and have made considerable progress towards civilisation'.[3] Even the darkest depths of the East End were somewhat improved during Victoria's reign. Take, for example, the opium den which Dickens depicts in the opening of *The Mystery of Edwin Drood*. The den was based upon a real place, a shoddy two-room cottage in New Court, Victoria Street, St George's-in-the-East, a district also known as 'Bluegate Fields' (immediately south of modern-day Shadwell station). The place was first described in *All the Year Round* in 1866, in an article by Joseph Charles Parkinson.[4] Various pieces then appeared in the press, telling the stories of the owners and their patrons, including a certain Mother Abdallah,

Lascar Sal and Cheeny (China) Emma. These were English women, two of whom were married to Asian husbands and managed the premises. Edmund Yates, one of Dickens's young journalist protégés, produced his own description of a trip to the opium den in 1867.[5] Dickens himself then visited in 1869 – partly as a tourist, partly because he was researching the work of lodging-house inspectors – and the place finally made its appearance in *Drood* in April 1870. Thanks to the novel, New Court briefly became one of the famous sights of London – if one could find, for safety's sake, an obliging local policeman. Prince Louis-Napoléon, son of the dethroned French Emperor, studying physics at King's College in 1872, arranged a visit to the house in the company of the journalist William Blanchard Jerrold.[6] New Court was the same opium den that Gustav Doré illustrated for his book with Jerrold, *London: A Pilgrimage* (1872). The Prince of Wales was also alleged to have paid calls there 'to witness the opium smoking'.[7] There were even press reports that the foul bed described by Dickens was sold by Lascar Sal (also known as Opium Sal) to an American collector.[8] The owner of these slum properties was a tailor from Pentonville called Summerfield, who reportedly let out rooms for two shillings a week. In 1874, he success-fully sued the East London Railway for £220 in damages caused by their tunnelling works, doubtless something of a pleasant windfall. By the end of the 1880s, the buildings had been demolished by the local authority to make way for public gardens.

The rapid disappearance of the slumland side of 'Dickens's London' was, in fact, noted very early on by M.D. Conway in his 'Footprints of Charles Dickens' (1870). Conway enjoined Dickens's fans to 'walk the streets and by-ways he had woven into the tissue of his work'. But his own brief travelogue includes a description of two walks round Field Lane and Saffron Hill, one undertaken in 1862 and the other in 1870. These two perambulations do not quite tally. In 1862, we are told, he found the district pretty much as it was portrayed in *Oliver Twist*. His travelling companion even informed him that he once had a handkerchief stolen by a local pickpocket and then discovered it for sale in a nearby shop window.[9] In 1870, however, Conway finds the district radically altered by the building of Holborn Viaduct and a 'very handsome Gothic church' (probably St Alban-the-Martyr, which was built to bring the gospel to local slum dwellers). Conway hopes that the solitary surviving section of Field Lane will soon, likewise, be swept away by slum clearance – or so he claims. For his description of the local inhabitants ('Bloated, diseased, filthy men, women and children still swarm at the doors like rats . . .') reads more like reassurance for the voyeuristic connoisseur of slumdom.[10] Something of the London which Dickens documented, he reassures the reader, still remains in this spot, in human form. There is a distinct tension between Conway's claim that real-life 'vestiges of Dickens' survive in the streets and the admission that those vestiges amount to 'bloated, diseased, filthy' individuals and their crumbling homes. Which is the fitter memorial to Dickens: that his books are so true to life that one can find the real-world equivalent slum, or that the reality has been swept away by social improvement and urban renewal? There is a nagging sense that the vanishing of these sites, however socially beneficial, represents a diminution or even obliteration of the author, and an anxiety that the author's work may not transcend the time and place of its origin.

Indeed, the creation of 'Dickens's London' as a literary territory in subsequent decades was, for some literary topographers at least, about creating a sort of living memorial to the great author. The buildings might vanish entirely, but the texts and practice of Dickensian literary pilgrimage – an apt term in this context – would, it was hoped, preserve his memory. Thus, for Percy Fitzgerald, there was some value in creating a sculpture of Dickens for the Prudential Assurance Company after their offices were built upon the site of the demolished Furnival's Inn, in order to bring Dickens pilgrims to the same spot in communal acknowledgement of his genius.[11] Scarcity also increases value; the less that remains, the more we are inclined to cherish it. The George Inn, as already discussed, became such a beloved 'Dickensian' destination precisely because there was nothing else like it remaining in the heart of the metropolis.

***

One reason for the survival of 'Dickens's London', of course, has been the author's enthusiastic fans – not least, transatlantic tourists. I have already highlighted the large numbers of keen Americans visiting Dickens's literary territory, from Louisa May Alcott onwards. It is worth remembering that the literary culture of England was seen by most Americans, at the turn of the twentieth century, as a common inheritance, a shared anglophone legacy.[12] Moreover, during this period, this cultural tie was being actively promoted as a common transnational property, a sort of cultural cement in the anglophone world, binding Britain to the increasingly powerful United States, a friendly rival rather than an enemy. A shared literary inheritance was offered as both a justification for asserting a collective transatlantic 'Anglo-Saxon patriotism' and a means of fixing such a notion in the public consciousness.[13] Some literary topographers even framed their work as an international endeavour, a means of uniting 'English-speaking peoples' ('England and America, whatever the differences between them, are one – one in ancestry, one in literature, and one in the future of the Anglo-Saxon race').[14] Equally, a collective literary heritage was offered by others as a whole or partial replacement for the lack of racial ties between Great Britain and non-Anglo-Saxon immigrants to the United States.[15] This idea of an anglophone collective literary and historical heritage, although not *the* driving force, undoubtedly was part of the broad cultural backdrop to the formation of 'Dickens's London'. More practically, of course, American money helped to maintain commercial destinations – such as the George Inn and the Old Curiosity Shop – and fund the creation of the Charles Dickens Museum. It also seems likely that, in the case of the Portsmouth Street shop, it was largely the enthusiasm of American fans, following up B.E. Martin's article in *Scribner's Monthly*, which engendered this alluring piece of fakery in the first place.

Dickens, in fact, has always attracted a particularly dedicated and obsessive fanbase. Consequently, those fans have often come in for a good deal of criticism and mockery. Hence Elbert Hubbard's *Little Journeys to the Homes of Famous People* (1895) singles out Dickensians alone for satirical treatment. Hubbard documents a lengthy encounter with a literary tour guide, Mr Hawkins, an off-duty policeman, a Dickens fan who 'knew no other author . . . soaked with Dickensology'. Mr Hawkins seems to believe not only that Dickens's characters lived, but also that they still live in the capital: he sees visions of them everywhere. Possibly this is a spoof of a certain type of tour guide who tries to conjure up imaginary incidents before one's very eyes. But the piece concludes with Hawkins running off, having heard news of a murder in Whitechapel, which prompts him to remark: 'I knew it. Bill Sykes has killed Nancy at last!' The ghost of Bill Sikes merges with that of Jack the Ripper in the feverish mind of this typical 'Dickensologist', blurring reality and fiction, and ultimately he seems like an utter lunatic. Even the most ardent Dickensians have occasionally objected to the obsessive nature of other fans. In 1916, J. Cuming Walters was taken to task by fellow members of the Dickens Fellowship, in the letters page of the society's magazine, for mocking pedantic Dickens tourism with its 'discussions on the location of a Pump or on the exact number of milestones on Dover road'. He conceded in the next issue that he had some interest in literary rambles, but not for the literary tourist's invariable obsession with 'unessential trivialities': 'I don't want to look at a pebble that Dickens's foot may have touched; I am not thrilled by a sight of his bootlaces; and the vision of a pump-handle in a yard he once visited dazzles in vain.'[16]

Others have seen Dickensian tourism as emblematic of the vapidity of the whole business of literary tourism. One of Virginia Woolf's earliest pieces of published writing was a review of Frederick Kitton's

The Dickens Country (1905) in the *Times Literary Supplement*, entitled 'Literary Geography'. She concluded that 'we run the risk of disillusionment if we try to turn such phantom cities into tangible brick and mortar...No city, indeed, is so real as this that we make for ourselves.'[17] For Woolf, and other like-minded critics, literary tourism can potentially be a reductive exercise, even an insult to the creative powers of the author. There is a suggestion that the literary topographer posits a naïve mimetic relationship between place and fictional place – that the author simply describes what they see in front of them – and this downplays the author's genius. Frank Marzials, commenting on Percy Fitzgerald's *Bozland*, wrote in 1895:

> Dickens, like Turner in the sister art of painting, like all real artists, indeed, used Nature, no doubt, but used it as being his slave, and in no wise his master. He was not content simply to reproduce the places, persons, things he had seen and known. He passed them through the crucible of his imagination, fused them, recombined their elements, changed them into something richer and rarer ... Are we not doing him some disservice when we try to reverse the process?[18]

Charles Dickens Jr made much the same point as Marzials, a couple of years later, describing his father as raising 'so considerable a superstructure on the basis of the original fact as to make it practically unrecognisable'.[19] The real-world place was merely the initial inspiration, the spark for the creative process, and thus, he suggested, 'Dickensian' localities could only ever be of minor interest. Some famous literary figures would express similar sentiments. Tennyson was said to have been vexed by a literary topographer who attempted to link landscapes from his Lincolnshire childhood to his published work, remarking: 'Why do they give me no credit for any imagination? The power of poetical creation seems totally ignored now.'[20]

Some critics of literary tourism went further. It is interesting to note that the *New York Times*, reviewing B.E. Martin's article 'In London with Dickens' in 1881, remarked disdainfully that both Balzac and Dickens had been 'subjected to the same process' (that is, their works had been made the subject matter of literary tourism).[21] 'Process' is an unusual and telling choice of word, suggesting uncreative factory-like (re)production. The suggestion is that works of literary tourism are mechanical and derivative, churned out for the masses. There is a strong hint of mass-market vulgarity in 'process'. Indeed, literary tourism was widely seen in certain circles – and perhaps still is – as antithetical to serious thought and serious literature. F.R. Leavis, for example, co-authoring a book on the state of literary education in the 1930s, included an aside on literary tourism, suggesting that students contemplate 'the kind of people they have seen visiting "shrines"' and the 'cheapness and vulgarity' of the sort of literature that had encouraged them.[22] Put this sort of attitude together with a degree of critical condescension about the populist nature of Dickens's own original work, and one could argue that the Dickens literary tourism boom helped to diminish his literary reputation. Class-based social unease about Dickens's subject matter and readership, however, was present from the start, with or without the literary tourist. There is, for instance, a curious copy of *The Pickwick Papers* in the British Library which originally belonged to a book club for City of London clerks, held at the George and Vulture Tavern (which Dickens also featured in *Pickwick*). A handwritten comment inside the cover notes: 'The motion [to purchase and read Pickwick] was opposed by Messrs. Musket and Beckwith, who considered the work vulgar.'

Dickens himself, however, would probably have felt some degree of sympathy with Woolf's criticism of literary tourism, and perhaps even Leavis's comments on the vulgarity of the literary pilgrimage. For there is a passage in *Nicholas Nickleby* where Mrs Wititterly, a character given to parading her Romantic sentiment and whose name hardly inspires confidence, discusses Shakespeare with the foppish Lord Verisopht:

'I find I take so much more interest in his plays, after having been to that dear little dull house he was born in! Were you ever there, my lord?'

'No, nayver,' replied Verisopht.

'Then really you ought to go, my lord ... I don't know how it is, but after you've seen the place and written your name in the little book, somehow or other you seem to be inspired; it kindles up quite a fire within one.'

'Ye—es!' replied Lord Verisopht, 'I shall certainly go there.'

'Julia, my life,' interposed Mr Wititterly, 'you are deceiving his lordship – unintentionally, my lord, she is deceiving you. It is your poetical temperament, my dear ... There is nothing in the place, my dear – nothing, nothing.'[23]

There is a strong hint here that literary tourism is foolish, chasing ghosts in an empty house. Visits to Shakespeare's birthplace heighten one's appreciation of the plays but only if one has the 'poetical temperament' of a Mrs Wititterly (which does not necessarily seem a very desirable thing at all, given what we know of her).

Yet Dickens himself *was* a literary tourist. He visited Shakespeare's Birthplace, signed the guestbook and sat in 'Shakespeare's chair'; and he also made sure to see Shakespearean sights in Verona during his tour of Italy. This included the so-called tomb of Juliet, which was widely believed to be an old water trough. He was conscious that visiting such places was following the herd, writing, in an ironic vein, of Verona: 'I read Romeo and Juliet in my own room at the inn that night – of course, no Englishman had ever read it there before.' Nonetheless, he still took in all the usual tourist destinations, even if he adopted a certain ironic distance. Towards the end of his life, he even took his American publisher and promoter James T. Fields to see literary sites in London, such as Dr Johnson's House in Bolt Court and – at Fields's request – his own old chambers at Furnival's Inn. This was only a couple of years after Louisa May Alcott had made the same pilgrimage.

The passage from *Nicholas Nickleby*, in fact, captures a polarity that continues to exist around the (lack of) appeal of literary tourism. For some, visiting literary sites is a richly satisfying imaginative experience, a chance to spiritually connect with the dead author, see the places that informed or shaped their life and work, and perhaps acquire a certain cultural kudos.[24] For others, like Mr Wititterly, there is 'nothing in the place'. Woolf's article characterises this, in part, as a difference between 'sentimental' pilgrims, for whom place evokes imaginary encounters with the author and his characters, and the 'scientific', who can only see historical context and detail. But, as noted above, she also suggests that literary territories simply cannot compete with the worlds we imagine as readers. I would argue, however, that this latter criticism misunderstands the relationship between real and fictional place for the literary tourist. The real-world place, paradoxically enough, becomes illustrative of the fictional. The real-world place actually prompts imaginative recall of that city which 'we make for ourselves' – the Dickensian city already lodged in our imagination.[25] The real-world building thus should not simply be conceived as the 'original' which the author merely copied and/or improved upon (although plainly that relationship does exist); nor should we necessarily consider it the poor relation to the imagined place (as Woolf suggests). Rather, the real-world building or locality, at least in part, serves as an illustration of the imagined one. This has the same capacity to influence (and be influenced by) the reader's perception of the original text as any other illustration. Some find that the illustration pleasingly colours or informs their pre-existing conception of 'Dickens's London', while others do not.

This illustrative quality goes some way to explaining the undoubted appeal of manufactured and misattributed sites. They lack a certain authenticity – they may even be in the wrong place entirely – but they potentially can serve equally well as illustrations. This is why the literary topographer's 'Dickens's London' bears some relation both to recreations, such as the Old London Street, and to recreated Dickensian scenery in theatre, film and television – even theme parks. The aim of such reproductions is to create an immersive experience, and the literary topographer has a very similar project: transforming ordinary metropolitan streets and buildings into three-dimensional illustrations of Dickens's fiction.

***

Dickens's literary territory, then, has weathered both the ravages of urban redevelopment (albeit losing a good deal of ground) and the barbs of sceptical critics. But has Dickens tourism changed during its long history? Certainly, there have been some highs and lows in terms of popularity. Touristic 'Dickens's London' was undoubtedly at its peak fame in the early 1900s. The 1900 Merrill & Baker 'Edition de Grande Luxe' of the novels even included photographs of the territory – for example, the Leather Bottle Inn at Cobham in *The Pickwick Papers*, and the Portsmouth Street shop in *The Old Curiosity Shop*. There were not only books, newspaper reports and magazine articles, Dickens bazaars, carnivals and pageants, but also – amongst other notable examples – collectible sets of cigarette cards, illustrated calendars, poster advertisements and short films. 'Dickens's London' was a multimedia cultural phenomenon.

The most striking poster was for the Underground Electric Railways Company of London (or 'UERL', forerunner of the London Underground), published in 1911, drawn by Sidney Thomas Charles Weeks. The poster, entitled 'Dickens' London', featured a wreathed portrait of the author and quaint paintings of the gateway to Lincoln's Inn, Staple Inn, Fountain Court in the Temple, the Spaniard's Inn in Hampstead and the Old Curiosity Shop of Portsmouth Street (all with accompanying quotes from the novels, and a note of the nearest

Tube stations). This was part of the vision of London as a modern metropolis of travel, opportunity and culture which was being promoted by Frank Pick of the UERL, under his newly designed 'UNDERGROUND' corporate branding, designed to boost passenger numbers. The poster's title, of course, was a reference back to all those earlier books and magazine articles, reminding potential visitors of what was, by now, a well-established tourist territory.[26]

The following decade saw the release of the short silent film *Dickens' London*, part of a series of cinematic London 'sketches' called 'Wonderful London' (with titles such as *London by Night* and *London's Free Shows*). The 1924 film begins with an (uncredited) Walter T. Spencer, an antiquarian bookdealer, standing outside his shop at No. 27 New Oxford Street, the window filled with first editions. Spencer was considered 'the chief living authority on Dickens from the collector's standpoint'.[27] The first proper literary shrine on this cinematic tour – and the most famous – is the Portsmouth Street Old Curiosity Shop, contrasted with a shot of bustling modern Kingsway, followed by a vignette of a spectral Little Nell and her grandfather quitting the property. The film accidentally provides a rare close-up view of the shop's windows, with the main visible object in the window being a large historical print of, naturally, the shop itself. An intertitle tells viewers 'To this day the Old Curiosity Shop preserves the spirit of Dickens' and then we see a (very literal) ghostly 'spirit of Dickens' – transparent, like Nell and her grandfather – emerge from the premises. The remainder of the film shows a range of Dickens sites, and the murder of Nancy (footage taken from Bentley's 1911 film of *Oliver Twist*, the only footage that now survives), before a peculiar collection of Dickens characters gather somewhere near the Spaniard's Inn in Hampstead and mount an omnibus, driven by Mr Pickwick. Their destination is the British Empire Exhibition at Wembley.[28]

This somewhat chaotic brief film was designed as filler between proper features; it does not necessarily bear minute scrutiny. Nonetheless, it has some interesting elements. There is a drawing of

Tudor houses beneath the title card – possibly meant to represent the Holborn exterior of Staple Inn – which do not appear in the film itself. Once again, we have the insistence on an association between 'Dickens's London' and 'Old London'. The film also ends with the following intertitle:

> Dickens' characters move among us to this day – their costumes have changed that is all . . .

Next we see the ghost of Dickens superimposed over modern London, then a picture of the Houses of Parliament, before, finally, the concluding text:

> . . . and while London exists, the spirit of Dickens will never die.

The film and its text thus link 'Dickens's London' to a supposedly unchanging national character or identity and, indeed, Britain's assumed imperial destiny. The implication is that both the British nation and Dickens have an empire on which the sun will never set, and that Dickens's work is a cultural jewel that, at least in part, underpins both these dominions.

The mid-1920s, however, with the opening of the Charles Dickens Museum in 1925, were arguably the high-water mark for 'Dickens's London'. The following decade certainly saw a marked decline in published material. Earlier in the century, hundreds of brief press articles, dozens of magazine articles and several books, all dedicated to Dickens's literary territory, might be published within the space of a single year. By the 1930s, this torrent of print had reduced to a mere trickle. 'Dickens's London' would, of course, also take some damage during the Second World War. The Dickens Museum collection was removed to the Bowes Museum in Barnard Castle for the duration of the war, and the museum itself, thankfully, narrowly escaped the falling bombs.[29] The wider territory, however, undoubtedly suffered.

The *Dickensian* contains four lengthy reports called 'Some Damage has Been Reported' which meticulously list every street with the slightest Dickensian association, alongside a damage rating, compiled by members of the Fellowship, a Lt Col. W.M.H. Spiller and Mrs Gwen Major.[30] Much was lost, although some areas – such as Staple Inn – were later meticulously restored. There was also, of course, a general sense in the post-war years that 'Victorian London' – 'Dickens's London' in the loosest sense – needed to be cleared away to create a brighter future. William Kent, however, a tour guide writing in 1948, believed that there was also a growing 'Laodicean attitude towards the London lore associated with Dickens', and that there were generally fewer readers of Dickens's work. He bemoaned the fact, for example, that, out of fourteen students at an adult education course he had conducted on London history, 'not one had read *Little Dorrit*'.[31] He suspected that the lack of interest in touristic 'Dickens's London' also reflected the passing of those who had their own personal nostalgic memories of the Victorian period.

This was also, of course, the same period in which cinematic depictions of 'Dickens's London' began to make a deep impression on the popular imagination. As discussed in the previous chapter, Lean's adaptations of *Great Expectations* and *Oliver Twist* helped to establish a cinematic lexicon of the Dickensian metropolis – cobbles, tiled rooftops, smoking chimneys, gaslights, illuminated shop windows, damp cobbles and bricks, winding crooked stairs and alleys. They also helped to bring about what is surely the biggest change in one hundred and fifty years of 'Dickens's London' – that is, that our collective visual sense of 'Dickens's London' increasingly derives from cinematic and televisual adaptations. For, to put it bluntly, many more people watch television and go to the cinema than read the books.

That is not to say the cinematic version of Dickens's metropolis diverges massively from that depicted in the novels. One journalist, writing in 1887, described 'Dickens's London' in the following terms:

To the readers of DICKENS, London is a veritable City of Dismal Night. Within its narrow streets mist and gloom and fog – the celebrated 'London particular' – reign perennial. The houses are black, the trees are black, the people are splashed, and mud-stained and dirty. It is a forbidding place altogether, and even its amusements are sad. When the Londoner of those days wanted to dine, he 'dived' into a steaming eat-house, where ill-cooked steaks and greasy puddings were served to him over a dingy table cloth by a boy in his shirt-sleeves. When he wanted to drink – which seems to have been pretty frequently – he went to a public house and regaled himself beside cab-drivers and hot-piemen. There is a perpetual air of squalor, dirt, bad beer, and general discomfort about the London of DICKENS.[32]

One could, in other words, obtain a generic vision of the 'forbidding' Dickensian city as a place of gloom, mud and dirt long before the advent of cinema and television. But it is visual media that now embed a vision of 'Dickens's London' in the public imagination. Symptomatic of this, as discussed in Chapter 6, is the relocation of Nancy's murder to Nancy's Steps (or, rather, their modern surrogate). This is assuredly an instance of the media warping Dickens's legacy, changing public perception of even the original plot of his book. But one could also say that it is the very thing which keeps the book alive. How many people would know the plot of *Oliver Twist* if the film adaptations did not exist? How many people would be interested in the real-world Nancy's Steps? The answer is plainly far fewer. Moreover, some viewers will undoubtedly be prompted to read the novel. Film and television can also be very positive for places that rely on tourism: they certainly do not necessarily erase an interest in real-world place. The Charles Dickens Museum, for example, when it featured costumes, props and production material from the *Dickensian* television series, experienced a notable boost in visitor numbers.[33] Interestingly, the Museum's guestbook from this period contains comments both from people who came to see the show's costumes and from those who came to learn about Dickens and were now interested in seeing the series – a two-way traffic.

There is, admittedly, an argument that the cinematic visual lexicon is reductive, that the complexity of Dickens's fiction, his view of human nature, the richness of his poetics, is diminished to a few visual ticks and tricks. Filmmakers, moreover, as we have seen, often refer back to previous adaptations, borrowing their scenes and imagery. There must be a fear that something fundamental may be lost in these endless copies of copies. Dickens himself surely would have been very wary of both literary tourism and film reducing his work to a series of 'sights' for the real-world or armchair tourist. Indeed, Dickens repeatedly expresses qualms about tourists and tourism. There are several tourists in his work, for instance, who cannot see the forest for the trees, including Mrs Skewton in *Dombey and Son*, who admires the 'dear old dungeons' of Warwick Castle (blind to the reality of brutality and torture); the rather annoying Mr and Mrs Davis, part of a tour party of Rome in *Pictures from Italy* (she with no seeming interest whatsoever in her surroundings; he indiscriminately poking into nooks and corners, removing the covers of ancient urns 'as if they were pickles'); and Mr Pickwick at Cobham, who fantasises about antiquarian discoveries and mistakes a labourer's idle chisellings for a Roman inscription. Dickens also evinces a particular disdain for the prescriptive imagination-crushing weight of guidebooks. In *Little Dorrit*, we learn that English tourists see Rome solely through the prism of the tourist handbook ('Everybody was walking about St Peter's and the Vatican on somebody else's cork legs, and straining every visible object through somebody else's sieve').[34] The prim Mrs General, a paid travelling companion, obsessed with Eustace's guidebook to Italy, is likewise aghast that Amy Dorrit should 'wonder' at Venice, when 'Mr Eustace, the classical tourist, did not think much of it; and ... compared the Rialto, greatly to its disadvantage, with Westminster and Blackfriars Bridges'.[35] In 1854,

Dickens also took issue with the guidebooks to the various 'Courts' at the recreated Crystal Palace at Sydenham, zones themed by architectural and historical period, representing the progress of mankind. In his private correspondence, he memorably described them as 'flatulent botheration'.[36]

Tangentially, we also have Betsy Trotwood in *David Copperfield* and her enduring obsession with donkeys trespassing on the grass outside her cottage at Dover. Copperfield describes his Aunt Betsy and her maidservant Janet engaged in regular skirmishes:

> Janet came running up the stairs as if the house were in flames, darted out on a little piece of green in front, and warned off two saddle-donkeys, lady-ridden, that had presumed to set hoof upon it; while my aunt, rushing out of the house, seized the bridle of a third animal laden with a bestriding child, turned him, led him forth from those sacred precincts, and boxed the ears of the unlucky urchin in attendance who had dared to profane that hallowed ground.[37]

The donkeys are not merely a nuisance but are representatives of the intrusive outside world. Betsy Trotwood is a reclusive spinster and the donkeys are a sort of proxy for the unspeakable trouble and worry that other people bring, and thus they must be banished. But who is actually riding these vexatious animals? We know next to nothing, since Miss Trotwood focuses so intently on the four-legged intruders and their drovers. But the fact that donkeys are led by boys suggests that they are ridden by irritating tourists. Donkey rides were part of the British seaside experience and there were certainly donkeys at Dover. An aggrieved visitor writing in the *Dover Telegraph* in 1866, for example, would take a very Trotwood-esque stance on the 'dirty state of the Dover donkeys and their saddles, and the insolence and bad language of the donkey boys'.[38] Dickens, admittedly, does not make direct mention of tourism, but we also know Miss Trotwood had a real-life 'original' in the form of a certain Mary Pearson Strong, a resident of Broadstairs. The Dickens family frequented this Kentish seaside resort during the 1840s, where they encountered the old lady, perpetually vexed by tourists' donkeys trampling the green in front of her house. Charley Dickens recalled one unfortunate occasion from his childhood, when he was enjoying a ride and found her 'making vigorously hostile demonstrations at me with the hearth-broom'.[39]

Miss Trotwood herself, of course, soon turns out to be an admirable character, imbued with much strength of purpose. The same manic self-assurance which enables her to box the ears of unlucky 'donkey boys' ensures that she can face down David's vile stepfather, Mr Murdstone. There is no doubting her moral fibre and determination; she has a good heart and Dickens, like Copperfield, seems very fond of her. But I end with the nagging suspicion that Dickens, too, faced with an endless stream of sightseers, searching for the nooks and crannies of 'Dickens's London', would raise the cry of 'Donkeys!' and demand the literary topographers stay off his patch. He would not have welcomed his work being reduced to a parade of picturesque 'sights', a sourcebook of quaint 'historic' localities for the literary tourist, strained through 'somebody else's sieve'. The nadir of this trend was perhaps the cigarette cards I mentioned earlier: 'Historic Places from Dickens' London', two series of collectible cigarette cards produced by the Spinet House, issued in 1926 and 1934, from watercolours by James Lawson Stewart. The paintings and their reproductions are all eerily homogeneous, sanitised and twee. Stewart's representation of the 'pestiferous neighbourhood now happily gone' of Field Lane, for instance, looks as picturesque and sanitary as everywhere else in his vision of 'Dickens's London'.[40] The text on the reverse of the cards, meanwhile, gives bland summaries of events in the author's life and works and reminds us that these are all *historic* places. Dickens would not have appreciated this peculiar dilution of his work, even if he welcomed tokens of its ongoing popularity and ubiquity. Indeed, there is an 1857 letter to fellow writer

Sir Edward Bulwer-Lytton on the writing of place, which seems apt, where Dickens, in editorial mode, states that it is important that 'all these scenic appliances are subdued to the Piece, instead of the Piece being sacrificed to them'.[41] The spectacle of 'Dickens's London', howsoever it is illustrated, may be dazzling, but it is nothing without the stories.

A DICKENS CHRONOLOGY

For quick reference, this timeline provides a very brief chronology of Dickens's life and publications, as touched upon in this book.

1812 Charles Dickens (CD) born in Portsmouth on 7 February
1814 Navy Pay Office recalls John Dickens (and family) to London
1817 Navy Pay Office sends John Dickens to Chatham
1822 John Dickens recalled again to London
1824 John Dickens in debt; CD sent to work in blacking warehouse; John Dickens imprisoned for debt in Marshalsea Gaol but freed after receiving legacy; family move to Johnson Street in Camden Town (they leave *c.* 1829/30)
1827 CD begins employment as a lawyer's clerk
c. 1831 CD begins work as parliamentary reporter for the *Mirror of Parliament* (and later works for the *True Sun* and the *Morning Chronicle*)
1834 CD takes lodgings in Furnival's Inn

1836 CD marries Catherine Hogarth; *The Pickwick Papers* begins publication as a serial (dates of novels below all mark beginning of serialisation)

1837 Charley Dickens is born; CD and his young family move to 48 Doughty Street; his sister-in-law Mary Hogarth dies suddenly; *Oliver Twist*

1838 *Nicholas Nickleby*; CD tours Midlands and visits Shakespeare's birthplace

1839 CD and family move to Devonshire Terrace, Marylebone

1840 *The Old Curiosity Shop*

1841 *Barnaby Rudge*

1842 CD tours America and publishes *American Notes*; also begins *Martin Chuzzlewit*

1844–5 CD tours Italy and publishes *Pictures from Italy* the following the year

1846 *Dombey and Son*

1849 *David Copperfield*

1850 CD founds/edits the magazine *Household Words*

1851 CD and family move to Tavistock House, Tavistock Square

1852 *Bleak House*

1854 *Hard Times*

1855 *Little Dorrit*

1856 CD buys Gads Hill Place in Kent, moves in the following year

1858 CD publicly separates from his wife Catherine; begins giving commercial public readings of his work

1859 CD founds/edits the magazine *All the Year Round*; *A Tale of Two Cities*

1864 *Our Mutual Friend*

1867–8 CD undertakes a second tour of America with public readings

1870 *The Mystery of Edwin Drood*; CD dies on 9 June 1870

ENDNOTES

1 Dead: To Begin With

1. See, for example, *Daily Telegraph*, 10 June 1870. The magazine *Chit-Chat* ran a commemorative article in which the exclamatory refrain *Charles Dickens is dead!* began every paragraph (*Chit-Chat*, July 1870, p. 73).
2. *Liverpool Daily Post*, 9 April 1869.
3. *London City Press*, 11 October 1870.
4. For the machinations which brought Dickens to Westminster Abbey, contrary to his own expressed wishes, see Leon Litvack, 'Even in Death, Charles Dickens Left Behind a Riveting Tale of Deceit', *Smithsonian Magazine*, 5 February 2020, https://www.smithsonianmag.com/history/untold-story-charles-dickens-death-and-burial-180974126/ (accessed 13 March 2023).
5. Robert Langton, *Charles Dickens and Rochester* (Chapman and Hall, 1880), p. 19. Chapman and Hall, Dickens's final publishers, sold 'prodigious' quantities of his work after his death, so much so that it underpinned their whole business, as discussed by Arthur Waugh, *One Man's Road* (Chapman and Hall, 1931, p. 307). Other publishers gradually got in on the act, as copyright expired forty-two years after initial publication. For a useful summary, see Lucinda Hawksley, 'Charles Dickens, Copyright Pioneer', Authors' Licensing and Collecting Society, 24 June 2015, https://www.alcs.co.uk/news/charles-dickens-copyright-pioneer (accessed 13 March 2023).
6. The earliest mention I have come across of a purely Dickensian fancy dress ball was at the Freemason's Tavern in February 1886 (*Daily News*, 4 February 1886). Female attendees were generally less keen to portray Dickens's grotesques than their male counterparts; and, indeed, they had fewer characters to choose from. Thus, at that first event there were seven Dolly Vardens (the attractive young heroine of *Barnaby Rudge*), as noted in the *Sheffield Independent*, 18 February 1886. Numerous similar

balls would follow, although rarely on roller skates. See also Takko Sakai, 'Dickens's Characters at Fancy Dress Balls in Late-Victorian and Edwardian Britain', *Dickensian* (Summer 2022), pp. 174–89, who notes the general popularity of Dolly Varden as a fancy dress character.

7. F.G. Kitton scrapbooks, Charles Dickens Museum.
8. Advertisements in the *Queen* and the *Sphere*, 7 December 1912. One could collect a set of six pipe-stoppers, including Pickwick, Mrs Bardell, Sam Weller, the Fat Boy, Perker and Tony Weller (which nowadays can still be found on eBay). This was, of course, also the year of Dickens's centenary.
9. 'The Posthumous Papers of the Pickwick Club', *Quarterly Review* (October 1837), pp. 484–518, p. 484.
10. Such shows were also popular further afield. Robert James Lee, for example, lectured in New York, promising 'Through London with Charles Dickens, Illustrated with eighty-three faithfully colored views thrown upon a surface measuring 900 square feet'. *Brooklyn Daily Eagle*, 27 November 1886.
11. Thomas Edgar Pemberton, *Dickens's London* (Samuel Tinsley, 1876); John R.G. Hassard, *A Pickwickian Pilgrimage* (James Osgood & Company, 1881); J. Ashby-Sterry, 'Charles Dickens in Southwark', *The English Illustrated Magazine* (November 1888), pp. 105–15; Edith Capper, 'The Haunts of Sarah Gamp', *Good Words* (April 1904), pp. 277–80; H. Snowden Ward and Catherine Weed Barnes Ward, *The Real Dickens Land* (Chapman and Hall, 1904).
12. *St. James Gazette*, 5 November 1903.
13. See, for example, 'Transformation Scenes: How They Are Made and Worked', *Strand* (December 1893), pp. 705–10.
14. John Forster, *The Life of Charles Dickens*, Vol. 1 (Chapman and Hall, 1872), 181.
15. See, for example, J.T. Wilson's 1869 watercolour of the pub. London Metropolitan Archives, record 315853, https://www.londonpicturearchive.org.uk/view-item?i=315995 (accessed 24 March 2019).
16. John Ruskin, *Letters of John Ruskin to Charles Eliot Norton* (Houghton Mifflin, 1904), Vol. 2, p. 5.
17. Walter Bagehot, 'Charles Dickens', *National Review*, 7 (1858), pp. 458–86, p. 468.
18. Collected in book form as *A Pickwickian Pilgrimage* (James Osgood & Company, 1881).
19. Louisa May Alcott, 'A Dickens Day', *Independent*, 26 December 1867. 'On the rampage', of course, is a nod to Pip's irascible older sister in *Great Expectations*, whom Joe Gargery repeatedly describes as 'on the rampage'.
20. Elizabeth Williams Champney, *Three Vassar Girls in England* (Estes and Lauriat, 1884), p. 174.
21. Susan Coolidge, *What Katy Did Next* (Roberts Brothers, 1887), p. 113.
22. 'Daily Magazine', *Daily Mail*, 16 February 1898.
23. *Northern Whig*, 29 January 1890.
24. I am grateful for Andrea Zemgulys's *Modernism and the Locations of Literary Heritage* (Cambridge University Press, 2008) for the term 'newly old', which perfectly captures how heritage sites seemed to suddenly appear fully formed in the late nineteenth century.
25. Harald Hendrix, 'From Early Modern to Romantic Literary Tourism: A Diachronical Perspective' in *Literary Tourism and Nineteenth-Century Culture*, ed. Nicola Watson (Palgrave Macmillan, 2009), p. 16.

26. Some core academic texts on literary tourism include Nicola Watson, *The Literary Tourist: Readers and Places in Romantic & Victorian Britain* (Palgrave Macmillan, 2006); Paul Westover, *Necromanticism: Travelling to Meet the Dead 1750–1860* (Palgrave Macmillan, 2012); Alison Booth, *Homes and Haunts: Touring Writers' Shrines and Countries* (Oxford University Press, 2016). Westover, in particular, writes how British literary tourism 'internalized, romanticized, and democratized the Grand Tour'. Westover, *Necromanticism*, p. 41.

27. Trains ran, for example, from Newcastle to Greenock, with 'ample time … for visiting the Falls of Clyde, Loch Lomond, Loch Katrin, the Trossachs, and many other highly interesting localities, which are so admirably described by Sir Walter Scott'. *Newcastle Journal*, 28 August 1852.

28. *Bradford Observer*, 2 July 1857.

29. Harry Johnson, 'The Story of My Life', *Graphic*, 22 September 1923.

30. Ednah D. Cheney, ed., *Louisa May Alcott: Her Life, Letters and Journals* (Roberts Brothers, 1889), p. 174.

31. 'Minor notices', *Saturday Review*, 8 January 1876, p. 59. The initial articles were M.D. Conway, 'Footprints of Charles Dickens', *Harper's New Monthly Magazine* (September 1870), pp. 610–16; Barton Hill, 'A Pilgrimage', *Lipincott's Magazine* (September 1870), pp. 288–93; 'Charles Dickens's Birthplace', *Ballou's Monthly Magazine* (November 1870), pp. 413–14.

32. Robert Allbut, *London Rambles 'en zigzag' with Charles Dickens* (Edward Curtice, 1886), includes an 'Important Notice' offering the author's service as a 'Well-qualified metropolitan guide' on 'Dickensian Rambles' (p. 110). By the early 1900s, he offered a complete day's tour round London, with lunch at the 'Baronial Hall' of the City of New York Restaurant in Hand Court, Holborn (a flier survives in the Charles Dickens Museum's scrapbooks). Thomas Cook seem to have started tours of 'Dickensland' around the turn of the century. They would boast in 1905 that they had 'special men who can identify the spots associated with the various London scenes depicted in his works, and they frequently conduct pilgrimages of this sort' (*Daily News*, 26 August 1905).

33. Percy Fitzgerald, *Rochester and Charles Dickens* (reprinted from the *Rochester and Chatham Journal*, 1903), p. 45.

34. Percy Fitzgerald (1830–1925) had begun life as a barrister in Ireland but moved to England to become a writer. He initially found employment writing pieces for Dickens's magazine *Household Words* and its successor *All the Year Round* and thus got to know Dickens personally. His prodigious literary output included *Bozland: Dickens' Places and People* (Downey and Co., 1895) and numerous other Dickens-related articles in magazines and journals.

35. William Godwin, 'Essay on Sepulchres', in *Political and Philosophical Writings of William Godwin*, Vol. 6: *Essays*, ed. Mark Philp (Pickering & Chatto, 1993), pp. 1–30, p. 28. See Westover's *Necromanticism* for a full discussion.

36. *Standard*, 4 September 1883, p. 4.

37. *Belfast News-Letter*, 15 November 1897, p. 5.

38. For example, *Penny Illustrated Paper*, 28 December 1901, p. 10; *Southern Reporter*, 30 July 1903, p. 2.

39. J. Ashby-Sterry, 'The Wooden Midshipman', *All the Year Round*, 29 October 1881, pp. 173–9, p. 177.

40. *Yorkshire Evening Press*, 27 October 1888, p. 2, referring back to an expedition in 1872.

41. Julia Thomas, *Shakespeare's Shrine* (University of Pennsylvania Press, 2012), p. 52.

42. Betram Matz scrapbook, No. 2. Charles Dickens Museum. The trains stopped at Gravesend, where horse-drawn carriages were available to convey visitors to Rochester, Gads Hill, Cobham and Strood. The tours were advertised as 'Inclusive Fare, First Class Only, Rail, Carriage Drive and Luncheon' and cost one guinea.
43. Advertisement for the Bean Tourer car, *Illustrated London News*, 27 November 1920.
44. Bagehot, 'Charles Dickens', p. 468.
45. Forster, *The Life of Charles Dickens*, Vol. 1, p. 99.

2 Great Rambling Queer Old Places

1. *The Pickwick Papers*, chapter 10.
2. Joseph Forsyth, *Remarks on Antiquities, Arts and Letters during an excursion in Italy in the years 1802 and 1803* (P. G. Ledouble, 1820), p. 353. Or, as Hunt puts it, ruins 'have [always] invited the mind to complete their fragments'. John Dixon Hunt, 'Ut Pictura Poesis, the Picturesque, and John Ruskin', *MLN* (December 1978), pp. 794–818, p. 797.
3. Stanley Harris, *The Coaching Age* (Richard Bentley and Son, 1885), p. 3.
4. *Galaxy: An Illustrated Magazine of Entertaining Reading*, 1870, p. 294.
5. B.E. Martin, 'Mr Pickwick and Nicholas Nickleby', *Scribner's Monthly Magazine* (September 1880), pp. 641–56, p. 651; Charles G. Harper, 'Pickwickian Inns', *London Magazine* (December 1905), pp. 584–90; Alfred Rimmer, *About England with Dickens* (Chatto and Windus, 1883), pp. 42, 92, 94; B.W. Matz, *The Inns and Taverns of 'Pickwick'* (Cecil Palmer, 1921), p. 6; Charles G. Harper, 'Mr Pickwick's Inns', *Autocar*, 22 March 1913, pp. 490–4.
6. *Standard*, 1 December 1886, p. 5. The limited edition, 'Edition de Grande Luxe' of *The Pickwick Papers*, published by Merrill & Baker in 1900, would also include photographs of the interior and exterior of the Leather Bottle at Cobham, as if inviting readers to visit the pub and its well-known 'Pickwick Room'.
7. John Camden Hotten, *Charles Dickens: The Story of His Life* (Harper and Brothers, 1870), p. 14.
8. [Albert Smith], 'Hotels: Chapter III. Of the good old coaching days', *The Month* (August 1851), pp. 83–6.
9. Dickens and Smith were well acquainted and moved in the same literary circles. Smith helped to dramatise two of Dickens's Christmas books, *The Cricket on the Hearth* (1845) and *The Battle of Life* (1846) (see *Dickensian Dramas: Plays from Charles Dickens*, Vol. 1, ed. J. Bratton (Oxford University Press, Oxford Scholarly Editions Online, 2018).
10. *The Pickwick Papers*, chapter 51.
11. *The Pickwick Papers*, chapter 35.
12. *The Pickwick Papers*, chapter 22.
13. *The Pickwick Papers*, chapter 10.
14. 'The Pickwick Papers: A Contemporary Review', *Dickensian* (August 1907), pp. 205–12, p. 208 (from *The Eclectic Review*, March 1837).
15. The setting for Act 1 Scene 1, as described in the published version of the play. William Thomas Moncrieff, *Sam Weller, Or, The Pickwickians: A Drama in Three Acts* (n.p., 1837).
16. *Examiner*, 28 October 1871.
17. *Express*, 6 February 1869.

18. Rimmer, *About England with Dickens*, p. 56.
19. James Pidgeon had been there some time. A newspaper article from 1861 mentions a fire in his premises, noting that the old inn had been let out as 'warehouses and workshops'. *Daily News*, 6 July 1861.
20. Percy Fitzgerald, 'Betwixt Tavern and Tavern', *Magazine of Art* (October 1884), pp. 485–9, p. 487.
21. *Barnaby Rudge*, chapter 1.
22. *Barnaby Rudge*, chapter 1.
23. *Barnaby Rudge*, chapter 10.
24. *Barnaby Rudge*, chapter 25. *Barnaby Rudge* opens in 1775, a decade before fast mail coaches, carrying both post and passengers, were introduced by the Post Office, but presumably even the older type of coach is too much for the landlord.
25. *Barnaby Rudge*, chapter 26.
26. *Barnaby Rudge*, chapter 1.
27. *Martin Chuzzlewit*, chapter 1.
28. *Little Dorrit*, Book II, chapter 17.
29. 'The Bemoaned Past', *All the Year Round*, 24 May 1862, pp. 257–61, p. 258. See also Patrick Brantlinger, 'Did Dickens Have a Philosophy of History? The Case of Barnaby Rudge', *Dickens Studies Annual*, 30 (2001), pp. 59–74, p. 64, for further examples.
30. *Dombey and Son*, chapter 27. Nancy Hill makes a strong case for *The Pickwick Papers* also containing numerous parodic references to picturesque tourism; she notes, for instance, that advertising copy for the first issue joked that Pickwick had managed to 'penetrate to the very borders of Wales in the height of summer' – a reference to the popularity of the picturesque Wye valley among tourist parties. Nancy K. Hill, *A Reformer's Art: Dickens' Picturesque and Grotesque Imagery* (Ohio University Press, 1981), p. 20.
31. Humphrey House, *The Dickens World* (Oxford University Press, 1942), p. 35. See also Dickens's satirical song 'The Fine Old English Gentleman', written in 1841, which describes a similar barbaric past unworthy of commemoration, as discussed in John Bowen, *Other Dickens: Pickwick to Chuzzlewit* (Oxford University Press, 2000), p. 27. See also Sally Ledger, '"God be thanked: a ruin!" The Rejection of Nostalgia in *Pictures from Italy*', *Dickens Quarterly*, 26 (2009), pp. 79–85.
32. James Payn, 'An Adventure in the Forest; or Dickens's Maypole Inn', *Harper's New Monthly Magazine* (July 1878), pp. 298–302.
33. See, for example, Christian Tearle, *Rambles with an American* (Mills & Boon, 1910), a droll account of showing an American tourist round London, in which the would-be guide regularly finds himself stumped by the tourist's detailed knowledge of all things Dickens.
34. Payn, 'An Adventure in the Forest', p. 298.
35. 'To John Forster, 25 March 1841', in *The Pilgrim Edition of the Letters of Charles Dickens*, Vol. 2: *1840–1841*, ed. Madeline House and Graham Storey (The Clarendon Press, 1969).
36. The first mention in the press I have found is in the *Chelmsford Chronicle*, 23 July 1875. A letter outlining the historical and literary associations of Chigwell in the *Chelmsford Chronicle*, 6 October 1871, merely describes the pub as 'ancient and pretty' whilst mentioning Dickens's novel in an entirely separate context.
37. 'Barnaby Rudge and Chigwell', *Dickensian* (Spring 1927), pp. 122–6.
38. 'Barnaby Rudge and Chigwell'.

39. *Graphic*, 22 July 1876.
40. Luke Sharp [pseud. of Robert Barr], 'The Old Maypole', *Detroit Free Press*, 14 July 1884, p. 18.
41. *Boxing World and Mirror of Life*, 22 December 1897.
42. Bransby Williams, *An Actor's Story* (Chapman and Hall, 1909).
43. 'Mr Bransby Williams' Charles Dickens Matinee'. Matz Dickens Scrapbook, No. 2. Charles Dickens Museum.
44. *Era*, 19 May 1900.
45. *Era*, 12 May 1900.
46. 'In the Footsteps of Barnaby Rudge', *Royal Magazine* (August 1900), pp. 173–8.
47. *The King's Head Chigwell. A Short Account of the historic 'Maypole' of Charles Dickens in 'Barnaby Rudge'* (Mann, Crossman & Co., 1912).
48. See https://sheeshbooking.co.uk/about-sheesh/ (accessed 8 March 2023).
49. Peter Brown, *Shakespeare's Local* (Macmillan, 2012), pp. 45ff. Brown notes that a National Trust survey from 2009 also found substantial refurbishment in the eighteenth and nineteenth centuries (hardly surprising, since hospitality venues have always been regularly remodelled).
50. The building itself was also listed by English Heritage in 1950.
51. Ashby-Sterry, 'Charles Dickens in Southwark', p. 114.
52. Mildred Roelker, 'A Visit to Some of Dickens' Landmarks', *Journal of Education*, 44 (1) (1896), pp. 16–18.
53. Roelker, 'A Visit to Some of Dickens' Landmarks'.
54. Amelia's tenancy may have dated from the late 1860s. Agnes recalled her mother succeeding George Grinslade, who died on 22 November 1868 (*Morning Advertiser*, 1 March 1869). An anonymous pamphlet in Southwark Archives describes Amelia as the ward of John East, tenant of the stables at the George from 1822–78, entrusted with the running of the pub by Grinslade in the latter's will.
55. B.W. Matz, *The George Inn, Southwark: A Survival of the Old Coaching Days* (Chapman and Hall, 1918), pp. 10, 14.
56. William Owen, 'Old Rochester', *Architecture* (September 1896), pp. 389–400, p. 392; Walter Dexter, 'Through Dickens-land with Cycle and Camera', *Boy's Own Paper* (May 1900), pp. 59–62, p. 60; E.S. Duncan-Davies, letter to the *Daily Chronicle*, 5 January 1901.
57. 'Haunt of visiting Americans, it is one of the literary show-places of London.' *Lewisham Borough News*, 11 August 1836.
58. Matz, *The George Inn, Southwark*, p. 11.
59. Matz, *The George Inn, Southwark*, p. 14.
60. G.F. Young, 'Charles Dickens' Southwark Re-visited', *St. Saviour with S. Peter, Southwark The Parish Paper and The Diocesan Gazette* (January–December 1930), p. 5.
61. *Daily News*, 27 November 1926.
62. *Kent and Sussex Courier*, 20 May 1927.
63. *Liverpool Echo*, 17 July 1935.
64. Miss Murray was posthumously quoted to this effect in an article on the George from *What's on in London*, 18 June 1971, held in Southwark Archives. I have been unable to locate the original remark.
65. *Dickensian* (Winter 1934), p. 40.
66. *Guardian*, 6 November 1934.
67. *Liverpool Echo*, 17 July 1935.
68. O. Sack [B.W. Matz], 'In Dickens's London', *Dickensian* (February 1915), p. 45.

69. Leslie C. Staples, 'Reflections of an Innkeeper', *Dickensian* (Fall 1937), pp. 288–90.
70. BBC Internal Circulating Memo, 8 February 1936. NN477 Charles Dickens Museum. The answer, scribbled on the memo, is 'Only on the <u>actual</u> broadcast, I think, don't you?!!!' (that is, no free drink during rehearsals).
71. 'Tabard Players', *Stage*, 17 February 1949; Obituary, Ross Barrington, *Stage*, 28 December 1951.
72. *Daily Mail*, 24 July 1930.
73. *The Pilgrim Edition of the Letters of Charles Dickens*, Vol. 1: *1820–1839*, ed. Madeline House and Graham Storey (The Clarendon Press, 1982).
74. W.J. Carlton, 'Dickens's Insurance Policies', *Dickensian* (January 1955), pp. 133–7.

3 The Burial Ground

1. *Bleak House*, chapter 11.
2. Lynn MacKay, *Respectability and the London Poor, 1780–1870: The Value of Virtue* (Routledge, 2013), p. 74.
3. Lee Jackson, *Dirty Old London* (Yale University Press, 2014), chapter 3.
4. *Public Ledger and Daily Advertiser*, 3 August 1832.
5. *True Sun*, 22 August 1832.
6. *Era*, 27 October 1839.
7. George Walker, *Gatherings from Graveyards* (Longman, 1839), p. 163.
8. *Shipping and Mercantile Gazette*, 4 August 1848.
9. 'To Miss Palfrey, 4 April 1868' in *The Pilgrim Edition of the Letters of Charles Dickens*, Vol. 12: *1868–1870*, ed. Graham Storey (The Clarendon Press, 2002), 4 April 1868.
10. James T. Fields, 'Some Memories of Charles Dickens', *The Atlantic* (August 1870), pp. 235–45, p. 238.
11. 'It was always known and accepted as such – even in Dickens's life-time ... an intimate friend of his assured me that it was always known as the site, and that full thirty years ago.' *Westminster Gazette*, 29 August 1894.
12. *Era*, 13 August 1848.
13. *Morning Advertiser*, 4 January 1838, for example, notes that the room has been 'furnished with a piano and stage ... The Keanites Social Harmonic Meeting takes place every Tuesday. – A Judge and Jury Society held every Sunday evening.'
14. 'Dickens's sentimental deaths should be read not as embarrassing failures of literary nerve by a writer who was unequal to the stern task of depicting mortality with fidelity, but rather as sites of literary experiment in which he sought to apply to fiction the psychological principles that had informed the construction of garden cemeteries.' David McAllister, 'Dickens's "School of Affliction": Learning from Death in *Nicholas Nickleby* and *The Old Curiosity Shop*', *Victoriographies*, 10 (3) (2020), pp. 228–47, p. 229.
15. Charles Dickens, *The Speeches of Charles Dickens* (Chatto and Windus, 1884), p. 128.
16. *Weekly Despatch*, 3 June 1849.
17. [J.R.G. Hassard], 'Haunted London', *New York Tribune*, 3 September 1879.
18. See, for a full discussion, Philip Bolton, 'Bleak House and the Playhouse', *Dickens Studies Annual*, 12 (1983), pp. 81–116.
19. Lee's year of birth is hard to pin down and she seems to have exaggerated. For instance, in an interview for the *Sketch*, 10 May 1896, she mentions that she was ten years old in 1870. This is highly unlikely, given that, in 1875, she was already

divorced and marrying a second husband. Census data from 1881 for 'Emily Burnett' (her maiden name) suggests that she was born *c.* 1849.

20. *Lloyd's Weekly Newspaper*, 30 November 1873, records the divorce in *Scott v Scott and Burnett* on the grounds of adultery. See also https://theatreheritage.org.au/on-stage-magazine/general-articles/item/537-jennie-lee-and-bleak-house (accessed 10 March 2023) for an excellent biography.

21. The well-known Victorian playwright Dion Boucicault was also in San Francisco at the time and was said to have urged Jennie Lee to undertake the project (Malcolm Morley, 'Bleak House SCENE', *Dickensian* (January 1953), pp. 175–82, p. 177).

22. Joseph Knight, *Theatrical Notes* (Lawrence & Bullen, 1893), p. 109.

23. A young Vesta Tilley did a turn as a dying 'Poor Jo' in 1878. See Alan Sutcliffe, 'Dickens and the Music Hall', *Dickensian* (Summer 2010), pp. 101–17 for a full list.

24. *Weekly Despatch*, 1 October 1876.

25. '... minuteness in painting costume, the common error of the followers of Sir Walter Scott' (review of *The Pilot* by Fennimore Cooper). [Anon.], 'Notices of New Books', *Tatler*, 7 April 1831, p. 757; 'the details of costume and pageant glitter are working up with great labour – perhaps more than is looked for or will be appreciated in a novel' (review of W. G. T. Power *The King's Secret*). [Anon.], 'The King's Secret', *The Mirror Literature, Amusement and Instruction*, 14 May 1831, pp. 330–2, p. 331.

26. John T. Page, 'Dr. Barnardo and Dickens', *Dickensian* (November 1916), p. 301.

27. Bolton, 'Bleak House and the Playhouse', p. 93.

28. Matthew 27:7. The priests in the Temple buy a field owned by a potter with Judas Iscariot's discarded pieces of silver, to be used as a site to bury strangers.

29. Morley, 'Bleak House SCENE', p. 175.

30. See also 'Music sheet cover for "Poor Jo!" written by H.B. Farnie and C.H.R. Marriott and performed by Jenny Lee, published by J. Scrutton, ca. 1883.' V&A (S.53-2012), which likewise features Jo in front of the gate.

31. *Daily News*, 20 May 1886.

32. *Daily News*, 20 May 1886.

33. *Exeter and Plymouth Gazette*, 22 May 1886.

34. *Daily News*, 28 August 1891.

35. *Birmingham Daily Post*, 17 January 1893.

36. *Westminster Gazette*, 14 August 1894.

37. It is possible, however, that the 'preserved' gate was not the same one that existed in the 1840s. An anonymous author reviewing 'Dickens's London' for the *St. James's Gazette*, 27 June 1892, was convinced that the gate in question was 'not the one depicted by H.K. Browne'.

38. *Gentlewoman*, 22 August 1925.

39. *Era*, 27 February 1897.

40. Dan H. Laurence and Martin Quinn, eds, *Shaw on Dickens* (Fredrick Ungar, 1985), p. 104.

41. *Great Expectations*, chapter 31.

42. *Morning Post*, 24 February 1876.

43. Lee was fondly remembered. She finally retired in 1906, shortly after playing Mrs Bedwin (Mr Brownlow's housekeeper) in Beerbohm Tree's *Oliver Twist* at His Majesty's Theatre. She reappeared briefly on stage in 1921 in a *Bleak House* tableau (doubtless seated before the usual prop gateway) at 'Dickens Birthday Matinee' – a theatrical event to support the creation of a children's library at Dickens's former

childhood home, 13 Johnson Street in Camden (a scheme I discuss in Chapter 5). She was greeted, this elderly woman clad as a Victorian street urchin, with unbounded applause, as if her fame was undimmed. Her death, which bizarrely had been successively misreported in 1893 and 1925, before being accurately recorded in 1930, produced dozens of column inches in the press. Many obituarists referenced her usual valediction to the audiences who had feted her at endless curtain calls: 'For you were always very good to me, you were.'

4 Kingsgate Street to Dickens Avenue

1. Moses Coit Tyler, *Moses Coit Tyler 1835–1900: Selections from His Letters and Diaries* (Doubleday, Page and Company, 1911), p. 32.
2. Moncure Daniel Conway, writing in 1870, retrospectively claimed to have walked the streets of Saffron Hill or thereabouts in the early 1860s, but it is not clear whether he was on a planned Dickens tour, or he simply happened to give some thought to Dickens while exploring the district. See Conway, 'Footprints of Charles Dickens'; see also Moncure Daniel Conway, *Autobiography: Memories and Experiences* (Houghton Mifflin and Company, 1904), Vol. 2, p. 40, where he writes that he saw 'an uninhabited old shanty . . . pointed out as the very house of Fagin, and I tried to make out the itinerary of Oliver Twist and the Artful Dodger'. Conway was a radical American clergyman and campaigner for the abolition of slavery, who moved to London in 1863. Conway Hall in Red Lion Square, Holborn, is named in his honour. Conway also acted as literary agent for Louisa May Alcott in London, and she stayed with his family for a couple of weeks during her time in the capital. We can probably assume that Dickens, whom Conway met at Thackeray's funeral in 1863, was discussed. Conway was also well acquainted with Alcott's guide round Dickens's London, Moses Coit Tyler.
3. Madeleine B. Stern, *Louisa May Alcott* (Peter Nevill, 1952), p. 55.
4. Daniel Shealy, ed., *Alcott in Her Own Time* (University of Iowa Press, 2005), p. 95.
5. Tyler, *Moses Coit Tyler 1835–1900*, p. 32.
6. 'A Dickens Day' would be republished in Louisa May Alcott, *Aunt Jo's Scrap-Bag*, Vol. 2: *Shawl-Straps* (Roberts Brothers, 1873), pp. 214ff, from which I take the quote used in this chapter.
7. Louisa May Alcott, *Aunt Jo's Scrap-Bag*, Vol. 2, p. 216.
8. Maria S. Porter, 'Recollections of Louisa May Alcott', *New England Magazine* (March 1892), pp. 3–19, p. 11; Shealy, *Alcott in Her Own Time*, p. 107.
9. 'Mr Pecksniff on his mission', *Martin Chuzzlewit*, chapter 19.
10. Tyler, *Moses Coit Tyler 1835–1900*, p. 31.
11. 'On the rampage' is a Dickens reference, repeatedly used by Jo Gargery of Pip's short-tempered sister in *Great Expectations*.
12. Tyler, *Moses Coit Tyler 1835–1900*, pp. 32–3.
13. John R.G. Hassard, *A Pickwickian Pilgrimage* (James Osgood & Company, 1881), p. 70.
14. *Chicago Tribune*, 16 June 1901.
15. *Martin Chuzzlewit*, chapter 19.
16. *Lloyd's Weekly Newspaper*, 20 March 1898; *Derby Mercury*, 28 December 1898.
17. *Pall Mall Gazette*, 5 July 1899.
18. Multiple adverts in the *Daily News* in 1900 featured this content; see, for example, 3 October 1900, p. 9.

19. Zemgulys, *Modernism and the Locations of Literary Heritage*, pp. 71–104; David Frisby, *Cityscapes of Modernity* (Polity, 2001), p. 215.
20. *Queen*, 5 April 1902, p. 61.
21. Mark Westgarth, *The Emergence of the Antique and Curiosity Dealer in Britain 1815–1850* (Routledge, 2020), p. 118.
22. Charles Knight, ed., *London*, Vol. 2 (Charles Knight & Co., 1842), p. 182.
23. One letter-writer to the RSA's journal mused, in passing, 'why not of women, too?'. Edward Jones, *Journal of the Society of Arts*, 5 August 1864, p. 612. Only four women had received plaques by 1900. [English Heritage], 'Pioneering Women in London', https://www.english-heritage.org.uk/visit/blue-plaques/blue-plaque-stories/women-pioneers/#?theme=358&page=1 (accessed 5 April 2021).
24. *Journal of the Society of Arts*, 11 May 1866, pp. 437–9, p. 437.
25. Tony Bennett, 'The Exhibitionary Complex', *new formations*, 4 (Spring 1988), pp. 73–102.
26. Sophie Thomas, *Romanticism and Visuality* (Routledge, 2008), p. 78.
27. As noted above, women were not excluded from the scheme, with a plaque to Sarah Siddons erected in 1876. Nonetheless men predominated. English Heritage have tried to redress this imbalance in recent years. See English Heritage's press release, 'English Heritage Want More Blue Plaques for Women', 30 October 2018, https://www.english-heritage.org.uk/about-us/search-news/more-blue-plaques-for-women/ (accessed 20 March 2023).
28. *Daily Telegraph & Courier*, 13 December 1871, p. 5, where the anonymous journalist proposes 'a series of plain tablets' to mark Dickens's homes in London for literary pilgrims.
29. *Journal of the Society of Arts*, 19 November 1897, p. 19.
30. 'Dickens in Furnival's Inn', *New York Times*, 4 April 1886, p. 12, contains an unattributed quote from the *London World* newspaper claiming that the unnamed author wrote to the RSA to propose Furnival's Inn as a location for a plaque and received enthusiastic cooperation from the building's owner – the property then being 'Wood's Hotel' – who drew upon old rent rolls to establish a correct location for the tablet on the exterior.
31. *Norfolk Chronicle*, 11 December 1886.
32. 'Woods' Hotel' advertisement, in *Wyman's Commercial Encyclopedia* (Wyman & Sons, 1888), p. 317.
33. *Birmingham Daily Post*, 19 April 1889.
34. Charles Eyre Pascoe, *London of To-Day* (Roberts Brothers, 1893), p. 67.
35. Whaley disposed of the lease in July 1894, and an auction of the 'furniture, fixtures and effects' was announced in the *London Evening Standard*, 31 July 1894.
36. Marks, who died in 1912, would be remembered as a highly successful banker in the City of London, as well as being an enthusiastic amateur antiquarian, contributing regularly to *Notes and Queries* and authoring books and pamphlets such as *Tyburn Tree: Its History and Annals* (1908). *Daily News*, 9 September 1912; 16 September 1912.
37. The originators were described as 'a few artists and others' in the *Nation*, 1 July 1880, p. 13.
38. *The Times*, 6 March 1875, p. 10. The annual subscription was 10s. 6d., as noted in the *Academy*, 12 May 1877, p. 425.
39. The pictures are best viewed online in the Royal Academy's collection of photographs, https://www.royalacademy.org.uk/art-artists/search/works-of-art?works_associated_with=C17010 (accessed 6 June 2019).

40. Abigail Solomon-Godeau, *Photography at the Dock* (University of Minnesota Press, 1991), p. 155. The *Nation* article, cited above, notes that the Society also secured 'a few portable relics' for the South Kensington Museum, but this seems to have been incidental rather than planned. The power of photography to capture architectural detail was, of course, recognised from its inception, with Fox Talbot noting in 1844 that artists could use the photograph to record 'endless details of Gothic architecture which a whole day would hardly suffice to draw'. Helmut Gernsheim, *Focus on Architecture and Sculpture: An Original Approach to the Photography of Architecture and Sculpture* (Fountain Press, 1949), p. 15.

41. Alfred Marks's letterpress to accompany the photograph: Henry Dixon & Son, 'Old Houses in Aldersgate Street', 1879, 226 mm x 178 mm, https://www.royalacademy.org.uk/art-artists/work-of-art/old-houses-in-aldersgate-street (accessed 6 June 2019).

42. Elizabeth Edwards, *The Camera as Historian* (Duke University Press, 2012), p. 11.

43. The photographer William Strudwick – best remembered for recording the streets and wharves of the Lambeth shore in the 1860s – had hitherto photographed scenes of ordinary London life. He was also asked in 1868 by the South Kensington Museum to photograph 'residences of remarkable persons and other buildings of interest likely to be affected by the changes now going on in the metropolis' (see *Illustrated London News*, 4 July 1868, p. 23). Strudwick, indeed, contributed a photograph to the SPROL project, of the York Water Gate on the Embankment. Photography aside, John Wykeham Archer (1806–64) had previously sketched a handful of historic shops and houses in his *Vestiges of Old London* (David Bogue, 1849) and documented many more in his unpublished watercolours privately produced for the antiquarian William Twopeny, donated to the British Museum in 1874. This work was akin to the earlier obsessive urban sketching of George Scharf (1788–1860). Both Scharf's and Wykeham's work provides a fascinating portrait of mid-Victorian streets, and their sketches can be found searching by the artists' names via the museum's website, https://www.britishmuseum.org/collection/ (accessed 13 March 2023). See also the sections on 'Domestic Architecture' in John Thomas Smith, *Ancient Topography of London* (John Thomas Smith, 1815).

44. Again, this is not to claim that Dickens's work was Marks's sole inspiration. The *Builder* in 1852, for example, featured an antiquarian look at the metropolis entitled 'The Houses and Shops of Old London', featuring lithographs of lost and surviving buildings: *Builder*, 1852, pp. 342–5, 391–3, 471–3, 566–9, 799–801, 809–10, 813. For an interesting discussion of shifting representations of London streets, see Alex Potts, 'Picturing the Modern Metropolis: Images of London in the Nineteenth Century', *History Workshop Journal*, 26 (1988), pp. 28–56.

45. Alfred Marks's letterpress to accompany the photograph: A. & J. Bool, 'Old Houses in Holborn', *c.* 1878, 180 mm x 227 mm, https://www.royalacademy.org.uk/art-artists/work-of-art/old-houses-in-holborn (accessed 6 June 2019).

46. Alfred Marks's letterpress to accompany the photograph: Henry Dixon & Son, 'Barnard's Inn, the Inner Courtyard', 1878–9, 179 mm x 225 mm, https://www.royalacademy.org.uk/art-artists/work-of-art/barnards-inn-the-inner-courtyard (accessed 6 June 2019).

47. Alfred Marks's letterpress to accompany the photograph: Henry Dixon & Son, 'White Hart Inn Yard, Southwark', *c.* 1881, 180 mm x 225 mm, https://www.royalacademy.org.uk/art-artists/work-of-art/white-hart-inn-yard-southwark-1 (accessed 6 June 2019).

48. See the previous chapter. Ruth Livesey notes that coaching inns gained an 'intense affective charge as sites of memory' when they were made redundant by the growth of the railway. Ruth Livesey, *Writing the Coaching Nation* (Oxford University Press, 2016), p. 18.

49. Nostalgic exploration of coaching inns was a subgenre of Dickens literary topography. B.W. Matz claimed in 1921 that 'No writer has done more than Dickens to reflect the glory of that era, and the glamour and comfort of the old inns of England . . .'. Matz, *The Inns and Taverns of 'Pickwick'*, p. 6.

50. Marks on one occasion asks readers to imagine famous figures populating the historic city ('Here Dr Johnson worshipped; his seat in the north gallery is still pointed out') and briefly imagines the occupants of opposing houses shaking hands across a narrow medieval street when describing Cloth Fair. See Marks's letterpress to accompany the photograph: A. & J. Bool, 'Old Houses in Wych Street, formerly a continuation of Drury Lane., ca. 1876', 228 mm x 176 mm, https://www.royalacademy.org.uk/art-artists/work-of-art/old-houses-in-wych-street-formerly-a-continuation-of-drury-lane (accessed 6 June 2019); and A. & J. Bool, 'Cloth Fair', 1877, 227 mm x 178 mm, https://www.royalacademy.org.uk/art-artists/work-of-art/cloth-fair (accessed 6 June 2019). The great majority of the letterpress, however, avoids the imaginary. Prescott lists two dozen credited authors from whom Marks quotes antiquarian, historical and topographical information (often no more than a sentence, sometimes with a full citation, sometimes without). Gertrude Mae Prescott, 'Architectural Views of Old London', *Library Chronicle of the University of Texas at Austin* (1981), pp. 9–31, p. 29.

51. *The Times*, 26 September 1882.

52. 'A City of Transformations', *Graphic*, 31 January 1874, p. 13.

53. Percy Fitzgerald, 'Sentimental Journeys in London: Dickens and Old London – The "Inns"', *Tinsleys' Magazine* (April 1884), pp. 385–92, p. 385.

54. Bertram Wallis, 'Charles Dickens as an Antiquary', *The Antiquary* (June 1901), pp. 165–70, p. 168.

55. *The Pickwick Papers*, chapter 10.

56. 'To W. W. F. De Cerjat, 1 February 1861', in *The Pilgrim Edition: The Letters of Charles Dickens*, Vol. 9: *1859–1861*, ed. Graham Storey (The Clarendon Press, 1997).

57. *Illustrated London News*, 16 July 1864, pp. 30–1.

58. *Manchester Courier and Lancashire General Advertiser*, 13 September 1864, p. 4; *Orkney Herald*, 13 September 1864, p. 4; *Dorset County Chronicle*, 15 September 1864, p. 10.

59. *Birmingham Daily Gazette*, 22 August 1864, p. 6; *Brecon County Times*, 21 July 1866, p. 3.

60. 'Nooks and Corners of Old England: The House of Milton and Tree Planted by Him in Petty France, Westminster', *Illustrated London News*, 9 January 1847, p. 5.

61. See, for example, *Leigh's New Picture of London* (Leigh and Son, 1834), p. 351; 'Local Memories of Great Men: Milton', in *The Guide to Knowledge*, ed. Robert Sears (Walker & Co., 1845), pp. 129–31; William Howitt, *Homes and Haunts of the Most Eminent British Poets* (Richard Bentley, 1847), pp. 106–7; *Limbird's Handbook Guide to London* (John Limbird, 1851), p. 56.

62. Letter from the clerk of the Historical Records and Buildings Committee, LCC, to Kitton, 27 March 1902. Kitton scrapbooks, Volume 3, Charles Dickens Museum. The LCC brochure documenting the tablet's history notes that 'the Council's attention was directed particularly to No. 48 Doughty Street' – as reprinted in

London County Council, *Indication of Houses of Historical Interest in London*, Vol. 1 (LCC, 1907), p. 22.

63. Robert Gomme, 'Laurence Gomme', in *Oxford Dictionary of National Biography*, online edn, 23 September 2004 (Oxford University Press, 2004), https://doi.org/10.1093/ref:odnb/38353 (accessed 14 November 2020). See also Kota Ito, 'Municipalization of Memorials: Progressive Politics and the Commemoration Schemes of the London County Council, 1889–1907', *The London Journal*, 42 (2017), pp. 273–90.

64. London County Council, *Indication of Houses of Historical Interest in London*, Vol. 1, p. 32.

65. *Dickensian* (May 1911), p. 116; *Dickensian* (September 1911), p. 228.

66. *The Survey of London: Being the First Volume of the Register of the Committee for the Survey of the Memorials of great London, containing the parish of Bromley-by-Bow* (P. S. King, 1900), p. iv; cited in Zemgulys, *Modernism and the Locations of Literary Heritage*, p. 215.

67. See, for example, Clerk of the Council, *Returns of Outdoor Memorials in London* (LCC, 1910). For a good summary of the Council's interest in historic buildings, see Sir Anthony Wagner, 'Preserving Historic Buildings', *The Times*, 8 December 1964, p. 13.

68. For the complex history of this building, see https://www.cityoflondon.gov.uk/things-to-do/attractions-museums-entertainment/prince-henrys-room (accessed 2 May 2023).

69. *The Survey of London*, pp. xxv, xxxvi.

70. Georges-Eugène Haussmann drove through the public works schemes of Napoleon III in Paris in the 1850s and 1860s, destroying medieval streets and replacing them with wide modern boulevards.

71. *Daily Mail*, 17 October 1902, p. 3.

72. *Saint Paul Globe*, 2 October 1904, p. 364.

73. Elizabeth Robins Pennell, 'Vanishing London', *Atlantic Monthly* (December 1903), pp. 796–804, p. 804.

74. Zemgulys notes, for example, the Council's insistence on prominently branding the LCC name on its plaques, to the consternation of London's wealthy landowners. Zembulys, *Modernism and the Locations of Literary Heritage*, pp. 77, 88.

75. *The Times*, 14 October 1905, p. 7.

76. Ito, 'Municipalization of Memorials', p. 279.

77. David Rooney, 'Visualization, Decentralization and Metropolitan Improvement: "Light-and-Air" and London County Council Photographs, 1899–1908', *Urban History*, 40 (2013), pp. 462–82, p. 479.

78. Culler notes Whiggish praise for the 'democratic' Anglo-Saxons in the work of Henry Hallam, Macaulay and others. A. Dwight Culler, *The Victorian Mirror of History* (Yale University Press, 1985), pp. 154–5.

79. 'Why Not King's Gate?', *Westminster Gazette*, 23 February 1901, p. 4.

80. *London Daily News*, 9 February 1903, p. 10.

81. *Literature*, 8 September 1900, p. 166.

82. *Graphic*, 30 July 1892, p. 15; 6 August 1892, p. 13; 20 August 1892, p. 13; 2 July 1898, p. 13; 21 October 1899, p. 6; 22 September 1900, p. 29.

83. Arnold Wright, 'London Homes and Haunts of Dickens', *London Argos*, 13 December 1901, pp. 145–51, p. 151. See also 'A Lost London Thoroughfare: Disappearance of Kingsgate Street', *London Argos*, 2 August 1901, p. 1.

84. 'The Last of Another Bit of Dickens Land', *Daily Graphic*, 5 September 1903, in Kitton scrapbooks, Volume 3, Charles Dickens Museum.

85. Kitton scrapbooks, Volume 3, Charles Dickens Museum.
86. For example, *Westminster Gazette*, 3 October 1900, p. 12; *Birmingham Daily Gazette*, 4 January 1901, p. 2.
87. Leigh Hunt argued for continental-style naming of streets after the great and the good in an 1833 essay, noting it was virtually unknown in London, in *Townsman*, 17 November 1833, republished in *Leigh Hunt's Political and Occasional Essays*, ed. Lawrence Huston Houtchens and Carolyn Washburn Houtchens (Columbia University Press, 1962), pp. 312–17.
88. Joanna Hofer-Robinson, *Dickens and Demolition* (Edinburgh University Press, 2018), pp. 91–129. See also Jamieson Ridenhour, *In Darkest London* (Scarecrow Press, 2013), p. 51.
89. Fitzgerald, 'Sentimental Journeys in London', p. 385.
90. *Standard*, 29 December 1887.
91. *Morning Advertiser*, 10 February 1903 (bound cuttings collection of Dickens Fellowship, Vol. 2, May 1903, DF2, Charles Dickens Museum).
92. *Standard*, 29 December 1887.
93. *Scraps: Literary and Pictorial; Curious and Amusing* was a magazine that ran from 1883 to 1910, largely containing cartoons. The cartoon preserved by Kitton (Kitton scrapbooks, Volume 3, Charles Dickens Museum) is undated, but, based upon the content and surrounding material in Kitton's scrapbook, it is likely to date from 1903 or 1904.
94. *Nicholas Nickleby*, chapter 4.
95. 'London Made Hideous', *Spectator*, 5 August 1893, pp. 173–4.
96. Jane Martin, 'The Role of Women in the Education of the Working Classes: 1870–1904', doctoral thesis, Open University, 1992, p. 230.
97. Peter Doyle, *First World War Britain* (Shire, 2012), p. 73.
98. Catalogue of Raphael Tuck & Sons cards available online at TuckDB Postcards, https://tuckdbpostcards.org/ (accessed 29 June 2020). Four of the cards are reproductions of the work of the artist Pilford Fletcher Watson (1842–1907).
99. The Charles Dickens Museum also holds a Dickens calendar from 1906, also published by Raphael Tuck & Sons, which uses the same images.
100. 'Gateway, Lincoln's Inn'; 'Marsh Lock, Henley'; 'Rochester from Strood Pier'.
101. See Walter Besant, *London* (Chatto & Windus, 1892), p. 216.
102. Francis Miltoun, *Dickens' London* (L.C. Page & Company, 1903), p. 42.

5 A Tale of Two Houses

1. Diary, *The Pilgrim Edition of the Letters of Charles Dickens*, Vol. 1: *1820–1839*.
2. Barton Hill, 'A Pilgrimage', *Lipincott's Magazine* (September 1870), pp. 288–93.
3. The chalet was an extravagant gift from the Swiss actor Charles Fechter, delivered in fifty-eight boxes – an early flat-pack – for Christmas 1864. It currently stands re-erected in the grounds of Eastgate House, Rochester.
4. Forster, *The Life of Charles Dickens*, Vol. 1, p. 24.
5. A description from the 10 December 1870 edition of the *Graphic*; the article was actually published on 25 December 1870.
6. See Richard Scully, 'William Henry Boucher (1837–1906): Illustrator and Cartoonist', *Victorian Periodicals Review*, 46 (4) (2013), pp. 441–75, p. 451.
7. Another drawing showing Dickens at his desk, surrounded by airy versions of his characters, appeared in *Fun* on 26 June 1870, four days after Boucher's work was published, drawn by Fred Barnard.

8. *Morning Post*, 11 August 1870.
9. Charley told Georgina that he was not aware of the reserve price (at which, if unsold, it was intended by Hogarth and Forster that the house should be bought back by the estate and retained in the family). He claimed he was only motivated by trying to prevent the house going cheap. Georgina seems to have harboured some doubts, calling it a 'dishonest transaction'. For more detail, see Arthur Adrian, *Georgina Hogarth and the Dickens Circle* (Oxford University Press, 1957), pp. 158–9. Charley and his aunt would also be at loggerheads when he arranged for the writing chalet to be re-erected at the Crystal Palace as an exhibit. See Emily Bell, 'Changing Representations of Dickens, 1857–1939', doctoral thesis, University of York, 2017, pp. 21–5.
10. Walter T. Stephenson, 'A Dickens Pilgrimage', *Vogue*, 23 May 1907, pp. 858, 860.
11. Nicola Watson, *The Literary Tourist: Readers and Places in Romantic & Victorian Britain* (Palgrave Macmillan, 2006), p. 25; see also Westover, *Necromanticism*, p. 14.
12. The reasons for this change are unknown, but it was common in the early nineteenth century for there to be disputes about street numbering, and renumbering, after new properties were built.
13. An advertisement placed in the *Morning Chronicle*, 29 April 1819, by a Henry Wilson, offered leases on 19, 22, 26, 27, 28 and 29 Johnson Street, described as currently let to tenants at thirty guineas per annum, with more than sixty years to run on the leases (suggesting a build date some thirty years earlier, given the prevalence of one-hundred-year leases in the metropolis).
14. 'Recollections of Charles Dickens', *Dickensian* (September 1911), pp. 229–31, p. 229.
15. 'A Laundress who has an eligible situation adjoining the fields of Somers Town … No.34, Johnson Street, Somers Town.' *Morning Advertiser*, 22 September 1822.
16. The (somewhat garbled and incomplete) rate-book evidence for the Dickens family in the house from 1824–7 is well summarised in the LCC's booklet *Indication of Houses in London of Historical Interest*, Vol. 3 (LCC, 1912).
17. For Augustus's birth, see *Sun*, 13 November 1827, p. 4. John Dickens had a Royal and Sun Alliance insurance policy for 13 Johnson Street, taken out on 12 February 1829 (London Metropolitan Archives, LMA CLC/B/192/F/001/MS11936/521/1086718). The precise date when they finally left is unknown. Dickens gave his address at 10 Norfolk Street in 1830 when applying for a British Museum reader's ticket; but a recent article has suggested that this may have been only a convenient address for collecting mail (Helena Kelly, 'Evidence that the Dickens Family May Not Have Lived in 10 Norfolk Street', *Dickens Quarterly*, 37 (2) (2020), pp. 186–8. This is possible, but it is noteworthy that a legal notice published in the *Morning Herald* on 11 April 1833 by John Dodd (owner of the Norfolk Street house), regarding a dividend on the debts of John Dickens, lists his recent addresses as 'No.13, Johnson Street, Somers Town, then of No.10 Norfolk-street, Middlesex Hospital, then of No.21 George-street, Adelphi, and of North End Hampstead and last of Bell Vue, Hampstead'.
18. Harriet Dickens was previously assumed to have died in infancy, but more recent discoveries show that she lived until 1827. See William F. Long, 'Defining a Life: Charles's Youngest Sister, Harriet Ellen Dickens (15 September 1818–19 August 1827)', *Dickensian* (Spring 2014), p. 24.
19. Walter Dexter, 'One Hundred Years Ago', *Dickensian* (January 1926), pp. 45–7, p. 45.
20. 'Our School', *Household Words*, 11 October 1851, pp. 49–52.

21. Forster, *The Life of Charles Dickens*, Vol. 2, p. 518.
22. *St Pancras Gazette*, 16 December 1871.
23. Frederick Kitton, *Charles Dickens: His Life, Writings and Personality* (T.C. & E.C. Jack, 1902), p. 19.
24. C. Pilkington, '"Little Dorrit" as She Is Today', *Black & White*, 14 February 1903, p. 240.
25. London County Council, *Indication of Houses of Historical Interest in London*, Vol. 3, pp. 97–104, p. 98
26. *Dundee Evening Telegraph*, 1 July 1920. One Oxford alumnus who regularly attended the library was Arthur Bryant, later a well-known historian whose work was admired by Churchill. He had recently finished his undergraduate degree at Queen's College and worked as a teacher for the London County Council, visiting the library and reading to children in the evening. Charles Douie, *Beyond the Sunset* (John Murray, 1935), p. 28.
27. John Brett Langstaff, *David Copperfield's Library* (George Allen & Unwin, 1924), p. 23. Anne Carroll Moore, who ran children's library services at the New York Public Library, likewise found the child visitors to the library to be 'children who might have stepped that very day from the pages of Charles Dickens, so little is Somers Town changed from the days of the Micawbers'. Anne Carroll Moore, *New Roads to Childhood* (George H. Doran Co., 1923), p. 18.
28. Langstaff claimed that the children themselves had decided not to allow books to be taken home. Anne Carroll Moore was impressed by this, writing: 'Their library was a safer place for books than their homes, and they knew it'. Moore, *New Roads to Childhood*, p. 22. Another visitor, however, recorded that 'Mr Langstaff's intention was always to have them [the books] circulated as soon as a trained librarian can be employed'. Caroline M. Hewins, 'David Copperfield's Library', *Library Journal*, 1 November 1922, pp. 918–19.
29. J.W.T. Ley, 'Dickens and Children', *Dickensian* (April 1905), pp. 87–90, p. 88.
30. London County Council, *Indication of Houses of Historical Interest in London*, Vol. 3 (1912), p. 98.
31. William Sibbald, 'Charles Dickens Re-Visited', *Westminster Review* (January 1907), pp. 62–73, p. 63.
32. *Diss Express*, 27 August 1926.
33. *Staffordshire Sentinel*, 1 February 1929.
34. Forster, *The Life of Charles Dickens*, Vol. 1, p. 34.
35. Langstaff, *David Copperfield's Library*, p. 96.
36. *Daily News*, 12 November 1921.
37. Alfred Noyes, *Two Worlds for Memory* (J.B. Lippincott Company, 1953), p. 160.
38. Noyes, *Two Worlds for Memory*, p. 99.
39. *Observer*, 6 February 1921. A letter from Langstaff confirms that the matinee made the charity the substantial sum of £400. Camden Local Studies Library, 'David Copperfield Library, Somers Town: information including photocopies from St Pancras Council minutes relating to the library' 52.112. Performers included the child actress Monica Disney, Bransby Williams, Jennie Lee and Russell Thorndike (as Scrooge).
40. *Daily News*, 29 December 1921.
41. For the full cast, see *Pall Mall and Globe*, 15 November 1821. Cast members were also photographed for *Sketch*, 7 December 1921.
42. *Portsmouth Evening News*, 14 December 1920; William Pett Ridge, *A Story Teller: Forty Years in London* (Hodder and Stoughton, 1923), p. 40.

43. The original 'Council' for the project, in a prospectus issued by Langstaff, included famous literary figures such J.M. Barrie, Lord Dunsany, John Galsworthy, Kenneth Grahame and H.G. Wells, not to mention Robert Baden Powell. Brett Langstaff, *David Copperfield's House as a Children's Free Library* [*c.* 1920], uncatalogued item, Charles Dickens Museum.
44. Noyes, *Two Worlds for Memory*, p. 156.
45. *Westminster Gazette*, 10 June 1922.
46. *Daily News*, 20 October 1920; *Westminster Gazette*, 2 May 1922.
47. *Weekly Dispatch*, 7 December 1924.
48. Langstaff, *David Copperfield's Library*, p. 92
49. *Daily News*, 27 November 1920.
50. *Bookman*, February 1922, p. 209, documents the full contents of the letter, which begins: 'I began to love Charles Dickens and to read him when I was a little "country mouse" eight years old and when I was eleven (Oh! wonderful good fortune!) I travelled with him on a certain railway journey between Maine and Massachusetts. It was a magical, a miraculous trip of two hours, during which my child's hand was in his, and his arm around my waist, so that in that long talk we became real friends.' Wiggin concludes by noting that Annie Carroll Moore, of the New York Public Library, has organised the 'representative selection' of books donated by American publishers which she has forwarded on their behalf. The NYPL also sent six illustrations by Leslie Brooke to decorate the library: 'The Babes in the Wood'; 'Puss in Boots' and drawings of children from India, China, Canada and Russia.
51. Formal presentation to St Pancras occurred on 1 November 1922. *Scotsman*, 2 November 1922.
52. *St. Pancras Gazette*, 1 June 1923; St Pancras Borough Council Minutes, 1923, pp. 360ff. Camden Local Studies Library.
53. He took the position of Associate Rector at St John's Church, Getty Square in New York. *Times Union*, 22 January 1923.
54. *Dickensian* (October 1923). Mrs Tate organised a tea dance in aid of the library at the American Women's Club in Grosvenor Street on 12 November 1927. *Daily Telegraph*, 25 October 1927. Both Ord Marshall and Tate were members of the 'Executive Board' listed in Langstaff's initial prospectus, *c.* 1920.
55. *Westminster Gazette*, 23 June 1926. The likes of Stacy Aumonier, Michael Sadleir, Temple Thurston and Ian Hay contributed to a fundraising book reading event, organised by Pett Ridge, in November 1926. *Dundee Courier*, 8 November 1926.
56. *Not So Bad as We Seem* programme. Camden Local Studies and Archive Centre. 52.112.
57. See *Dickensian* (Fall 1935), pp. 241ff. for the text of Dickens's tenancy agreement.
58. 'Rate books show that Dickens' house was occupied in June, 1809, but before that the entries are confused. There is no doubt, however, that it was built between 1801 and 1809, as leases were being granted by Elizabeth Doughty to various builders in the street at this time. The house is not marked on Horwood's map (1799).' *Survey of London*, Vol. 24: *The Parish of St Pancras Part 4: King's Cross Neighbourhood*, ed. Walter H. Godfrey and W. McB. Marcham (LCC, 1952) pp. 25–55. British History Online, http://www.british-history.ac.uk/survey-london/vol24/pt4, pp. 25–55 (accessed 13 March 2023).
59. For a claim about the gate, see William R. Hughes, *A Week's Tramp in Dickens-Land* (Chapman and Hall, 1891). Compare 'Return from Paving Boards or Districts in Parish of St Pancras (Middlesex), 1847–49', *House of Commons* Paper No. 585, p. 13 (which explicitly shows that Doughty Street had no barrier, in a tally of the

state of the roads in the district) with 'Returns of all gates, bars …', *House of Commons* Paper no. 369, 1882, p. 7, which mentions a gate on Doughty Street, with a notice regarding rules and regulations dated 1856 (i.e. the gate was likely erected in that year).

60. *Sketches by Boz*, Tales: The Boarding House, chapter 2.
61. Quoting Dickens from a letter 'To Mrs George Hogarth [24 October 1841], in *The Pilgrim Edition of the Letters of Charles Dickens*, Vol. 2: *1840–1841*, p. 408.
62. 'To John Forster [?8 January 1841]', in *The Pilgrim Edition of the Letters of Charles Dickens*, Vol. 2: *1840–41*.
63. Forster, *The Life of Charles Dickens*, Vol. 1, p. 187.
64. Emily Valia Smith, 'Charles Dickens and Literary Tourism: His Experiential Encounters and Legacy', doctoral thesis, Royal Holloway, University of London, 2022, p. 146; *Willesden Chronicle*, 8 February 1884.
65. Hughes, *A Week's Tramp in Dickens-Land*, p. 29.
66. *Daily Mail*, 18 May 1897.
67. *Daily Telegraph*, 12 June 1902.
68. *Warder and Dublin Evening Mail*, 18 May 1901; [J. Ashby-Sterry], *Graphic*, 31 January 1903.
69. *The Times*, 11 March 1914.
70. F. Hopkinson Smith, *In Dickens's London* (Smith, Elder & Co., 1914), pp. 30ff.
71. Mary Richardson, *Laugh a Defiance* (George Weidenfeld & Nicholson, 1953), p. 158.
72. 1914 is the last year in which Lyons appears on the electoral register. My thanks to Norma McGilp for sending me this information, along with much other useful material.
73. 'A Dickens Museum of London', *Daily Chronicle*, 3 January 1901.
74. *Daily Chronicle*, 5 January 1901.
75. *Sphere*, 20 December 1913.
76. The initial membership was Lord Acton, Lord James of Hereford, Sir H. Drummond Wolff, Sir Henry Irving, Sir Walter Besant, Andrew Lang, Marcus Stone, Luke Fildes, Augustine Birrell, W. Warren Vernon, Charles Kent, Rev. Professor Bonney, Henry Fielding Dickens and Percy Fitzgerald ('of the above, eight at least have been acquainted with Dickens', wrote Fitzgerald, in a prospectus for the club). *The Boz Club* [two-page leaflet], Guildhall Museum, Rochester.
77. Emily Bell, 'The Dickens Family, the Boz Club and the Fellowship', *Dickensian* (Winter 2017), pp. 219–32, pp. 225–7.
78. Waugh, *One Man's Road*, p. 304.
79. *Dickensian* (October 1925).
80. *Dickensian* (October 1925).
81. J.T. Ley, 'The Dickens Fellowship: 1902–23. A Retrospect', *Dickensian* (October 1923), pp. 178–95, p. 179.
82. *Daily News*, 7 October 1902.
83. *Yorkshire Evening Post*, 16 May 1903; *St. James's Gazette*, 25 May 1903.
84. For example, the inaugural meeting of the Lewisham branch promised 'a short illustrated lecture on "Dickens Land"'. *Kentish Mercury*, 16 January 1903. A meeting of the central group of the Fellowship at the Memorial Hall in 1903 also included a slideshow of photographs by H. Snowden Ward, showing 'The Real Dickens Land', which would be published in book form the following year. *Sevenoaks Chronicle and Kentish Advertiser*, 13 February 1903. The Fellowship had a library of 1,000 lantern slides, 'all of which illustrate some Dickens subject'. *Dickensian* (July 1924).

85. *New York Tribune*, 29 March 1903.
86. 'Dickens Shrine in London', *Daily Mail (Atlantic edition)*, 26 July 1923; *Dickensian* (July 1924), p. 149.
87. B.W. Matz, 'Charles Dickens and Reform', *Bookman* (November 1910), pp. 79–86, p. 86. Brett Langstaff also listed him as a 'Council' member of the David Copperfield Library but he does not seem to have been heavily involved in the project. His name appears in a flyer for *Not So Bad as We Seem* (an uncatalogued item held in the Charles Dickens Museum).
88. *Daily Telegraph*, 17 March 1921.
89. *Graphic*, 19 August 1922.
90. *Dickensian* (January 1923), p. 4.
91. The Fellowship was originally based in the offices of Chapman Hall in Henrietta Street, Covent Garden, then moved in 1911 to 13 Cockspur Street, SW1 (shortly afterwards demolished); then relocated to 33 Craven Street the same year; then moved to Whitehall House, Charing Cross in 1914; and finally settled in 14 Clifford's Inn in 1915, after the previous building was commandeered by the War Office. *Dickensian* (January 1951), p. 90.
92. *Dickensian* (January 1923), pp. 13–14.
93. *Dickensian* (April 1923), p. 79; *Birmingham Post*, 19 June 1922, states that 48 Doughty Street cost £3,000 and its neighbour £1,500.
94. *LCC Staff Gazette*, October 1926, p. 262.
95. *Dickensian* (April 1923), p. 73.
96. *Dickensian* (July 1923), p. 149. The two firms in question were Keen, Robinson & Co., manufacturers of mustard, and Fortnum & Mason.
97. Edmonds was a local government assessor, whose entire estate was valued at $15,000 when he died in 1935. *Brooklyn Daily Eagle*, 7 September 1935. The conversion rate between the dollar and the pound in the early 1920s was roughly 5:1.
98. *Western Chronicle*, 27 February 1925. Matz died shortly after the house's opening in 1925. The collection, only held on loan, was purchased by Sir Charles Wakefield and given to the museum in 1927.
99. Unknown newspaper from scrapbook, *c.* 1922–5, Charles Dickens Museum.
100. 'The Dickens House', *American Women's Club Magazine* (July 1925), pp. 228–9, p. 228; *Queen*, 17 June 1925.
101. The fires were all by John Wright & Co., Aston, who produced an advertising booklet to accompany this coup, 'a little booklet they are distributing in various ways to lovers of Dickens, which deals with this period of Dickens' life in a way that makes fascinating reading'. *Gas Journal* (June 1925), p. 324.
102. William Pett Ridge, 'A Dickens Museum for London', *Graphic*, 7 February 1925.
103. *Dickensian* (April 1925).
104. It is unclear when the shift from tavern scene to Dingley Dell occurred. In the Dickens Fellowship minutes for 29 October 1924, held at the Charles Dickens Museum, it is likewise described as presenting an 'old English Tavern Kitchen'.
105. Sherwood's obituary records that he made his money in the Montana gold rush of the 1860s and was Chairman of the Nassau Union Bank in Glen Cove. *Times Union*, 10 March 1934. See also *Dickensian* (April 1925).
106. *Dickensian* (April 1925). The architect was one Reginald C. Fry.
107. Dickens Fellowship Minutes, 14 March 1925.
108. For more detail about the Bayham Street window, see Malcolm Andrews, 'Windows into Dickens's World', *Dickensian* (Summer 2022), pp. 124–39.

109. Advertisement for the Bean Tourer car, *Illustrated London News*, 27 November 1920; for Johnnie Walker whisky, *ILN*, 8 December 1923; for Buchanan's 'Black & White' whisky, *Sphere*, 2 June 1928; for Sharp's Toffee, *ILN*, 5 August 1922; for Fox's Glacier Mints, *Daily Mirror*, 28 December 1929; for Trident Salmon & Shrimp Paste, *Daily Mirror*, 1 April 1927; for Heinz Baked Beans, *Daily Mirror*, 27 February 1923; for Hudson's Soap, *Weekly Dispatch*, 1 March 1925.
110. *Sphere*, 21 February 1925.
111. Mr Gradgrind, the miserable utilitarian in Dickens's *Hard Times*, begins the novel by demanding school children learn 'nothing but facts'. The Museum guidebook cost one shilling and the contents would remain unchanged for several decades: a description of Dickens's life at Doughty Street, including paragraphs on the death of Mary Hogarth and his friendship with Forster; extracts from his diary and letters; a list of literary works completed during Dickens's time in the house; pictures of Dickens and family; and photographs of a couple of pages from his manuscripts.
112. *Weekly Dispatch*, 30 August 1925.
113. *Glasgow News*, 5 July 1927.
114. *Philadelphia Inquirer*, 1 May 1912.
115. 'Sixty Years at Dickens House', *Dickensian* (Summer 1985), pp. 66–71, p. 68.
116. *Liverpool Post and Mercury*, 21 December 1927.
117. David Parker, 'The Reconstruction of Dickens's Drawing-Room', *Dickensian* (Spring 1982), pp. 8–18, p. 17. I am grateful to Emily Smith for drawing this to my attention in her thesis, 'Charles Dickens and Literary Tourism', p. 204.

6 The Haunted Bridge

1. *Oliver Twist*, chapter 39.
2. *Oliver Twist*, chapter 46.
3. Westover, *Necromanticism*.
4. 'The Uncommercial Traveller', *All the Year Round*, 20 June 1860, pp. 274–87, p. 274.
5. Dickens refers to 'Timpson's Blue-Eyed Maid', which may actually refer to the coach run by a Mr Simpson, who operated in Chatham. *Dickensian* (January 1922), p. 21.
6. Forster, *The Life of Charles Dickens*, Vol. 1, p. 51.
7. *David Copperfield*, chapter 11.
8. *Oliver Twist*, chapter 50.
9. *Oliver Twist*, chapter 40.
10. 'New London Bridge', *Literary Chronicle*, 18 June 1825, p. 396.
11. 'An Antiquary', *Chronicles of London Bridge* (Smith Elder and Co., 1827), p. 2. See also Lucy Peltz, 'Aestheticizing the Ancestral City: Antiquarianism, Topography and the Representation of London in the Long Eighteenth Century', *Art History*, 22 (1999), pp. 472–94, who discusses antiquarians' anxieties about the disappearance of London's historic buildings in the eighteenth century.
12. London Metropolitan Archives (ref. q6888682). George Scharf also sketches a similar contrasting picture of pedestrians on the finished bridge, looking at demolition work. (British Museum 1862,0614.507)
13. *Oliver Twist*, chapter 46.
14. Iain Crawford, 'Time and Structure in "Oliver Twist"', *Dickensian* (Spring 1981), pp. 23–31, p. 29
15. *Oliver Twist*, chapter 46.
16. *Oliver Twist*, chapter 46.

17. John R. Reed, *Dickens and Hyperrealism* (Ohio State University Press, 2010), p. 42.
18. *Morning Advertiser*, 5 September 1846.
19. *Oliver Twist*, chapter 16.
20. National Portrait Gallery, NPG 6251(2), drawn by Harry Furniss, the noted illustrator of Dickens's novels.
21. B.W. Matz, 'Joseph Ashby-Sterry' [obituary], *Dickensian* (July 1917), pp. 185–7.
22. J. Ashby-Sterry, *The River Rhymer* (Charles Scribner's Sons, 1913), pp. 30–9.
23. Ashby-Sterry, 'Charles Dickens in Southwark'.
24. Ashby-Sterry even copies Dickens's style when picturing the reader standing under London Bridge: 'with scarce a sound to be heard but the lapping of the tide on the steps, the rush of the river through the arch, the muffled rumble of a late hansom going citywards; as the punctual clocks chime the quarters with querulous distinctness and laggard clocks, in their anxiety to be in time, trip one another up and cause a quaint discord . . .'. Ashby-Sterry, 'Charles Dickens in Southwark', p. 107.
25. Victoria and Albert Museum (image reference S.23–1982), https://collections.vam. ac.uk/item/O1248744/oliver-twist-drawing-buchel-charles/ (accessed 13 March 2023). Others would also select this scene as emblematic of the production; for example, a full-page illustration appeared in *Black & White*, 9 September 1905. Tree was also, as it happens, the illegitimate father of Carol Reed, the director of the film *Oliver!*.
26. *Daily Telegraph*, 11 July 1905; *Stage*, 13 July 1905.
27. Thanks to Lionel Wright for pointing out this plaque to me.
28. *Little Dorrit*, Book 1, chapter 12.
29. The brown plaque is mentioned in Richard Jones, *Walking Dickensian London* (New Holland, 2004), p. 160, the earliest reference I can find; the blue plaque was erected in 2019.

7 An Old Curiosity Shop

1. *Echo*, 31 December 1883, p. 2.
2. *Stage*, 8 February 1884, p. 12.
3. P.T. Barnum, *Struggles and Triumphs, or the Recollections of P.T. Barnum* (Ward Lock & Co., 1882), p. 120.
4. *London Daily News*, 1 December 1896, notes: 'When it was in imminent danger of suddenly collapsing like a pack of cards, Mr Bruce Smith, the eminent scene-painter, was called in at Christmas time to exercise his skill in carpentry on it, for no other reason than that of preserving a Dickens landmark.'
5. *Morning Call*, 21 May 1902, p. 3.
6. *Nicholas Nickleby*, chapter 32.
7. *Sketches by Boz*, 'Seven Dials'.
8. *Bleak House*, chapter 5.
9. *Oliver Twist*, chapter 26.
10. Forster, *The Life of Charles Dickens*, Vol. 1, p. 43.
11. *Dombey and Son*, chapter 4.
12. *Bleak House*, chapter 32 and chapter 5.
13. *Old Curiosity Shop*, chapter 1.
14. *Old Curiosity Shop*, chapter 3.
15. 'To George Cattermole, 22 December 1840'; 'To Richard Monckton Miles, 10 March 1841', in *The Pilgrim Edition of the Letters of Charles Dickens*, Vol. 2: *1840–1841*.
16. Charles Dickens, *Speeches: Literary and Social* (John Camden Hotten, 1870), p. 50.

17. Hawthorne writes of his delight in the 'sight and actual presence of almost all the objects and renowned localities that I had read about, and which had made London the dream-city of my youth'. Nathaniel Hawthorne, *Our Old Home* (Smith Elder & Co., 1863), Vol. 2, p. 82.

18. Tesseyman owned the shop from 1868 to 1877, according to a letter written by his brother, printed in the *Echo*, 31 December 1883, p. 2 (mistakenly cited as 21 December 1883 in O. Sack [B.W. Matz], 'The Legend of "The Old Curiosity Shop"', *Dickensian* (October 1923), p. 224).

19. *Illustrated London News*, 5 January 1884.

20. B.E. Martin, 'In and Out of London with Dickens: "Splendid Strolling"', *Scribner's Monthly Magazine* (May 1881), pp. 32–45, p. 32

21. Tesseyman formerly had a shop in 5 Broad-court, Covent Garden (for the Broad Street address, see *Post Office London Directory* (Frederic Kelly, 1843), p. 397) and, as a bookbinder, reportedly had a fund of anecdotes about famous actors and numbered Thackeray amongst his customers (*Hampstead and Highgate Express*, 21 April 1877). An article in the *Illustrated London News*, 5 January 1884, claimed 'John Forster was one of his patrons, and brought Charles Dickens, with other friends who had a taste for quaint reminiscences of London life, or who cared for chance purchase of old play-bills, broadsheets, caricature drawings, and autographs, to visit the odd little shop'.

22. *Dickensian* (May 1911), p. 115. Another editorial in 1921 described it as a 'false shrine'. *Dickensian* (April 1921), p. 61.

23. Elizabeth Robins Pennell, 'Vanishing London', *Atlantic Monthly* (December 1903), pp. 796–804, p. 804.

24. Henry James, *Transatlantic Sketches* (James R. Osgood and Company, 1875), p. 10, cited in James Buzard, *The Beaten Track: European Tourism, Literature, and the Ways to 'Culture', 1800–1918* (Oxford University Press, 1993), p. 199. James suggests that English writers, such as Dickens and Eliot, write vividly about childhood thanks to 'having had the happiness of growing up among old, old things'.

25. *American Notes*, Book I.

26. *Dombey and Son*, chapter 19, 'The Wooden Midshipman on the Look-out'.

27. Susan Stewart, *On Longing* (Duke University Press, 1993), pp. 56, 62.

28. 'Tudor' being American English for a Tudor-style property. Advertisement in the *Sacramento Bee*, 29 October 1987, p. 240.

29. *Bystander*, 10 August 1910.

30. 'A Real Dickens Romance', *Penny Illustrated Paper*, 24 August 1912.

31. *London Daily News*, 21 March 1881, p. 4. This association of the Tudors with the coming glories of Empire was merely one of several rather rosy visions which the Victorians had of the Tudor period. Peter Mandler, for instance, outlines how the Tudor period was portrayed as possessing a particularly cosy English domesticity and, indeed, as the foundational period for various aspects of English social and cultural life. Peter Mandler, 'In the Olden Time: Romantic History and the English National Identity: 1820–50', in *A Union of Multiple Identities*, ed. Laurence Brockliss and David Eastwood (Manchester University Press, 1997), pp. 78–92.

8 Down Newgate Lane

1. *Queen*, 30 June 1888.

2. *Programme of the Charles Dickens Bazaar in aid of the Fund for the Restoration of St. Peter's Church . . . June 27th, 28th, and 29th, 1888* [1888].

3. *Preston Herald*, 7 July 1888.
4. Programme, p. 100 of 115 (not numbered).
5. Programme, pp. 108–11 of 115 (not numbered).
6. Various press advertisements and reviews advertised the bazaars; see, for example, *Leamington Spa Courier*, 24 April 1880, p. 5; *Coventry Times*, 3 November 1880, p. 8; *Nottinghamshire Guardian*, 17 December 1880, p. 2.
7. *Hearth and Home*, 2 February 1899. It is likely to have been a modest affair, as I have found no surviving images or detailed visual description.
8. Programme, p. 12 of 115.
9. For a more detailed historical account of the Old London Street, see Dory Agazarian, 'Buying Time: Consuming Urban Pasts in Nineteenth-century Britain', doctoral thesis, City University of New York, 2018, pp. 437–57.
10. Obituary, *Telegraph*, 13 May 1904, p. 7.
11. Douglas Galton, 'International Health Exhibition', *Art Journal* (June 1884), pp. 161–4, p. 161.
12. *Sporting Gazette*, 17 May 1884, p. 19.
13. *Telegraph*, 16 May 1884, p. 5.
14. 'The I. H. E. Examination Paper', *Punch*, 22 November 1884, p. 249.
15. *Myra's Journal of Dress and Fashion*, 1 July 1885, p. 350.
16. 'Our Ladies Column', *Nottinghamshire Guardian*, 25 April 1884, p. 9.
17. *Sporting Gazette*, 21 June 1884, p. 789.
18. *Aberdeen Weekly Journal*, 5 July 1884, p. 2.
19. *Daily News*, 25 December 1884, p. 4.
20. Thomas P. Collins, *Arizona on Stage* (Twodot, 2016), p. 31.
21. See *Atlanta Constitution*, 26 October 1890, p. 12; *New York Tribune*, 27 October 1890. The building's interior was left empty for several years, then demolished to make way for a gym in 1896 (*New York Sun*, 26 August 1896).
22. *London Evening Standard*, 31 May 1911.
23. The half-timbered look, in fact, was something of a contemporary fixation. For example, both the Staple Inn in Holborn and the Leather Bottle at Cobham in Kent, picturesque sites associated with *Edwin Drood* and *The Pickwick Papers*, were returned to a half-timbered appearance in the late 1880s and early 1920s respectively, having been previously entirely covered in plaster. Tourists professed themselves gratified by their thoroughly 'Dickensian' appearance, even though Dickens himself would have found them quite changed.
24. *The Pickwick Papers*, chapter 10. Warren's was a rival blacking company, for which Dickens's himself was famously briefly obliged to work as a youth. A Dickens Fellowship scrapbook from 1922 contains a colour advertisement for Day & Martin's Boot Polish, showing Sam Weller at work in the White Hart Inn yard. NN122, Scrapbook concerning the Dickens House 1922–1929. Charles Dickens Museum.
25. A 'Dickens Fair' at Hartlepool Independent Church, for example, is pictured in the *Northern Echo* on 3 March 1927, with a replica of the Portsmouth Street facade clearly visible. Dickens Fellowship Scrapbook, 1927. Charles Dickens Museum.
26. Clara E. Laughlin, *So You're Going to Merrie England* [1934], [p. 6].
27. Laughlin, *So You're Going to Merrie England*, [p. 16]; see also the advertisement 'Do Not Fail to See Merrie England's [. . .]', *Chicago Tribune*, 1 July 1934, p. 50.
28. Readers will know the gesture even if not linking it to the phrase: placing one's thumb in front of one's nose and wiggling one's fingers. The film can be viewed online, courtesy of BFI National Archive, https://www.youtube.com/watch?v=yqufG89Jlyc (accessed 13 March 2023).

29. The first Bentley performance I can find in the press is at the Empress, Brixton. *People*, 24 October 1909. Although often later referred to as an exponent of 'Dickensian characters', he seems to have mainly restricted himself to portraying the characters and telling the story of *The Old Curiosity Shop*, which he would also bring to the screen on three separate occasions (1914, 1921 and 1934). The *Stage* remarked that the act was 'somewhat novel', in as much as he confined himself to characters from a single book and attempted to work through the narrative. *Stage*, 29 September 1910. Bransby Williams and other rivals tended to provide a selection of set pieces from different books.

30. *Kinematograph Weekly*, 11 January 1912.

31. Thomas Bentley, 'Ten Years of Dickens Films', *The Picturegoer*, July 1922, pp. 16–17 (p. 16)

32. *New Castle Herald*, 9 October 1915.

33. Cecil M. Hepworth, *Came the Dawn: Memories of a Film Pioneer* (Phoenix House, 1951), p. 111.

34. Hepworth, *Came the Dawn*, p. 125.

35. *Dickensian* (November 1914), p. 284.

36. *Western Mail*, 6 March 1915.

37. *Kinematograph Weekly*, 24 December 1914.

38. Mark Napolitano notes how Lean's film reflects the disorderly chaos of post-war London ridden with bomb sites but offsets this with Dickens and his work as a form of enduring 'national heritage' immortalised on screen, and perhaps Oliver himself as a symbol of national endurance. Mark Napolitano, *Oliver!* (Oxford University Press, 2014), Kindle Edition, p. 16.

39. Interview with John Box, *Journal of British Cinema and Television*, 2 (1) (2005), pp. 137–47, p. 144.

40. This was partly thanks to the set being built around well-established real trees that were growing on the Shepperton lot. Ian Christie, *The Art of Film: John Box and Production Design* (Wallflower Press, 2008), p. 88.

41. Michael Billington, 'Dickens Transformed', *Illustrated London News*, 5 October 1968.

42. Napolitano, *Oliver!*, Kindle edition, p. 86.

43. Napolitano, *Oliver!*, Kindle edition, p. 189.

44. The viaduct plainly owes a lot to Gustav Doré's drawing of Ludgate Hill in *London: A Pilgrimage* (n.p., 1872), which Box turned to when he heard it had inspired John Bryan.

45. An image of a gang of paviours using heavy weights, resembling milk churns with handles, to flatten macadam paving, inspired one of the dancing groups in 'Consider Yourself'. Indeed, the original drawing, which appeared in the *Illustrated London News*, 26 April 1851, shows the men coordinating their movement, the weights all carefully held at the same angle – synchronised like a group of dancers.

46. See, for example, William Marshall Craig, *The Itinerant Traders of London* (1804). See https://www.bl.uk/romantics-and-victorians/articles/the-cries-of-london (accessed 13 March 2023).

47. *Oliver Twist*, chapter 12.

48. Christie, *The Art of Film*, p. 88.

49. In a 2005 interview, Box said: 'We made it a crescent because we did not want to build a whole square. With careful use of camera angles, you could make it look like you were shooting on a whole crescent.' 'Interview with John Box', p. 145.

50. Reviews in *Daily Mail*, 28 October 2005; *Sunday Telegraph*, 30 October 2005.

51. *A Christmas Carol*, stave I

52. 'A New Chapter for a Dickens Classic', *Coventry Evening Telegraph*, 15 October 2005.

53. The ease with which film units can set up camp in these semi-private corners of the capital also helps. The more eagle-eyed viewer will have noticed portions of Lincoln's Inn incorporated not only into multiple Dickens adaptations but also into the likes of *Sherlock Holmes: A Game of Shadows* (2011); *Wonder Woman* (2017), albeit transformed somewhat by CGI; and *The Sandman* (2022).

54. See the series press pack at http://downloads.bbc.co.uk/mediacentre/dickensian-media-pack.pdf (accessed 13 March 2023).

55. *Birmingham Post*, 24 October 1972.

56. *Stage*, 9 August 1979.

57. 1980 flyer for Charles Dickens Centre, Southwark Archives.

58. Tom Fordy, 'Hard Times at Dickens World: The Curious Saga of Kent's £62 Million Literary Theme Park', *Daily Telegraph*, 1 December 2017, p. 4.

59. 'Forget Disneyland, Try Dickens World', *Evening Standard*, 6 April 2005; *Time Out*, 15 June 2005.

60. 'Theme Park with a Little Bit of a Twist', *Evening Standard*, 2 April 2007; *Guardian*, 18 April 2007.

51. 'RMA/O'Sullivan-Beare Theme for Dickens World', *Design Week*, 21 April 2005.

62. Lee Jackson, *Palaces of Pleasure* (Yale University Press, 2019), p. 172.

63. 'Bemusement Park', *Christian Science Monitor*, 25 May 2007. 'Buildings straight out of an Oliver Twist film set', remarked another reviewer. 'A Dickens of a Place', *Daily Mail*, 14 April 2007.

64. 'Dickens's work was like a soap opera for Victorian times. You know, if he were alive now, I bet he'd love Dickens World. He'd probably be a shareholder.' 'Bemusement Park', *Christian Science Monitor*, 25 May 2007. 'If he was writing now, he'd be writing for television.' *Daily Mail*, 14 April 2007.

65. Vincent van Gogh, letter to Anthon van Rappard, *c.* 5 March 1883. Online via Van Gogh Museum, https://vangoghletters.org/vg/letters/let325/letter.html (accessed 13 March 2023). Sutherland notes Dickens's own use of 'picture' in his working notes as shorthand for intended descriptive passages in his novels. John Sutherland, 'Visualizing Dickens', in *Palgrave Advances in Charles Dickens Studies*, ed. John Bowen and Robert Patten (Palgrave Macmillan, 2006), pp. 111–30, p. 113. For cinema, see generally Grahame Smith, *Dickens and the Dream of Cinema* (Manchester University Press, 2003).

66. S. Eisenstein, 'Dickens, Griffith, and the Film Today', in *Film Form* (Dennis Dobson, 1951), p. 195. Griffith was, indeed, quoted as saying: 'All that I know of motion picture technique I owe to Dickens' during a visit to the United Kingdom in 1922. *Leeds Mercury*, 20 April 1922.

67. *Oliver Twist*, chapter 50

68. Alison Byerly, *Are We There Yet?*, University of Michigan Press, 2013, p. 70.

9 Somebody Else's Sieve

1. Richard Jones, 'Virtual Tours of Dickens London', https://www.dickenslondontours.co.uk/virtual-dickens-walks.htm (accessed 13 March 2023).

2. *South London Journal*, 15 July 1856; *Globe*, 2 September 1871. A set of houses known locally as 'Sikes's dwellings' were pulled down in 1891, but the district had long since lost its slum character. *Eddowes's Journal*, 21 January 1891.

3. *Dickens's Dictionary of London* (Charles Dickens, 1879).

4. [Joseph Charles Parkinson], 'Lazarus, Lotus-eating', *All the Year Round*, 12 May 1866, pp. 421–5.
5. Edmund Yates, 'Going the Rounds', *Temple Bar*, 20 (1867), pp. 244–54.
6. 'Inspector Meiklejohn's Detective Experiences', *Blackburn Standard*, 27 October 1888.
7. *Cambridgeshire Times*, 28 February 1874.
8. *Newry Reporter*, 4 May 1876. See *Dundee Evening Telegraph*, 27 October 1888, where Inspector Meiklejohn says that he brokered the sale to 'Colonel Butler, who had been American consul at Alexandria, and was the brother of the famous General Butler, erstwhile Governor of New Orleans after the War of Secession. He had read about it in Dickens's works and took a fancy to it as a relic.' George Harris Butler was a colourful character, married to American actress Rose Eytinge, star of *Nancy Sikes*, a play which received disastrous reviews in London in 1878. See https://en.m.wikipedia.org/wiki/George_Harris_Butler (accessed 13 March 2023).
9. Conway, 'Footprints of Charles Dickens', p. 611. One is reminded of John Westlock's invention of a pickpocket for Tom Pinch, pointing out a random stranger as a thief, to live up to Pinch's preconceptions of 'notorious localities' (*Martin Chuzzlewit*, p. 568), a passage in which Dickens surely is reflecting on his own part in creating a 'criminal London' in the public imagination.
10. Conway, 'Footprints of Charles Dickens', p. 611.
11. Professor Ruth Livesey has argued that Dickens's portrayal of 'homely' places such as Dingley Dell in *The Pickwick Papers* presents to readers 'intensely localized places that offer native habitation to all who read or hear the story; the novel creates collective prosthetic memory of locality in a globally mobile world'. I suggest, likewise, that many literary topographers saw 'Dickensland' as a set of fixed points, a stable Dickens presence in the ever-changing city. Livesey, *Writing the Coaching Nation*, p. 20.
12. Westover, *Necromanticism*, p. 109. Dickens himself attended a public dinner at the Mansion House with US novelist Harriet Beecher Stowe, where a toast was raised to 'Mr Charles Dickens and the literature of the Anglo-Saxons'. Harriet Beecher Stowe, *Sunny Memories of Foreign Lands* (Phillips, Sampson and Company, 1854), p. xli. See also Joseph De Sapio, *Modernity and Meaning in Victorian London* (Palgrave Macmillan, 2014), pp. 81–2; and Nicola Watson, 'Rambles in Literary London', in *Literary Tourism and Nineteenth-century Culture*, ed. Nicola Watson (Palgrave Macmillan, 2009), pp. 139–49, pp. 147–8.
13. A phrase coined in a much-quoted speech by Balfour in 1896, urging cooperation with the United States. Arthur James Balfour, *Arthur James Balfour as Philosopher and Thinker* (Green & Co., 1912), p. 290; see also De Sapio, *Modernity and Meaning in Victorian London*, pp. 18–19, 77–8.
14. A.J. Faust, 'A London Literary Pilgrimage', *Catholic World* (February 1883), pp. 669–712, p. 712.
15. 'The unity of language, literature and law between England and America is a threefold cord that cannot be broken. To have our English Bible, our English Shakespeare, our English Blackstone all absolutely American in reverence and influence outweighs … all question of racial compositeness.' William Crosswell Doane, 'Patriotism', *North American Review*, 166 (March 1898), p. 318, quoted in Duncan Bell, *Reordering the World: Essays on Liberalism and Empire* (Princeton University Press, 2016), p. 193. See also Westover, *Necromanticism*, p. 112.
16. J. Cuming Walters, *Dickensian* (November 1916), p. 285; see also *Dickensian* (January 1917), p. 19.

17. [Virginia Woolf], 'Literary Geography', *Times Literary Supplement*, 10 March 1905, p. 81.
18. Frank Marzials, 'Bozland', *Academy*, 9 November 1895, p. 383, reviewing Fitzgerald's *Bozland*; however, Marzials confesses 'inconsistency' in himself 'having gone on pilgrimages . . . to many of the Dickens haunts, and stood with due emotion, in the ballroom of the Bull Inn'.
19. Charles Dickens Jr, 'Notes on some Dickens Places and People', *Pall Mall Gazette* (July 1896), pp. 342–55, p. 344.
20. Mrs Warre Cornish, 'Personal Memories of Tennyson', *Living Age* (1922), pp. 472–8, p. 478.
21. B.E. Martin, 'In London with Dickens', *Scribner's Monthly Magazine* (March 1881), pp. 649–64, reviewed in *New York Times*, 28 February 1881, p. 3. The latter concludes: 'There is no occupation that is more harmless or [intellectually] unprofitable.'
22. F.R. Leavis and Denys Thompson, *Culture and Environment* (Chatto & Windus, 1934), p. 51.
23. *Nicholas Nickleby*, chapter 27.
24. Charlotte Boyce writes about how the spiritual connection felt at literary sites – particularly biographical sites – gives visitors a feeling of an exclusive intimate relationship with the author and a sense of 'cultural distinction'. Charlotte Boyce, 'At Home with Tennyson', in Charlotte Boyce et al., *Victorian Celebrity Culture and Tennyson's Circle* (Palgrave Macmillan, 2013), pp. 18–52, p. 28.
25. [Virginia Woolf], 'Literary Geography', p. 81.
26. London County Council issued a similar promotion for its tram network in 1923, albeit as a newspaper advert, with simple cartoon sketches of Dickens's characters, a list of locations and the relevant tram services.
27. Thomas Moult, introduction to Walter T. Spencer, *Forty Years in my Bookshop* (1923), p. xxiii.
28. The film can be viewed via the British Film Institute website at https://player.bfi.org.uk/free/film/watch-dickens-london-1924-online (accessed 13 March 2023).
29. 'Sixty Years at Dickens House', *Dickensian* (Summer 1985), pp. 66–71, p. 70.
30. 'S.D.' slight damage; 'D.' damaged; 'B.D.' badly damaged; 'DEM' demolished and site cleared; 'DES' fragments only of the original building remaining, which may be restored or ultimately cleared away; 'W.S.' walls standing. 'Some Damage has been Reported', *Dickensian* (Spring 1946), pp. 92–7.
31. William Kent, *London for the Literary Pilgrim* (Salisbury Square, 1949), p. 4.
32. *Standard*, 29 December 1887.
33. 'We opened our special exhibition "Dickensian: Behind the Scenes of the New BBC Drama" on 19 January 2016, and this ran until 17 April 2016. During this period, our visitor numbers were up 28% on the same period the year before (2015).' Email from Dr Cindy Sughrue, Director of the Charles Dickens Museum, 11 November 2002.
34. *Little Dorrit*, Book 2, Chapter 7.
35. *Little Dorrit*, Book 2, Chapter 7.
36. 'To Mrs Watson, 1 November 1854', in *The Pilgrim Edition of the Letters of Charles Dickens*, Vol. 7: *1853–1855*, ed. Graham Storey, Kathleen Tillotson and Angus Easson (The Clarendon Press, 1993).
37. *David Copperfield*, chapter 13.
38. *Dover Telegraph*, 23 June 1866.
39. Charles Dickens Jr, 'Notes on Some Dickens Places and People', p. 350. The house is now Broadstairs' own Charles Dickens Museum.

40. James Lawson Stewart's watercolours for the cards were derived from a series of paintings he produced in the 1880s, equally picturesque and untroubling, showing 'Dickens's London'. Joanna Hofer-Robinsons writes of his depiction of Jacob's Island: 'Stewart's representation encourages the viewer to enjoy the scene, indicating a desire to linger in Dickens's London, like the strollers crossing the bridge in the painting.' Joanna Hofer-Robinson, ' "Once upon a time would not prove to be All-time or even a long time': From Sanitary Reform to Cultural Memory: The Case of Jacob's Island', in *Dickens after Dickens*, ed. Emily Bell (White Rose University Press, 2020), pp. 1–34, p. 28. The paintings, indeed, represent a rather bland idyllic visualisation of Dickensian literary tourism, focused upon a quaint 'Old London'.

41. 'To Lord Lytton, 17 September 1867', in *The Pilgrim Edition of the Letters of Charles Dickens*, Vol. 11: *1865–67*, cited in Smith, *Dickens and the Dream of Cinema*, p. 105.

SELECT BIBLIOGRAPHY

Primary Sources: Dickens's own works and Dickensian literary topography

A bibliography of Dickens's novels and journalism would serve little purpose here and take up a good deal of space. Individual works are briefly cited in the text. Scholars, however, may wish to know that I have used the Pilgrim Edition of the letters, and Oxford editions of the novels, where available. There is also already a substantial bibliography of Dickensian topography, compiled by Miller (William Miller, *The Dickens Student and Collector* (Chapman and Hall, 1946), Division XI, 'Topographical', pp. 257–74), which can be found online at archive.org. I have added to that list a couple of dozen items, and some more recent works, to form my own bibliography of Dickensian topography – but, again, it is too lengthy to reproduce here. Readers can refer to Miller or contact me on lee@victorianlondon.org if they would like a copy of my list.

Other Primary Sources

'An Antiquary', *Chronicles of London Bridge* (Smith Elder and Co., 1827).

Archer, John Wykeham, *Vestiges of Old London* (David Bogue, 1849).

Ashbee, C.R., *The Survey of London: Being the First Volume of the Register of the Committee for the Survey of the Memorials of great London, containing the parish of Bromley-by-Bow* (P.S. King, 1900).

Balfour, Arthur James, *Arthur James Balfour as Philosopher and Thinker* (Longmans, Green & Co., 1912).

Barnum, P.T., *Life of P. T. Barnum* (The Courier Company, 1888).

Beecher Stowe, Harriet, *Sunny Memories of Foreign Lands* (Phillips, Sampson and Company, 1854).

'The Bemoaned Past', *All the Year Round*, 24 May 1862, pp. 257–61.

Bentley, Thomas, 'Ten Years of Dickens Films', *The Picturegoer*, July 1922, pp. 16–17.

Besant, Walter, *London* (Chatto & Windus, 1892).

Blanchard, E. L., *Bradshaw's Guide through London* (W. J. Adams, 1859).

A brief historical sketch of the Old London Street erected at 728 and 730 Broadway, near 8th Street, New York (Souvenir Publishing Co., 1897).

Carlyle, Thomas, 'Sartor Resartus', *Fraser's Magazine*, July 1834, pp. 77–87.

[Carter, John], 'Of the Impropriety of Theatrical Representations, as They Relate to the Scenery, Dresses, and Decorations When Brought Forward as Illustrative of the Antient History of This Country', *Gentleman's Magazine*, February 1799, pp. 113–16.

Champney, Elizabeth Williams, *Three Vassar Girls in England* (Estes and Lauriat, 1884).

Cheney, Ednah D., ed., *Louisa May Alcott: Her Life, Letters and Journals* (Roberts Brothers, 1889).

Conway, Moncure Daniel, *Autobiography: Memories and Experiences* (Houghton Mifflin and Company, 1904).

Cook, E.T., ed., *The Works of John Ruskin* (George Allen, 1909).

Coolidge, Susan, *What Katy Did Next* (Roberts Brothers, 1887).

Craig, William Marshall, *The Itinerant Traders of London* (n.p., 1804).

Dickens's Dictionary of London (Charles Dickens, 1879).

'A Dickens Village at Broadstairs', *Pall Mall Gazette*, 8 July 1897, p. 8.

Dolby, George, *Charles Dickens as I Knew Him* (J.B. Lippincott & Co., 1885).

Douie, Charles, *Beyond the Sunset* (John Murray, 1935).

Fields, James T., 'Some Memories of Charles Dickens', *The Atlantic*, August 1870, pp. 235–45.

Fitzgerald, Percy, 'The Author of "Paul Pry"', *The Gentleman's Magazine*, September 1874, p. 339.

'Five Hundred Years Ago', *All the Year Round*, 6 October 1860, pp. 608–14.

Fletcher, Geoffrey, 'Where Did Little Nell Live?', *Daily Telegraph*, 25 March 1970, p. 15.

Fordy, Tom, 'Hard Times at Dickens World: The Curious Saga of Kent's £62 Million Literary Theme Park', *Daily Telegraph*, 1 December 2017, p. 4.

Forster, John, *The Life of Charles Dickens*, 3 vols (Chapman and Hall, 1874).

Forsyth, Joseph, *Remarks on Antiquities, Arts and Letters during an excursion in Italy in the years 1802 and 1803* (P. G. Ledouble, 1820).

Galton, Douglas, 'International Health Exhibition', *Art Journal* (June 1884), pp. 161–4.

'Gambling with Cigarette Cards', *Pearson's Weekly*, 30 March 1901, p. 12.

Godwin, William, 'Essay on Sepulchres', in *Political and Philosophical Writings of William Godwin*, Vol. 6: *Essays*, ed. Mark Philp (Pickering & Chatto, 1993), pp. 1–30.

Hall, Mrs S.C., *Pilgrimages to English Shrines* (Arthur Hall, 1850).

Harris, Stanley, *The Coaching Age* (Richard Bentley and Son, 1885).

Hawthorne, Nathaniel, *Our Old Home*, 2 vols (Smith Elder & Co., 1863).

Hepworth, Cecil M., *Came the Dawn: Memories of a Film Pioneer* (Phoenix House Limited, 1951).

'Hoary London "Fakes" That Fool American Visitors', *El Paso Times*, 6 November 1904, p. 9.

Horne, R.H., *A New Spirt of the Age*, 2 vols (Smith Elder and Co., 1844).

Howitt, William, *Homes and Haunts of the Most Eminent British Poets* (Richard Bentley, 1847).

Hughson, David, *Walks Through London* (Sherwood, Neely & Jones, 1817).

Hutton, Laurence, *Literary Landmarks of London* (T. Fisher Unwin, 1885).

'The I. H. E. Examination Paper', *Punch*, 22 November 1884, p. 249.

James, Charles, *Two on a Tandem* (Chapman and Hall, 1896).

James, Henry, *Transatlantic Sketches* (James R. Osgood and Company, 1875).

Kent, Charles, *Charles Dickens as a Reader* (Chapman and Hall, 1872).

Kent, William, *London for the Literary Pilgrim* (Salisbury Square, 1949).

Knight, Charles, ed., *London*, 6 vols (Charles Knight & Co., 1841–4).

— *Passages of a Working Life*, 2 vols (Charles Knight & Co., 1864).

Knight, Joseph, *Theatrical Notes* (Lawrence & Bullen, 1893).

Langstaff, John Brett, *David Copperfield's Library* (George Allen & Unwin, 1924).

Laughlin, Clara E., *So You're Going to Merrie England* [n.p., 1934].

Lee, Anna, 'Famous Old Curiosity Shop of London Saved for Twenty Years', *The Province*, 21 March 1926, p. 48.

'Local Memories of Great Men: Milton', in *The Guide to Knowledge,* ed. Robert Sears (Walker & Co., 1845), pp. 129–31.

London County Council, *Indication of Houses of Historical Interest in London*, 6 vols (LCC, 1907–38).

'London in Books', *All the Year Round*, 14 October 1865, pp. 270–6.

'London Made Hideous', *Spectator*, 5 August 1893, pp. 173–4.

[MacFarlane, Charles], *The Book of Table Talk*, 2 vols (Charles Knight, 1836).

Matz, B. W., 'Charles Dickens and Reform', *Bookman*, November 1910, pp. 79–86.

— *The Inns and Taverns of "Pickwick"* (Cecil Palmer, 1921).

— 'Joseph Ashby-Sterry' [obituary], *Dickensian*, 1 July 1917, pp. 185–7.

Moncrieff, William Thomas, *Sam Weller, Or, The Pickwickians: A Drama in Three Acts* (n.p., 1837).

Moore, Anne Carroll, *New Roads to Childhood* (George H. Doran Co., 1923).

'Mr Charles Dickens's New Reading', *Tinsley's Magazine* (February 1869), pp. 60–4.

'Nooks and Corners of Old England: The House of Milton and Tree Planted by Him in Petty France, Westminster', *Illustrated London News*, 9 January 1847, p. 5.

Noyes, Alfred, *Two Worlds for Memory* (J.B. Lippincott Company, 1953).

Ogilvy, James S., *Relics and Memorials of London City* (George Routledge & Sons, 1910).

'Old Bits of New Babylon: II. Clifford's and Staple's Inn', *Daily Mail*, 19 March 1897, p. 7.

'The Old Pump-Handle', *Quiver* (March 1865), pp. 370–2.

'Opium Sal', *Edinburgh Evening News*, 16 December 1875, p. 3.

Pascoe, Charles Eyre, *London of To-Day* (Roberts Brothers, 1893).

Pett Ridge, William, *A Story Teller: Forty Years in London* (Hodder and Stoughton, 1923).

Pocock, Tom, 'East End Loses a Dollar Harvest', *Daily Mail*, 14 May 1949, p. 4.

Porter, Maria S. 'Recollections of Louisa May Alcott', *New England Magazine* (March 1892), pp. 3–19.

'The Posthumous Papers of the Pickwick Club', *Quarterly Review* (October 1837), pp. 484–518.

Programme of the Charles Dickens Bazaar in aid of the Fund for the Restoration of St. Peter's Church [. . .] June 27th, 28th, and 29th, 1888 (n.p., [1888]).

Returns of Outdoor Memorials in London (LCC, 1910).

Rideing, William H., *Thackeray's London: A Description of his Haunts and the Scenes of his Novels* (J. W. Jarvis, 1885).

Rimmer, Alfred, *Ancient Streets and Homesteads of England* (Macmillan and Co., 1877).

[Robertson, John], 'My London Ghosts', *Household Words*, 11 April 1857, pp. 344–9.

Rogers, Samuel, *The Pleasures of Memory* (n.p., 1792).

'Round London with Cook', *Daily Mail*, 14 July 1900, p. 3.

Ruskin, John, *Letters of John Ruskin to Charles Eliot Norton*, 2 vols (Houghton Mifflin, 1904).

— *Modern Painters*, 5 vols, 2nd edn (Smith Elder & Co., 1867–9).

Sack, O., 'The Legend of "The Old Curiosity Shop", *Dickensian*, 1 October 1923, p. 224.

Shorter, Clement K., *Victorian Literature* (James Bowden, 1897).

[Smith, Albert], 'Hotels: Chapter III. Of the good old coaching days', *The Month* (August 1851), pp. 83–6.

Smith, John Thomas, *Ancient Topography of London* (John Thomas Smith, 1815).

— *Antiquarian Ramble in the Streets of London*, 2 vols (Richard Bentley, 1846).

Smollett, Tobias, 'Art. III – Essay on Sepulchres [. . .]', *The Critical Review, or Annals of Literature*, 19 (January 1810), pp. 29–34.

Sorgatz, Anne W., 'Dickens's Victorian London Lies in Wait on Portsmouth Street', *Albuquerque Journal*, 18 July 1982, p. 47.

Spencer, Walter T., *Forty Years in my Bookshop* (n.p., 1923).

'A Trip to Vienna or to India for a shilling', *Era*, 9 April 1848, p. 12.

Wagner, Sir Anthony, 'Preserving Historic Buildings', *The Times*, 8 December 1964, p. 13.

Walker, George, *Gatherings from Graveyards* (Longman, 1839).

Wallis, Bertram, 'Charles Dickens as an Antiquary', *The Antiquary* (June 1901), pp. 165–70.

Waugh, Arthur, *One Man's Road* (Chapman and Hall, 1931).

'Why Not King's Gate?', *Westminster Gazette*, 23 February 1901, p. 4.

Wilkinson, Robert, *Londina Illustrata* (Robert Wilkinson, 1819).

Williams, Bransby, *An Actor's Story* (Chapman and Hall, 1909).

Wordsworth, William, *The Prelude* (Edward Moxon, 1850).

Secondary Sources

Ackroyd, Peter, *Dickens* (Minerva, 1991).

— *London: The Biography* (Chatto & Windus, 2000).

Adrian, Arthur, *Georgina Hogarth and the Dickens Circle* (Oxford University Press, 1957).

Agathocleous, Tanya, *Urban Realism and the Cosmopolitan Imagination* (Cambridge University Press, 2011).

Agazarian, Dory, 'Buying Time: Consuming Urban Pasts in Nineteenth-century Britain', doctoral thesis, City University of New York, 2018.

Allen, Esther, '"Money and little read books": Romanticism, Tourism and the Rise of the Guidebook', *LIT*, 7 (1996), pp. 213–25.

Anderson, Benedict, *Imagined Communities* (Verso, 1991).

Andrews, Malcolm, 'Dickens, Turner and the Picturesque', in *Imagining Italy*, ed. Catherine Waters, Michael Hollington and John Jordan (Cambridge Scholars Publishing, 2010), pp. 177–94.

— *Dickensian Laughter* (Oxford University Press, 2013).

— 'The Metropolitan Picturesque', in *The Politics of the Picturesque*, ed. Stephen Copley and Peter Garside (Cambridge University Press, 1994), pp. 282–98.

— *The Search for the Picturesque* (Stanford University Press, 1989).

— 'Windows into Dickens's World', *Dickensian* (Summer 2022), pp. 124–39.

Auerbach, Jeffrey, and Peter Hoffenberg, *Britain, the Empire and the World at the Great Exhibition of 1851* (Ashgate, 2008).

Bachman, Maria K., 'Dickens's Evocative Objects: A Tale of Two Lockets', *Dickens Quarterly*, 33 (2016), pp. 38–54.

Bagehot, Walter, 'Charles Dickens', *National Review*, 7 (1858), pp. 458–86.

Bann, Stephen, *Romanticism and the Rise of History* (Twayne, 1995).

Battles, Kelly Eileen, 'The Antiquarian Impulse: History, Affect and Material Culture in Eighteenth- and Nineteenth-Century British Literature', doctoral thesis, Michigan State University, 2008.

Baumgarten, Murray, 'Calligraphy and Code: Writing in "Great Expectations", *Dickens Studies Annual*, 11 (1983), pp. 61–72.

— 'Fictions of the City', in *The Cambridge Companion to Charles Dickens*, ed. John O. Jordan (Cambridge University Press, 2001), pp. 107–19.

— 'Theatre of Homelessness: Dickens, London and the Technology of Representation', in *Representing London*, ed. Martin Zerlang (Spring Publishers, 2001), pp. 57–73.

Bell, Duncan, *Reordering the World: Essays on Liberalism and Empire* (Princeton University Press, 2016).

Bell, Emily, 'Changing Representations of Dickens, 1857–1939', doctoral thesis, University of York, 2017.

— ed., *Dickens After Dickens* (White Rose University Press, 2020).

— 'The Dickens Family, The Boz Club and the Fellowship', *Dickensian* (Winter 2017), pp. 219–32.

Bending, Stephen, 'Every Man Is Naturally an Antiquarian: Francis Grose and Polite Antiquities', *Art History*, 25 (2002), pp. 520–30.

Benjamin, Walter, *Arcades Project*, trans. by Howard Eiland and Kevin McLaughlin (Belknap Press, 1999).

— *The Work of Art in the Age of Mechanical Reproduction* (Penguin, 2008).

Bennett, Tony, *The Birth of the Museum* (Routledge, 1995).

— 'The Exhibitionary Complex', *new formations*, 4 (Spring 1988), pp. 73–102.

Bhandari, Kalyan, 'Touristification of Cultural Resources: A Case Study of Robert Burns', *Tourism*, 56 (2008), pp. 283–93.

Bodenheimer, Rosemarie, *Knowing Dickens* (Cornell University Press, 2007).

Bolton, Philip, 'Bleak House and the Playhouse', *Dickens Studies Annual*, 12 (1983), pp. 81–116.

Booth, Alison, *Homes and Haunts: Touring Writers' Shrines and Countries* (Oxford University Press, 2016).

Booth, Michael R., 'The Metropolis on Stage', in *The Victorian City: Images and Realities*, ed. H.J. Dyos and Michael Wolff, 2 vols (Routledge & Kegan Paul, 1973), Vol. 1, pp. 211–24.

Bowen, John, 'A Garland for "The Old Curiosity Shop", *Dickens Studies Annual*, 37 (2006), pp. 1–16.

— *Other Dickens: Pickwick to Chuzzlewit* (Oxford University Press, 2000).

[Box, John], 'Interview with John Box', *Journal of British Cinema and Television*, 2 (1) (2005), pp. 137–47.

Bramen, Carrie Tirado, 'A Transatlantic History of the Picturesque: An Introductory Essay', *Nineteenth-century Prose*, 29 (2002), pp. 1–19.

Brantlinger, Patrick, 'Did Dickens Have a Philosophy of History? The Case of Barnaby Rudge', *Dickens Studies Annual*, 30 (2001), pp. 59–74.

Brister, Lori N., 'Looking for the Picturesque: Tourism, Visual Culture, and the Literature of Travel in the Long Nineteenth Century', doctoral thesis, George Washington University, 2015.

Brooks, Peter, 'Repetition, Repression, and Return: Great Expectations and the Study of Plot', *New Literary History*, 11 (1980), pp. 503–26.

Brown, Bill, 'Thing Theory', *Critical Inquiry*, 28 (2001), pp. 1–22.

Brown, Peter, *Shakespeare's Local* (Macmillan, 2012).

Buckland, Adelene, '"The Poetry of Science": Charles Dickens, Geology, and Visual and Material Culture in Victorian London', *Victorian Literature and Culture*, 35 (2007), pp. 679–94.

Buzard, James, *The Beaten Track: European Tourism, Literature, and the Ways to 'Culture', 1800–1918* (Oxford University Press, 1993).

Byerly, Alison, *Are We There Yet?* (University of Michigan Press, 2013).

Carlton, W.J., 'Dickens's Insurance Policies', *Dickensian*, 1 January 1955, pp. 133–7.

Chesterton, G.K., *Appreciations and Criticisms of the Works of Charles Dickens* (J. M. Dent & Sons, 1911).

Chialant, Maria Teresa, 'The Shop in Dickens's Fiction', *e-Rea*, 13 (2016), pp. 1–43.

Christie, Ian, *The Art of Film: John Box and Production Design* (Wallflower, 2008).

Cohen, Erik, 'Authenticity and Commodization in Tourism', *Annals of Tourism Research*, 15 (1988), pp. 371–86.

Cohen, Margaret, 'Panoramic Literature and the Invention of Everyday Genres', in *Cinema and the Invention of Modern Life*, ed. Leo R. Cheney and Vanessa R. Schwartz (University of California Press, 1995), pp. 227–52.

Collins, Philip, 'Dickens's Reading', *Dickensian*, 1 September 1964, pp. 136–51.

Collins, Thomas P., *Arizona on Stage* (Twodot, 2016).

Cotsell, Michael, 'The Pickwick Papers and Travel: A Critical Diversion', *Dickens Quarterly*, 3 (1986), pp. 5–16.

Craig, David M., 'The Interplay of City and Self in Oliver Twist, David Copperfield and Great Expectations', *Dickens Studies Annual* (1987), pp. 17–38.

Crawford, Iain, 'Time and Structure in "Oliver Twist"', *Dickensian* (Spring 1981), pp. 23–31.

Cubitt, Geoffrey, *History and Memory* (Manchester University Press, 2007).

Culler, A. Dwight, *The Victorian Mirror of History* (Yale University Press, 1985).

Culler, Jonathan, 'Semiotics of Tourism', *American Journal of Semiotics*, 1 (1981), pp. 127–40.

Cutler, James, 'Remembering the Victorians: Cultural Memory, Popularity, Place', doctoral thesis, University of London, Royal Holloway, 2017.

De Cauter, Lieven, 'The Panoramic Ecstasy: On World Exhibitions and the Disintegration of Experience', *Theory and Culture*, 10 (1993), pp. 1–23.

De Certeau, Michel, *The Practice of Everyday Life*, trans. by Steven Rendall (University of California Press, 1988).

De Sapio, Joseph, *Modernity and Meaning in Victorian London* (Palgrave Macmillan, 2014).

De Stasio, Clotilde, 'The Traveller as Liar: Dickens and the "Invisible Towns" in Northern Italy', *Dickensian* (Spring 2000), pp. 5–13.

Dennis, Richard, *Cities in Modernity: Representations and Productions of Metropolitan Space, 1840–1930* (Cambridge University Press, 2008).

Dobraszczyk, Paul, 'City Reading: The Design and Use of Nineteenth-Century London Guidebooks', *Journal of Design History*, 25 (2012), pp. 123–44.

Doyle, Peter, *First World War Britain* (Shire, 2012).

Dubini, Renzo, *Geography of the Gaze* (University of Chicago Press, 2002).

Easley, Alexis, *Literary Celebrity, Gender, and Victorian Authorship, 1850–1914* (University of Delaware Press, 2011).

Edmondson, John, 'From a Distance: The Remote Cityscape as Dream and Nightmare', *e-Rea*, 13 (2016), pp. 1–37.

Edwards, Elizabeth, *The Camera as Historian* (Duke University Press, 2012).

Ellis, Markman, '"Spectacles within doors": Panoramas of London in the 1790s', *Romanticism*, 14 (2008), pp. 133–48.

Ellis, Patrick, 'The Panstereorama: City Models in the Balloon Era', *Imago Mundi*, 70 (2018), pp. 79–93.

Ellis, Stewart M., *Harrison Ainsworth and His Friends* (John Lane, 1911).

— *Mainly Victorian* (Hutchinson & Co., 1924).

Epstein Nord, Deborah, *Walking the Victorian Streets* (Cornell University Press, 1995).

Farrell, S. M., 'William Ewart', in *Oxford Dictionary of National Biography*, online edn, 9 January 2014 (Oxford University Press, 2014).

Flint, Kate, *The Victorians and the Visual Imagination* (Cambridge University Press, 2000).

Foster, Shirley, 'Americans and Anti-Tourism', in *Literary Tourism and Nineteenth-Century Culture*, ed. Nicola Watson (Palgrave Macmillan, 2009), pp. 175–83.

Frank, Lawrence, 'News from the Dead: Archaeology, Detection, and "The Mystery of Edwin Drood"', *Dickens Studies Annual*, 28 (1999), pp. 65–102.

Franklin, Stephen, 'Dickens and Time: The Clock without Hands', *Dickens Studies Annual*, 4 (1975), pp. 1–35, 167–71.

Fraser, Hilary, 'Writing the Past', in *The Cambridge Companion to English Literature 1830–1914*, ed. Joanne Shattock (Cambridge University Press, 2010), pp. 108–26.

Frisby, David, *Cityscapes of Modernity* (Polity, 2001).

Fulkerson, Richard P., '*Oliver Twist* in the Victorian Theatre', *Dickensian*, 1 May 1974, pp. 83–95.

Gardiner, John, 'Dickens and the Uses of History', in *A Companion to Charles Dickens*, ed. David Paroissien (Blackwell, 2008), pp. 240–54.

Gernsheim, Helmut, *Focus on Architecture and Sculpture: An Original Approach to the Photography of Architecture and Sculpture* (Fountain Press, 1949).

Gissing, George, *Charles Dickens: A Critical Study* (Doll, Mead and Company, 1898).

Gomme, Robert, 'Laurence Gomme', in *Oxford Dictionary of National Biography*, online edn, 23 September 2004 (Oxford University Press, 2004).

Goodwin, George, and H.C.G. Matthew, 'George Dodd', *in Oxford Dictionary of National Biography*, online edn, 12 November 2020 (Oxford University Press, 2020).

Gordon, Beverly, 'Woman's Domestic Body: The Conceptual Conflation of Women and Interiors in the Industrial Age', *Winterthur Portfolio*, 31 (1996), pp. 281–301.

Gould, Marty, and Rebecca N. Mitchell, 'Understanding the Literary Theme Park: Dickens World as Adaptation', *Neo-Victorian Studies*, 3 (2010), pp. 145–71.

Hales, S.J., 'Re-Casting Antiquity: Pompeii and the Crystal Palace', *Arion: A Journal of Humanities and the Classics*, 14 (2006), pp. 99–134.

Hammond, Mary, *Charles Dickens's Great Expectations: A Cultural Life, 1860–2012* (Routledge, 2015).

Handa, Rumiko, and James Potter, *Conjuring the Real* (University of Nebraska Press, 2011).

Harrison, Rodney, *Heritage: Critical Approaches* (Routledge, 2013).

Hendrix, Harald, 'From Early Modern to Romantic Literary Tourism: A Diachronical Perspective', in *Literary Tourism and Nineteenth-Century Culture*, ed. Nicola Watson (Palgrave Macmillan, 2009), pp. 13–24.

Herbert, David, 'Literary Places, Tourism and the Heritage Experience', *Annals of Tourism Research*, 28 (2001), pp. 312–33.

Hewison, Robert, *The Heritage Industry* (Methuen, 1987).

Hill, Nancy K., *A Reformer's Art: Dickens' Picturesque and Grotesque Imagery* (Ohio University Press, 1981).

Hillis Miller, J., 'The Fiction of Realism', in *Realism, Modern Literatures in Perspective*, ed. Lilian R. Furst (Longman, 1992), pp. 287–318.

Hofer-Robinson, Joanna, *Dickens and Demolition* (Edinburgh University Press, 2018).

— '"Once upon a time would not prove to be All-time or even a long time": From Sanitary Reform to Cultural Memory: The Case of Jacob's Island', in *Dickens after Dickens*, ed. Emily Bell (White Rose University Press, 2020), pp. 1–34.

Hoffenberg, Peter, *An Empire on Display* (University of California Press, 2001).

Holtorf, Cornelius, 'Perceiving the Past: From Age Value to Pastness', *International Journal of Cultural Property*, 24 (2017), pp. 497–515.

House, Humphrey, *The Dickens World* (Oxford University Press, 1942).

Hunt, John Dixon, '*Ut Pictura Poesis*, the Picturesque, and John Ruskin', *MLN* (December 1978), pp. 794–818.

Ito, Kota, 'Municipalization of Memorials: Progressive Politics and the Commemoration Schemes of the London County Council, 1889–1907', *The London Journal*, 42 (2017), pp. 273–90.

Jackson, Lee, *Palaces of Pleasure* (Yale University Press, 2019).

Janowitz, Anne, 'The Artificial Sublime: Making London Poetry', in *Romantic Metropolis: The Urban Scene of British Culture, 1780–1840*, ed. James Chandler and Kevin Gilmartin (Cambridge University Press, 2006), pp. 246–60.

Jansson, André, 'The Open-Ended Ruin: Imaginative Authenticity as a Driver of Alternative Tourism', in *Locating Imagination in Popular Culture*, ed. Nicky van Es et al. (Routledge, 2021), pp. 34–50.

John, Juliet, *Dickens and Mass Culture* (Oxford University Press, 2010).

— 'The Heritage Industry', in *Charles Dickens in Context*, ed. Sally Ledger and Holly Furneaux (Cambridge University Press, 2011), pp. 74–80.

— 'Things, Words and the Meanings of Art', in *Dickens and Modernity*, ed. Juliet John (D. S. Brewer, 2012), pp. 115–32.

Kalter, Barrett, *Modern Antiquities* (Bucknell University Press, 2012).

Kaufman, Edward N., 'The Architectural Museum from World's Fair to Restoration Village', *Assemblage*, 9 (1989), pp. 20–39.

Kelly, Helena, 'Evidence that the Dickens Family May Not Have Lived in 10 Norfolk Street', *Dickens Quarterly*, 37 (2) (2020), pp. 186–8.

Kingstone, Helen, *Victorian Narratives of the Recent Past: Memory, History, Fiction* (Palgrave Macmillan, 2017).

Korte, Barbara, and Sylvia Paletschek, 'Nineteenth Century Magazines and Historical Cultures in Britain and Germany', in *Popular History Now and Then: International Perspectives*, ed. Barbara Korte and Sylvia Paletschek (Transaction Publishers, 2012), pp. 73–104.

Lake, Crystal B., *Artifacts* (John Hopkins University Press, 2020).

— 'The Life of Things at Tintern Abbey', *Review of English Studies*, 63 (2012), pp. 444–65.

Lamb, John B., 'Wax Girl: Molding Little Nell in "The Old Curiosity Shop"', *Dickens Studies Annual*, 44 (2013), pp. 127–42.

Larkin, Jamie, '"All Museums Will Become Department Stores": The Development and Implications of Retailing at Museums and Heritage Sites', *Archaeology International*, 19 (2016), pp. 109–21.

Leavis, F.R., and Denys Thompson, *Culture and Environment* (Chatto & Windus, 1934).

Ledger, Sally, '"God be thanked: a ruin!" The Rejection of Nostalgia in *Pictures from Italy*', *Dickens Quarterly*, 26 (2009), pp. 79–85.

Lefebvre, Henri, *The Production of Space*, trans. by Donald Nicholson-Smith (Blackwell, 1991).

Leighton, Mary Elizabeth, and Lisa Surridge, 'The Illustrated Novel', in *Charles Dickens in Context*, ed. Sally Ledger and Holly Furneaux (Cambridge University Press, 2011), pp. 166–77.

Ley, J.W.T., 'Dickens and Children', *Dickensian*, 1 April 1905, pp. 87–90.

— *The Dickens Circle* (Chapman and Hall, 1918).

— 'The Dickens Fellowship: 1902–23. A Retrospect', *Dickensian*, 1 October 1923, pp. 178–95.

Livesey, Ruth, *Writing the Coaching Nation* (Oxford University Press, 2016).

Lockwood, Allison, *Passionate Pilgrims: The American Traveler in Great Britain, 1800–1914* (Cornwall Books, 1981).

Lolla, Maria Grazia, 'Ceci n'est pas un monument: Vetusta Monumenta and anti-quarian aesthetics', in *Producing the Past*, ed. Martin Myrone and Lucy Peltz (Ashgate, 1999), pp. 15–30.

Lowenthal, David, *The Heritage Crusade and the Spoils of History* (Viking, 1996).

MacCannell, Dean, *The Tourist: A New Theory of the Leisure Class* (University of California Press, 1999).

Mandler, Peter, 'In the Olden Time: Romantic History and the English National Identity: 1820–50', in *A Union of Multiple Identities*, ed. Laurence Brockliss and David Eastwood (Manchester University Press, 1997), pp. 78–92.

Marsh, Joss, 'Recreating London: Dickens, Cinema and the Imagined City', in *Representing London*, ed. Martin Zerlang (Spring Publishers, 2001), pp. 74–121.

Martin, Jane, 'The Role of Women in the Education of the Working Classes: 1870–1904', doctoral thesis, Open University, 1992.

McAllister, David, 'Dickens's "School of Affliction": Learning from Death in *Nicholas Nickleby* and *The Old Curiosity Shop*', *Victoriographies*, 10 (3) (2020), pp. 228–47.

McCann, Andrew, 'Ruins, Refuse and the Politics of Allegory in *The Old Curiosity Shop*', *Nineteenth-century Literature*, 66 (2011), pp. 170–94.

McKellar, Elizabeth, 'Tales of Two Cities: Architecture, Print and Early Guidebooks to Paris and London', *Humanities*, 2 (2013), pp. 328–50.

McKinney, Kayla Kreuger, 'Collecting Subjects/Objects: The Museum and Victorian Literature 1830–1914', doctoral thesis, West Virginia University, 2017.

McNees, Eleanor, 'Reluctant Source: Murray's Handbooks and Pictures from Italy', *Dickens Quarterly*, 24 (2007), pp. 211–29.

Melman, Billie, *The Culture of History: English Uses of the Past 1800–1953* (Oxford University Press, 2006).

Metz, Nancy Aycock, 'The "Something" that His Brain Required', in *Dickens and the Virtual City*, ed. Estelle Murail and Sara Thornton (Palgrave Macmillan, 2017), pp. 121–32.

Miller, Angela, 'The Panorama, the Cinema and the Emergence of the Spectacular', *Wide Angle*, 18 (1996), pp. 34–69.

Miller, William, *The Dickens Student and Collector* (Chapman and Hall, 1946).

Mitchell, Rosemary, *Picturing the Past* (Oxford University Press, 2000).

Morley, Malcolm, 'Bleak House SCENE', *Dickensian*, 1 January 1953, pp. 175–82.

Murail, Estelle, 'Re-envisioning Dickens' City: London Through the Eyes of the Flaneur and Asmodeus', in *Dickens and the Virtual City*, ed. Estelle Murail and Sara Thornton (Palgrave Macmillan, 2017), pp. 57–77.

Myrone, Martin, and Lucy Peltz, eds, *Producing the Past* (Routledge, 2018).

Napolitano, Mark, *Oliver!* (Oxford University Press, 2014).

Nead, Lynda, *Victorian Babylon* (Yale University Press, 2000).

Nelson, Harland, 'Dickens and the Shakespeare Birthplace Trust: 'What a Jolly Summer!'', in *A Humanist's Legacy: Essays in Honor of John Christian Bale*, ed. Dennis M. Jones (Luther College, 1990), pp. 72–80.

Ogden, John T., 'The Power of Distance in Wordsworth's *Prelude*', *PMLA*, 88 (March 1973), pp. 246–59.

Orestano, Francesca, 'The Magic Lantern and the Crystal Palace: Dickens and the Landscape of Fiction', in *Dickens: The Craft of Fiction and the Challenges of Reading*, ed. Rossana Bonadei et al. (Unicopli, 2000), pp. 249–72.

Ott, Kristin, 'Sublime Landscapes and Ancient Tradition', in *Romantic Localities: Europe Writes Place*, ed. Christoph Bode and Jacqueline Labbe (Routledge, 2010), pp. 39–50.

Otto, Peter, *Multiplying Worlds* (Oxford University Press, 2011).

Page, John T., 'Dr. Barnardo and Dickens', *Dickensian*, 1 November 1916, p. 301.

Parker, David, 'The Reconstruction of Dickens's Drawing-Room', *Dickensian* (Spring 1982), pp. 8–18.

Paroissien, David, 'Dickens the Historian, Carlyle the Novelist: Dickens, Carlyle and the French Revolution', in *The Fiction of History*, ed. Alexander Lyon Macfie (Routledge, 2015), pp. 72–82.

— 'Parallel Lives, Converging Destinies: Dickens and Thomas Babington Macaulay', in *Reading Dickens Differently*, ed. Leon Litvack and Nathalie Vanfasse (Wiley Blackwell, 2019), pp. 61–74.

Peltz, Lucy, 'Aestheticizing the Ancestral City: Antiquarianism, Topography and the Representation of London in the Long Eighteenth Century', *Art History*, 22 (1999), pp. 472–94.

Phelan, Joseph, 'Dickens' *Pictures from Italy:* The Politics of the New Picturesque', *Nineteenth-century Prose*, 29 (2002), pp. 120–37.

Piggott, Gillian, *Dickens and Benjamin* (Routledge, 2012).

Piggott, Stuart, *Ruins in a Landscape* (Edinburgh University Press, 1976).

Potts, Alex, 'Picturing the Modern Metropolis: Images of London in the Nineteenth Century', *History Workshop Journal*, 26 (1988), pp. 28–56.

Prescott, Gertrude Mae, 'Architectural Views of Old London', *Library Chronicle of the University of Texas at Austin* (1981), pp. 9–31.

Rampley, Matthew, 'Peasants in Vienna: Ethnographic Display and the 1873 World's Fair', *Austrian History Yearbook*, 42 (2011), pp. 110–32.

Reed, John R., *Dickens and Hyperrealism* (Ohio State University Press, 2010).

Ridenhour, Jamieson, *In Darkest London* (Scarecrow Press, 2013).

Riegl, Aloïs, 'The Modern Cult of Monuments: Its Character and Its Origin', trans. by Kurt W. Forster and Diane Ghirardo, *Oppositions*, 25 (1982), pp. 21–51.

Rigney, Ann, *Imperfect Histories: The Elusive Past and the Legacy of Romantic Historicism* (Cornell University Press, 2001).

Rogers, Philip, 'The Dynamics of Time in *The Old Curiosity Shop*', *Nineteenth-century Fiction*, 28 (1973), pp. 127–44.

Rooney, David, 'Visualization, Decentralization and Metropolitan Improvement: "Light-and-Air" and London County Council Photographs, 1899–1908', *Urban History*, 40 (2013), pp. 462–82.

Saint, Andrew, 'The Survey of London', lecture, 20 November 2012 at Gresham College, https://www.gresham.ac.uk/lecture/transcript/print/the-survey-of-london/ (accessed 5 April 2021).

Samuel, Raphael, *Theatres of Memory* (Verso, 1994).

Sanders, Andrew, *The Victorian Historical Novel: 1840–1880* (St Martin's Press, 1979).

Santesso, Aaron, 'The Birth of the Birthplace: Bread Street and Literary Tourism before Stratford', *ELH*, 71 (2004), pp. 377–403.

Scalia, Christopher, 'Romantic Antiquarianism: Representations of Antiquaries, 1776–1832', doctoral thesis, University of Wisconsin–Madison, 2007.

Schad, J., 'Dickens's Cryptic Church: Drawing on *Pictures from Italy*', in *Dickens Refigured: Bodies, Desires and Other Histories*, ed. J. Schad (Manchester University Press, 1996), pp. 5–21.

Schaff, Barbara, '"In the Footsteps of …": The Semiotics of Literary Tourism', *KulturPoetik*, 11 (2011), pp. 166–80.

— 'John Murray's Handbooks to Italy': Making Tourism Literary', in *Literary Tourism and Nineteenth-Century Culture*, ed. Nicola Watson (Palgrave Macmillan, 2009), pp. 106–18.

Schlicke, Paul, 'Embracing the New Spirit of the Age: Dickens and the Evolution of "The Old Curiosity Shop"', *Dickens Studies Annual*, 32 (2002), pp. 1–35.

— 'Revisions to Sketches by Boz', *Dickensian* (Spring 2005), pp. 29–38.

Schoch, Richard, 'Performing History on the Victorian Stage', in *Conjuring the Real*, ed. Rumiko Handa and James Potter (University of Nebraska Press, 2011), pp. 119–52.

Schwartz, Vanessa, *Spectacular Realities: Early Mass Culture in fin-de-siècle Paris* (University of California Press, 1998).

Schwarzbach, Frederick S., 'Dickens and Carlyle Again: A Note on an Early Influence', *Dickensian* (September 1977), pp. 149–53.

— *Dickens and the City* (Athlone Press, 1979).

Scully, Richard, 'William Henry Boucher (1837–1906): Illustrator and Cartoonist', *Victorian Periodicals Review*, 46 (4) (2013), pp. 441–75.

Sen, Sambudha, 'Bleak House, Vanity Fair, and the Making of an Urban Aesthetic', *Nineteenth-century Literature*, 54 (2000), pp. 480–502.

Shealy, Daniel, ed., *Alcott in Her Own Time* (University of Iowa Press, 2005).

Sicher, Efraim, *Rereading the City, Rereading Dickens: Representation, the Novel, and Urban Realism* (AMS Press, 2003).

Simmons, James C., *The Novelist as Historian* (Mouton, 1973).

Simon, Leslie S., 'The De-orphaned Orphan: Oliver Twist and Deep Time', *Dickens Quarterly*, 34 (2017), pp. 306–30.

Smith, Emily Valia, 'Charles Dickens and Literary Tourism: His Experiential Encounters and Legacy', doctoral thesis, Royal Holloway, University of London, 2022.

Smith, Grahame, *Dickens and the Dream of Cinema* (Manchester University Press, 2003).

Solomon-Godeau, Abigail, *Photography at the Dock* (University of Minnesota Press, 1991).

Sorensen, Colin, *London on Film* (Museum of London, 1996).

Spiller, Robert E., 'The English Literary Horizon: 1815–1835 (As Seen by the American Traveller)', *Studies in Philology*, 23 (1926), pp. 1–15.

Stern, Madeleine B., *Louisa May Alcott* (Peter Nevill, 1952).

Sternberger, Dolf, *Panorama of the Nineteenth Century* (Blackwell, 1977).

Stewart, Susan, *On Longing* (Duke University Press, 1993).

Sutcliffe, Alan, 'Dickens and the Music Hall', *Dickensian* (Summer 2010), pp. 101–17.

Sutherland, John, *The Longman Companion to Victorian Fiction* (Longman, 2009).

— 'Visualizing Dickens', in *Palgrave Advances in Charles Dickens Studies*, ed. John Bowen and Robert Patten (Palgrave Macmillan, 2006), pp. 111–30.

Sweet, Rosemary, 'Antiquaries and Antiquities in Eighteenth-Century England', *Eighteenth-century Studies*, 34 (2001), pp. 181–206.

— *Antiquaries: The Discovery of the Past in Eighteenth-century Britain* (Hambledon, 2004).

— 'The Preservation of Crosby Hall, c. 1830–1850', *The Historical Journal*, 60 (2017), pp. 687–719.

Tambling, Jeremy, *Going Astray: Dickens and London* (Routledge, 2008).

Thomas, Julia, *Shakespeare's Shrine* (University of Pennsylvania Press, 2012), p. 37.

Thomas, Sophie, 'Assembling History: Fragments and Ruins', *European Romantic Review*, 14 (2003), pp. 177–86.

— 'The Location of Vacancy: Pompeii and the Panorama', in *Romantic Localities: Europe Writes Place*, ed. Christopher Bode and Jacqueline Labbe (Routledge, 2010), pp. 169–96.

— *Romanticism and Visuality* (Routledge, 2008).

Townshend, Dale, *Gothic Antiquity: History, Romance and the Architectural Imagination, 1760–1840* (Oxford University Press, 2019).

Tracy, Robert, 'Clock Work: "The Old Curiosity Shop" and "Barnaby Rudge"', *Dickens Studies Annual*, 30 (2001), pp. 23–43.

Urry, John, and Jonas Larsen, *The Tourist Gaze 3.0* (SAGE, 2011).

Van Ghent, Dorothy, 'The Dickens World: A View from Todgers's', *The Sewanee Review*, 58 (1950), pp. 419–38.

Wang, Ning, 'Rethinking Authenticity in Tourism Experience', *Annals of Tourism Research*, 26 (1999), pp. 349–70.

Waters, Catherine, *Commodity Culture in Dickens's Household Words* (Routledge, 2008).

Watson, Nicola, 'At Juliet's Tomb: Anglophone Travel-writing and Shakespeare's Verona, 1814–1914', in *Shakespeare, Romeo & Juliet, and Civic Life*, ed. Silvia Bigliazzi and Lisanna Calvi (Routledge, 2016), pp. 224–37.

— *Literary Tourism and Nineteenth-Century Culture* (Palgrave Macmillan, 2009).

— *The Literary Tourist: Readers and Places in Romantic & Victorian Britain* (Palgrave Macmillan, 2006).

— 'Rambles in Literary London', in *Literary Tourism and Nineteenth-Century Culture*, ed. Nicola Watson (Palgrave Macmillan, 2009), pp. 139–49.

Watt, James, Dale Townshend and Nicola J. Watson, 'Writing the Ruined Abbeys of Netley, Tintern and Melrose', in *Writing Britain's Ruins*, ed. Michael Carter, Peter N. Lindfield and Dale Townshend (British Library Publishing, 2017), pp. 167–203.

Westgarth, Mark, *The Emergence of the Antique and Curiosity Dealer in Britain 1815–1850* (Routledge, 2020).

Westover, Paul, 'How America "Inherited" Literary Tourism', *Literary Tourism and Nineteenth-Century Culture*, ed. Nicola Watson (Palgrave Macmillan, 2009), pp. 184–95.

— 'Inventing the London of Literary Tourists: Walking the Romantic City in Leigh Hunt's "Wishing-Cap" Essays', *European Romantic Review*, 23 (2012), pp. 1–19.

— *Necromanticism: Travelling to Meet the Dead 1750–1860* (Palgrave Macmillan, 2012).

Williams, Raymond, *The Country and the City* (Paladin, 1975).

Winter, Sarah, *The Pleasures of Memory* (Fordham University Press, 2011).

Wolfreys, Julian, *Dickens' London: Perception, Subjectivity and Phenomenal Urban Multiplicity* (Edinburgh University Press, 2015).

Wood, Claire, 'Material Culture', in *The Oxford Handbook of Charles Dickens*, ed. Robert Patten, John Jordan and Catherine Waters (Oxford University Press, 2018), pp. 452–68.

[Woolf, Virginia], 'Literary Geography', *Times Literary Supplement*, 10 March 1905, p. 81.

Zemgulys, Andrea, *Modernism and the Locations of Literary Heritage* (Cambridge University Press, 2008).

Zerlang, Martin, 'London as a Panorama', in *Representing London*, ed. Martin Zerlang (Spring Publishers, 2001), pp. 30–56.

Zimmerman, Virginia, *Excavating Victorians* (State University of New York Press, 2008), pp. 143–77.

INDEX